The Memphis Diary
of Ida B. Wells

BLACK WOMEN WRITERS
SERIES

The Memphis Diary of

Ida B. Wells

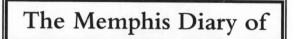

Edited by

MIRIAM DECOSTA-WILLIS

Foreword by Mary Helen Washington

Afterword by Dorothy Sterling

BEACON PRESS

Boston

Beacon Press
25 Beacon Street
Boston, Massachusetts 02108-2892

Beacon Press books
are published under the auspices of
the Unitarian Universalist Association of Congregations.

99 98 97 96 95   8 7 6 5 4 3 2

Text design by Margaret M. Wagner
Composition by Wilsted & Taylor

Library of Congress Cataloging-in-Publication Data

Wells-Barnett, Ida B., 1862–1931.
The Memphis diary of Ida B. Wells /
edited by Miriam DeCosta-Willis;
foreword by Mary Helen Washington;
afterword by Dorothy Sterling.
p.   cm. — (Black women writers series)
Includes bibliographical references and index.
ISBN 0-8070-7064-5 (cloth)
ISBN 0-8070-7065-3 (paper)
1. Wells-Barnett, Ida B., 1862–1931—Diaries.
2. Wells-Barnett, Ida B., 1862–1931—Homes and haunts—
Tennessee—Memphis.   3. Afro-American women civil rights
workers—United States—Diaries.   4. Civil rights workers—
United States—Diaries.   5. Memphis (Tenn.)—
Race relations.   I. DeCosta-Willis, Miriam.
II. Title.   III. Series.
E185.97.W55A3 1995
323'.092—dc20
[B]   94-9087

To the memor
my grandmoth
ANNA THERESA HARREN
(1868–1928
and
LILLIE OPHELIA JON
(1879–1932
two nineteenth-centu
of
great independ
and
indomitable sp

Contents

Foreword

Mary Helen Washington

*E*VERY woman who has ever kept a diary knows that women write in diaries because things are not going right. Although we may never know for certain why the young Ida B. Wells began keeping a diary in 1885, the internal evidence suggests that this was a particularly difficult time for her. Orphaned at sixteen, in 1878, and left to care for five younger brothers and sisters, Wells, an intelligent and talented young woman, had to give up her plans to finish school and take a teaching job in order to keep her family together. Eight years later, an extraordinarily mature Wells is a single professional woman without much money, trying to cope with siblings in various stages of adolescence and a teaching job she found tedious. The diary became a place for Wells to record those intimate thoughts she could not share with others, a place to "talk out" those issues she could not seem to resolve and a way of clarifying and affirming her own growth. We, of course, know Wells as a famous public figure—a dynamic journalist and a one-woman crusade against lynching—but the Wells we meet in the diary she began in 1885 is a twenty-four-year-old woman stuck in an unfulfilling job, struggling to make ends meet as she tries to keep up with the Black bourgeoisie in Memphis, and desperately trying to find a satisfying romantic relationship with a man.

While there is a remarkable continuity between the public Ida B. Wells and the private self that emerges in the diary, the most appealing aspect of the diary is the rare glimpse it gives us of the private Wells. It is probably the only unguarded moment in Wells's life, for, once she becomes a politically connected public figure, she will never again be so willing to expose herself without self-censorship.

I think of the diary as something like the Clearing in Black religious culture, a place where, physically and psychologically, Black people felt free to speak in a setting outside the boundaries of the official church, a private sanctuary where one's truer self is affirmed and authorized. In her private diary, Wells is able to express her anxiety over sexuality; she tells us about her fits of loneliness and depression, and she inadvertently reveals her own vanity and self-centeredness as well as her deep feelings of inadequacy. In an age when Black writers were straitjacketed into being examples of uplift to bring credit to the race, Wells's diary is a remarkable document, an honest and searching chronicle of a young woman's inner journey, the unexpurgated version of a Black woman's journey of personal and professional growth. The diary served a very useful purpose for Wells, allowing her to express what would surely have been unacceptable in a woman in the late Victorian 1880s (and in the refined world of Black Memphis society): a nonconforming, fiercely independent, often angry, powerful female self. In the clearing space that her diary provides, Wells wrote in private what could not be expressed publicly, thus ensuring that these qualities would continue to thrive in her life.

If there is a single recurring theme in Wells's diary, it is that a highly gifted and talented woman is in constant conflict with conventional female roles, which undermine and restrict a woman's desire for work and achievement. Sometimes that tension is expressed in Wells's lingering but inexplicable sense of dissatisfaction with life, feelings of melancholy that are typical of a young woman trying to live and work independently. She writes on Sunday, April 11, 1886:

> I am in as correspondingly low spirits tonight as I was cheerful this morning. I don't know what's the matter with me—, I feel so dissatisfied with my life, so isolated from all my kind. I cannot or do not make friends & these fits of loneliness will come & I tire of everything. My life seems awry, the machinery out of gear & I feel there is something wrong.

At this point in her life, Wells is trying to break into journalism, writing for every Black publication that will publish her work, sometimes getting small fees, but often getting no pay at all. She is boarding in other people's homes in Memphis, moving from place to place to find more suitable and affordable accommodations. With both parents dead and her brothers and sisters separated on her move to Memphis, there is no longer a stable family homestead to provide comfort and assistance. But this malaise that Wells reports, this sense of life being on hold, is not just the result of unfortunate family circumstances. Nearly every woman who has had dreams of a career and a life outside the boundaries prescribed for women reports this same sense of psychological stasis—Carolyn Heilbrun calls it the "female moratorium"—a period in which the young woman feels strongly that she has a vocation but is unable to recognize it or name it or move forward toward developing her career. As a freelance writer, Wells is praised as "brilliant" by her male colleagues, but she continues to downgrade her ability and to doubt her vocation: "I think sometimes I can write a readable article and then again I wonder how I could have been so mistaken in myself" (August 26, 1886).

In true female fashion, Wells keeps looking for the flaw in herself, and it never seems to occur to her that a passion for writing or work is not something that is supported in women. She did not have the freedom to travel that male journalists had, nor did she have models to emulate or the control of Black newspapers. Quite simply, a woman's passions in her day were to be directed toward men and marriage, not placed in the service of her own self-development.

Wells's discomfort with the societal roles that women were supposed to play is most clearly reflected in her rebellion against the courtship rituals of her day. Very few of the men with whom Wells is involved are a match for her intelligence, independence, and tough mindedness, and she is both disdainful of their failure to live up to her expectations and unwilling to play romantic games in order to "earn" their company: "I will not begin at this late day by doing that that my soul abhors; sugaring men, weak, deceitful creatures, with flattery to retain them as escorts or to gratify a revenge" (January 30, 1886).

Despite her scorn for the role of seductress and flatterer, Wells cannot entirely accept her own unconventional attitudes. Typically, she worries that there is something wrong with her. Later, she does marry—apparently quite happily—Chicago attorney Ferdinand Barnett, but it is the dilemma of these early years that is so revealing. Interpreters of women's fiction have termed this dilemma so common in women's lives the conflict between the romantic plot and the quest plot, the one being a plot in which the female "heroine" is the object of male attention, the other a plot in which the woman, as hero of her own story, searches for autonomy and self-fulfillment. Wells's tentativeness and self-doubt are echoed in women's fiction. That sense of being in a state of suspension, of "moratorium," could describe any number of fictional female characters. Helga Crane in Nella Larsen's first novel, *Quicksand* (1928), is never able to articulate her desires and dreams, and the novel is weighted down with images of numbness and suffocation. When Zora Neale Hurston's Janie in *Their Eyes Were Watching God* (1937) tries to understand the tumultuous feelings she experiences as she is about to enter womanhood, she uses images of passivity: "She felt an answer seeking her." Even such a powerful figure as Toni Morrison's Sula finds herself, after years of college and being in the world, and despite (or perhaps because of) her fertile imagination and aggressive intellect, "an artist with no art form," unable to find anything to engage her creativity.

Wells goes back and forth between these two poles, all the while aware of her own antipathy for "heroines" and her need for a self-directed life. In a critique of *Les Misérables*, she expresses admiration for the hero and intense dislike for its romanticized heroine. "I do not like his heroine," she writes; "she is sweet, lovely and all that, but utterly without depth, or penetration—fit only for love, sunshine & flowers." Perhaps at some level Wells desires the "sunshine and flowers" of love and marriage, but she also respects and admires the outlaw self that does not want to be subordinated in "wedlock." In one very painful encounter with a former lover who has married someone else, she concludes, somewhat arrogantly, that, since she herself does not have the necessary qualities of submission and meekness to be a good wife, he has made the right choice.

At the time that Wells was writing her diary, the courtship story—with all the anxiety that it produces for her, the fear that she will never marry because she is not sufficiently docile to attract and hold a man—must have seemed like the dominant story of her life. But often what is most meaningful in a woman's life is not discernible to the diarist herself and may be submerged beneath the welter of facts about daily life. Like any other narrative, diaries have subplots and subtexts, but, unlike the novelist or autobiographer who writes with confidence about destinations and arrivals, the diarist, who is merely laying the tracks, may be completely unaware of the subterranean meanings of her life as she records that life in daily increments. Readers are therefore called on to play an unusually active role in the interpretation of that life: what is unknown to the diarist is available to its readers, who can decode the signs and subplots because we know what happened later. We can see, as the twenty-four-year-old Wells could not have known, that the diary predicts the fearless and outspoken crusader against lynching and segregation whom Wells would become in the 1890s. In the diary she catalogs the growing violence against Blacks, noting with outrage the savagery of the attacks and the way even the flimsiest evidence serves to justify lynching. In her entry of September 4, 1886, Wells writes that the case of a brutal lynching of a Black woman accused of poisoning the woman she cooked for moved her to write a news article "almost advising murder!"

If the diary is a kind of second life, a dialogue with the self in which the diarist is working out the mysteries of her life, we can see in these entries a young Wells mapping out the psychic terrain of her future life as political activist. As early as this 1880s diary, Wells stakes out a staunchly militant position on the side of the Black victims of White mob rule. Her tone is the same militant and uncompromising one that will later get her run out of Memphis with a price on her head. When some Black leaders, among them even the esteemed Frederick Douglass, feared that lynchings might have been provoked by sexual assaults on White women by the "criminal element," Wells was convinced that lynching was an act of political terrorism designed to halt the tremendous economic and political gains that Blacks had made after slavery. She maintained consistently, as few other Black intellectuals of the 1890s did, that it was not necessary for Blacks to prove themselves worthy of White acceptance. Later, when she began a systematic investigation of lynchings, Wells would urge Blacks to resist violence, with force if necessary, arguing with characteristic intensity that a Winchester rifle should have a place of honor in every Black home.

Wells ends her diary with an account of the event that most clearly prefigures that future life: the loss of her legal suit against the railroad that tried to force her to sit in a Jim Crow railroad car.

Wells's suit goes back to May 1884, when she was forcibly ejected from the train on her way back from her teaching job in Shelby County, Tennessee, about ten miles from her home in Memphis. Like most of the Black people in Memphis, Wells was shocked at this attempt to establish a segregated railroad system in a state where Black people had been free to ride in whatever class they could afford (Black Memphis prided itself on being different from Mississippi); unlike many, Wells was prepared to protest. She hired a lawyer and took the case to court, arguing that the dirty smoking car was hardly "equal" accommodations. She was awarded $500.00 in damages, but three years later, in 1887, as she indicates in her diary, the Southern-dominated State Supreme Court, claiming that Wells's suit was intended to "harass" the railroad, sided with the railroad and ushered the Jim Crow era into Tennessee. By April 1887, when Wells learns of this reversal, she has been involved in litigation for three years, always believing that from the State Supreme Court she would get a fair and impartial hearing. The reversal was a stunning blow to her at the time, but we twentieth-century readers of the diary can see this defeat as a signpost on Wells's journey to political activism. Here is a twenty-five-year-old woman, boarding herself out in various Memphis homes, using her own money earned as a poorly paid schoolteacher to hire lawyers to take a major corporation all the way to the State Supreme Court. Like a great sob welling up from discouragement and anger, her response to the loss is the emotional high point of the diary. Nowhere else in the diary does Wells display such maternal warmth and protectiveness, not even for her orphaned brothers and sisters. While there is much that is omitted from the diary that would help us understand how and why she became a radical race woman, the diary does allow us to see that Wells's lifelong struggle for racial justice began with the pain and disillusionment of this early loss.

However uneasy and ambivalent Wells may have been about her role as a woman among the Black bourgeoisie of Memphis, she is clearly self-assured about taking a radical stand on behalf of the race. That split indicates that, even within the apparent privacy of her diary, the presence and pressure of an audience still exerts considerable influence on the shaping of the self. Even though the diarist seems to be writing for herself alone, the very act of writing shows that she is aware of and imagining an audience that enables her to say some things and dissuades her from saying others. Wells's imagined audience—her ideal audience—must have been the large Black communal network of journalists and friends that would have been supportive and encouraging of her racial views but would also have expected her to accept more conventional female roles of refinement and respectability. Certainly, there is a censor operating at some level, for Wells is evasive and silent about much of her personal life—she never writes about the scandal that made her unable to return to Rust College, and we never know the nature or extent of her romantic relationships with the many men in her life. Yet what is so precious and valuable about the diary are those very moments of personal revelation, those candid shots of Wells taken when no one seems to be looking—her admission that she is buying too many clothes, her fear that she is encouraging too many men, and her deep regret over her extravagance in both areas.

Without the venue of her diary, Wells would probably never have exposed this side of her life; it is the side that modern readers will probably value most because we can see in these ordinary problems someone much like ourselves. Contrary to public perception, we have almost no such record of how well-known Black women lived their daily lives, and, because Black women writing are so constrained by the pressures of race and gender uplift, we have very few honest accounts of these women's lives, very little sense of the daily events that have gone into the making of their lives. Letters, diaries, and journals, kept when the race and gender police were not operating at full force, provide rare glimpses into these lives, but Black women, without leisure time, financial independence, or access to the room with lock and key, have written or published very few such documents.

The two most well-known journals of famous Black women are Charlotte Forten's journals, kept during the mid-nineteenth century, and Alice Dunbar-Nelson's diary, which she kept from 1921 to 1931. Like Wells, Forten and Dunbar-Nelson came from socially prominent families, and it was their social class and education that provided them the freedom, the inclination, and the tools to record their lives. What makes these diaries and journals so compelling is that, like Wells's 1885–87 diary, what gets written in them are the socially unsanctioned aspects of women's lives: their desires, conflicts, relationships—even their humor—which the writers obviously felt they could not safely express publicly. Forten, for example, inadvertently reveals her passion for a young White doctor, a married man, with whom she spent time when she was in South Carolina teaching the newly freed slaves after the war. In her journal entry of February 19, 1863, she recounts "the loveliest horseback ride" with Dr. Rogers, "just he and I": "I shall never forget how that rosy light, and the moon and stars looked to us as we caught them in glimpses, riding through the dark pines. How wild and unreal it all seemed and what happiness it was" (Billington 1953, 187). Although Forten is captured by the "magnetism" of the man and is obviously sexually attracted to him, she is also aware of his married status and of the barriers of race. In another context she writes, "Although he is very good and liberal, he is still an *American*, and w'ld of course never be so insane as to love one of the proscribed race" (p. 207). Dunbar-Nelson's diary is even more unguarded than either Forten's or Wells's; evidently, she meant for her diary to be the place where she could write about those thoughts and ideas and feelings that she could not afford to expose elsewhere: her financial problems, her attraction to other women, her suicidal thoughts, her ambitions for social and professional success. Although her public face may have projected self-assurance and class privilege, Dunbar-Nelson's diary tells us about bounced checks, encounters with bill collectors, and unpaid mortgages. The diary also shows us a woman with a bawdy sense of humor and an earthy delight in her own sensuality. In one entry, she declares that she is tired of schools and newspaper offices and longs for flesh pots. On July 19, 1929, her fifty-fourth birthday, she writes, "I am fifty-four, feel twenty-five, look forty. What will the New Year bring? Beauty and good fortune" (Hull 1984, 325).

Wells's Memphis diary, like these other two, tells us something about the mystery and complexity of the private person. But one of the most intriguing things about her diary is that even as it exposes a private side of Wells—her vulnerability and hesitancy—it also reveals the tenacity, intellectual power, and self-determination that are the hallmarks of her public persona. In 1892, seven years after she began writing the diary, Wells began her antilynching work, publishing a series of editorials in the *Memphis Free Speech* that urged Blacks to arm and defend themselves against White mob brutality. Wells went even further, suggesting that relationships between Black men and White women, which had made Black men the target of lynching, were most often consensual, a stance that even Black male leaders were afraid to take. Because the leading White male citizens of Memphis threatened to kill her in retaliation, Wells bought and carried a pistol and vowed, if she were attacked, "to sell my life as dearly as possible" (Duster 1970, 62). In an era of growing Jim Crow despotism and Black conservatism, Wells was one of the most defiantly militant voices by any standard. In the Memphis diary, we have only a partial record of the independent and courageous activist she would become, but it contains nearly all the clues. Here in the pages of this fragmented diary are the sparks that ignited that fire.

Editor's Note

$\mathcal{I}$ FIRST learned of Wells's diary in 1984, when I read the excerpt published in Dorothy Sterling's *We Are Your Sisters: Black Women in the Nineteenth Century* (1984), the same year in which I also read *Crusade for Justice: The Autobiography of Ida B. Wells* (1970), edited by Alfreda M. Duster, and Paula Giddings's *When and Where I Enter: The Impact of Black Women on Race and Sex in America* (1984), which begins with an account of Wells's first antilynching campaign. I spent that year reading the little-known works, including the first-person narratives, of early Black women writers under a grant from the United Negro College Fund, and, in 1986, I presented a paper, "Native Daughters as Writers and Witnesses: Ida B. Wells and Anne Moody," at the University of Mississippi. I did not realize then that I would be engaged in research on Ida B. Wells for almost a decade.

What fascinated me so much about Wells's diary was not only its rarity but also its depiction of people, places, and events in Memphis that I had been researching for years. Wells and I were connected in many ways: I taught at LeMoyne-Owen College, once LeMoyne Normal Institute, where she attended Lyceum meetings; I had visited churches—Second Congregational, Collins Chapel, Beale Street Baptist, and Avery Chapel A.M.E.—where she had worshiped; and I had written about Julia Hooks, Robert Church, Green Polonius Hamilton, and others who appear in her diary. Finally, through her travel journal, Ida B. Wells introduced me to Dr. Georgia E. L. Patton, the first Black woman doctor in Memphis, whose life I continue to explore.

In the fall of 1989, I ordered a copy of Wells's diary from the University of Chicago's Regenstein Library. Both the 1885 and the

1930 diaries are in the Wells Papers, a collection of letters, articles, photographs, and documents that Alfreda M. Duster donated to the library in 1975. When the brown cardboard folder containing the photocopy arrived, I could barely contain my excitement. I stopped whatever I was working on and read the diary straight through, struck by her words, "I thought I had exorcised the demon of unrest and dissatisfaction," which evoked my own feelings of restlessness and disorientation at that point in my life. I had just left Memphis—in body, if not spirit—to accept a job in the Washington, D.C., area but was constantly moving back and forth between those two places that I inhabit. Ida B. Wells and I, clearly, were pursued by the same demons.

That fall, I was invited to present a paper at the Southern Conference of Afro-American Studies, which was meeting in Memphis, so I thought that a paper on Wells, a former Memphian, would be appropriate. I did extensive research that winter and, in 1990, gave a paper, "Ida B. Wells's *Diary*: A Narrative of the Black Community of Memphis in the 1880s," which was published a year later (see DeCosta-Willis 1991). In September 1990, I began transcribing the diary, a slow and tedious process because I wanted to render as accurate and accessible a version as possible.

The manuscript includes a three-page, handwritten poem, "Song of the Mystic," by Father Ryan, followed by a six-line proverb by Confucius, and the 202-page diary, which begins on December 29, 1885, and ends on September 18, 1887. The Regenstein Library also sent me a copy of Wells's fourteen-page diary, dated January 1–May 19, 1930, which begins with a list of names and addresses and ends with a catalog of cash receipts and expenditures for January and February. An assistant at the library recently provided me with the following physical descriptions of the diaries:

> Ida B. Wells diary, 1885, has been rebound in modern buckram (pale tan) on cardboard backing. The pages are of ruled white paper, yellowing at the edges, and the script is written in unevenly faded black and violet inks. Its dimensions are 19.4 ht. × 12.4 w. × 2 cm d.
>
> Ida B. Wells pocket diary, 1930, is bound in dark green embossed paper on thin cardboard. The pages are of ruled, yellowed white paper, and the script is written in faded black ink. Its dimensions are 13.5 ht. × 6.5 w. × .6 cm d.

I always begin a research project convinced that I can finish it in a summer, but, inevitably, the summer stretches into three years. So it was with Wells's diary, but each time I returned to it, after a hiatus of several months, I came back with additional material, renewed enthusiasm, and deeper insights. At various stages in the process, I decided to divide the diary into three sections and include the 1893 travel journal, the 1930 diary, and newspaper articles that she wrote in the mid-1880s. The process of editing such a work can best be described by the term *quilted narrative*, which Carole Boyce Davies uses in *Out of the Kumbla* (Davies and Fido 1990) to characterize the writing of Black women, because so much of what we—critics as well as creative writers—do is piecework completed piecemeal in the bits of time, stolen from work and family, that we have to write. At any rate, I spent my summers in Memphis reading census reports, city directories, obituaries, nineteenth-century newspapers, court documents, and cemetery plot books, visiting historic sites, and collecting photographs. I believe that visual images are very important in reconstructing the life—or, in this case, the life story—of a writer, particularly one who lived more than a hundred years ago, so I searched diligently for sketches and photographs that would illuminate the text: the people Wells knew and the places she visited. On August 7, 1991, I wrote this (excerpted) entry in my own journal:

> On the road again—this time to Holly Springs to do research on Ida B. Wells. I went first to Rust College, where I found an interesting paper on the early history of the college. . . . I have a good "feel" for the foundation that enabled Wells to develop her independence, morality, and religious beliefs. Afterwards, I spent an hour and a half at the Marshall County Library conducting a futile search through 19th c. cemetery lists, and then went to the Marshall County Museum, where I found four photographs from the 19th c. that the curator will have copied for me. It was hot as hell in that Mississippi town, and I felt drained after all the moving around and exertion.

My ties to Wells were somewhat tangled: I was both a reader of her diary and the writer of a diary in which she appears!

Intent on increasing my understanding of her diary through concentrated reading and writing, I prepared a paper, "Exorcising the Demon of Her Unrest: Self-Representation in Ida B. Wells's *Di-*

ary," which I presented at the October 1991 convention of the Association for the Study of Afro-American Life and Literature. I belonged to a five-woman group of literary critics, which included my friends Janet Hampton, Yvonne Captain-Hidalgo, Marie Racine, and Priscilla Ramsey, who critiqued the paper and offered helpful suggestions for revision. The previous May, I had met Mary Helen Washington, who, much to my surprise, had also done considerable research on Wells's diary. She shared with me the letters, maps, handwritten notes, copies of photographs, and newspaper articles that she had collected or that were given to her by Dorothy Sterling. Through Washington, I communicated with Dorothy Sterling and Sarah Ducksworth, who is preparing a collection of Wells's journalistic writing. I am grateful to these three writers and scholars for their generous support and assistance, for editing Wells's diary has truly been a collaborative project. Ducksworth sent me her transcriptions of articles that Wells wrote in the mid-1880s, while Washington and Sterling agreed to write the foreword and afterword.

Most of the diary entries begin at the top of the page. Wells seldom wasted space by indenting paragraphs and often crowded several sentences together at the bottom of the page to complete an entry. She left narrow, often nonexistent, margins at the sides and bottom of the page, while retaining the half-inch margin at the top. There is a neat orderliness to her writing that bespeaks a clear and uncluttered mind. Her beautifully crafted script—large, well-formed letters, open *a*'s and *o*'s, crossed *t*'s and dotted *i*'s, words written precisely on each line and slanted slightly to the right, and defined spaces between words—suggests that she was a good penmanship student. Her text is illegible in only one or two places, and I have used ellipses to indicate the omission or indecipherability of words or phrases.

Because Wells wrote quickly and seldom reread or revised her entries, there are numerous errors in grammar, spelling, and punctuation—errors that do not appear in her more carefully written newspaper articles. I have not corrected these (in most cases, very obvious) errors because I want the reader to feel the personality of the diarist and the flavor of her writing: the anger, passion, and quick wit that emerge on the page, unchecked by attention to minor details. I have, however, filled out Wells's abbreviations (in brackets).

One of the real challenges in editing the Memphis diary was to identify the people to whom Wells refers simply with letters or abbreviations. Those who appear frequently in the text or prominent figures like T. Thomas Fortune and William Simmons were relatively easy to identify in context, but obscure individuals in Memphis, Holly Springs, and the other cities to which she traveled in the summers of 1886 and 1887 were very difficult to place. I searched through census reports, city directories, newspaper articles, Wells's autobiography, and books such as *The Bright Side of Memphis* (Hamilton 1908), *Nineteenth-Century Memphis Families of Color* (Church and Walter 1987), *Blacks in Topeka, Kansas, 1865–1915* (Cox 1982), *Life behind a Veil* (Wright 1985), *Afro-Americans in California* (Lapp 1979), *The Afro-American Press and Its Editors* (Penn 1891), and *Men of Mark* ([1887] 1968). I was able to identify many of the figures in the 1885–87 diary and even made one or two serendipitous discoveries, such as the identity of Mr. C., the Holly Springs man who broke Wells's heart, and Stella B., a cousin, who moved from Holly Springs to Memphis, boarded with Wells, and married a mutual friend.

Like most diarists, Wells did not write for readers or editors; she wrote only for herself, quickly, not bothering to identify, clarify, explain, or elaborate. In editing the text for publication, then, it was necessary to provide information that would help the reader understand and appreciate the context within which Wells wrote this most important and unique work of literature. Although I was reluctant to intrude in Wells's story, I felt that the diary should be fully accessible to the contemporary reader, so I took an active role in interpreting the text and even in creating its meaning. I examined many edited works and found that the ones I had most enjoyed (had, in fact, read from cover to cover) were *Give Us This Day: The Diary of Alice Dunbar-Nelson* (Hull 1984) and *We Are Your Sisters* (Sterling 1984), a collection of letters, essays, and narratives. Because the editors provided comprehensive introductions to the entire work and to each section as well as running commentaries between entries (Hull) or between texts (Sterling), I did not have to interrupt the flow of my reading to consult notes at the bottoms of pages or at the end of the book. Each narrative, it seemed to me, was structured like a dialogue between the writer and the editor.

The Memphis Diary of Ida B. Wells, then, is like a conversation between five women: Ida B. Wells, whose voice is loud and clear and powerful; Alfreda M. Duster, Wells-Barnett's daughter, speaking through the words of Dorothy Sterling; Mary Helen Washington, who first presents Wells to the reader with loving insight into her person; and the editor.

I AM indebted to the descendants of Ida B. Wells-Barnett, Donald, Troy, Benjamin, and Charles Duster and Alfreda Duster Ferrell, for granting me permission to publish the diary of their grandmother. On behalf of his sister and brothers, Donald L. Duster wrote, "All of us would like for information about Ida B. Wells to be widely distributed and look forward to your publication." Thanks also to Carlotta Stewart Watson, a descendant of Wells's and a sister Memphian, for her encouragement.

Many librarians and curators assisted with this project. These include Daniel Meyer, Betsy Bishop, and Paula Y. Lee of the University of Chicago Library; James R. Johnson, Patricia M. LaPointe, and Heather Tankersley of the Memphis/Shelby County Public Library; Anita Moore of Rust College; Lois Swaney of the Marshall County Historical Museum; and Patricia A. Michaelis of the Kansas State Historical Society.

My research on Wells began in 1984, when I received a Distinguished Scholars Grant from the United Negro College Fund, which enabled me to take a year's leave from teaching. The grant came at an important point in my professional life, and I will always appreciate the support of Lea E. Williams and the UNCF staff.

Finally, I want to thank my family: my mother, Beautine DeCosta Lee, and stepfather, Richard Lee; my children, Tarik Sugarmon, Elena Williams, Erika Echols, and Monique Sugarmon; and my grandchildren, Gregory, Kenny, Angelique, and Nile, who give me the love and support that are so necessary for my work.

Introduction

*Nearly a month has elapsed since I scratched a pen in
my diary! Four days only is lacking to make it out;
during that time I have seen much and got about
briskly. On the Tuesday following my last entry, I
came out here. . . .*

July 13, 1887

THOSE of us who live in the 1990s cannot imagine what it was
like to live in the South in the 1890s, in backwater towns like Holly
Springs, Mississippi, and Elaine, Arkansas, and even in urban centers like Memphis, Tennessee, capital of that vast region of flatlands
and cottonfields and shotgun houses known as the Mississippi
Delta. Novelists and filmmakers have captured the images of that
period: night riders cloaked in white, crosses aflame on hilltops,
sudden awakenings at midnight, the piercing screams of women
and children, two-room plantation shacks burned to the ground,
and bodies mutilated and charred beyond recognition—the strange
fruit of a violent terrain. That was the world into which Ida Bell
Wells was born on July 16, 1862. Just four years later and forty miles
to the northwest, a White mob swept through the streets of Memphis, pillaging, burning, raping and murdering innocent people.
The three-day rampage ended with

46 Black men, women, and children killed
75 wounded
 5 women raped
100 robberies
91 houses burned
 4 churches burned
12 schools burned (U.S. Congress 1866, 36)

In testimony before a Select Committee of the United States Congress, Frances Thompson, a rape victim, reported, "They drew

their pistols and said they would shoot us and fire the house if we did not let them have their way with us. All seven of the men violated us two. Four of them had to do with me, and the rest with Lucy." Robert Church, a saloon owner, testified, "They ordered me to shut up my house; they fired at me and struck me in the neck; another ball glanced past me, and another ball struck me; in all they shot twelve to fifteen shots at me" (U.S. Congress 1866, 196, 226).

Twenty-six years later, Memphians were again traumatized by the infamous lynching at the Curve, where the streetcars turned off of Mississippi onto Walker Avenue. Three Black men, Tom Moss, Calvin McDowell, and Henry Stewart, had opened a grocery store in a predominantly White neighborhood near the Curve. A White grocer across the street smoldered over the competition. One day, after a minor disturbance, some policemen shot at the Black grocers, who fired back, injuring one of the policemen. The three Blacks were jailed and then carried to Cubbins Brick Yard, where they were shot to death. Others were injured or jailed when a mob descended on the Black community with guns, pistols, and knives. Ida B. Wells wrote blistering editorials in her *Free Speech*, while a witness reported the reactions of Memphians:

> She was branded by her own people here as a courageous and brave woman. When the news was circulated, a mob had planned, as her punishment, to take her to Court Square and tie her to a tree, without clothing and whip her to death, but she was too wise to stay here and eluded the mob. They searched everywhere for her but as I understand she was in the East when they went to her office looking for her. They smashed up everything in her place for revenge. After all, she did well to have left Memphis. Memphis was no place for a woman of that calibre. (Hutchins 1963)

Those two traumatic events—the Riot of 1866 and the 1892 lynching at the Curve—frame the early life of Ida B. Wells and prefigure the antilynching crusade that she would launch in the last decade of the century. The two-year diary that she began in 1885, however, tells a different story of Memphis. It is a personal and intimate account of a Black woman's social and political coming-of-age in this city, but between the lines of her story is an eyewitness account of the violence and indignities that Blacks suffered in the post-Reconstruction South: she writes passionately about lynchings, segregated churches, colored-only railroad cars, laws against interracial marriage, and persecution in the courts.

Ida B. Wells imagined that Memphis would be just the place for a "woman of [her] calibre." When she moved there in the early 1880s, a young, intelligent, and ambitious young woman in search of greater opportunities and a richer cultural life, she was probably unaware of the city's dark underside. She was excited by the glitter: the gaslit theaters, cobblestone streets, railroad terminals, department stores, churches and synagogues, schools and hospitals, and the waterfront, teeming with steamboats and cotton barges. By 1880, the city had recovered from two decades of trauma: war, military occupation, defeat, a huge influx of freedmen and Irish immigrants, and three devastating yellow fever epidemics, which left the city without a charter and $5 million in debt. By 1880, however, the river town was booming again, with ten railroads, three hundred factories, and a population of 33,952, which would double in ten years. Nestled in a bend of the Mississippi River, Memphis was a transportation center as well as a major market for cotton, hardwood, and wholesale groceries.

There was, of course, another Memphis, what those of us who live in the city call, euphemistically, South Memphis because, in the 1860s, Black soldiers and freedmen settled south of Beale Street, close to Fort Pickering and other Union camps. After the 1866 Riot, Blacks began the slow process of community building, establishing churches, schools, benevolent societies, and small businesses. During Reconstruction, they executed their right to vote, electing Blacks to city, county, and state offices. And, when Whites fled the city in droves, they served heroically in the yellow fever epidemics, nursing the sick, distributing supplies, patrolling streets, and burying the dead. It is this Memphis that Wells captures in the diary that she began on December 29, 1885.

The Memphis diary describes the intimate day-to-day life of a young Black teacher and journalist, who struggles in the mid-1880s with personal, financial, and professional problems. Although she is active and energetic, she often complains of exhaustion and frequent bouts of sickness: catarrh, neuralgia, depression, ear problems, and colds. Her most difficult struggle, however, is internal. She portrays herself as a fiery, ambivalent, and fiercely independent woman, at war constantly with contrary instincts: an incipient feminism, countered by a straitlaced Victorian femininity; a desire for male companionship, but no wish for marriage; and a longing for personal freedom, checked by a sense of duty to her family. She provocatively juxtaposes her private life, her relationships with friends and associates, social and cultural activities, and domestic arrangements against her public life as teacher and journalist. Wells rejects the prescribed domestic roles of wife and mother; she notes in her diary that she does not wish to be married, and she writes in her autobiography that she does not have the "same longing for children" that other women have, perhaps because her activism has smothered the "mother instinct" (Duster 1970, 251).

Eventually, she chooses, instead of domesticity, an active, male-related career while following a Victorian script in her personal life. The tension between these two ways of being is apparent in the diary, as Wells struggles to be a "lady," using the polite language that defines that type, without compromising her strong "unladylike" qualities, such as pride, ambition, outspokenness, assertiveness, and rebelliousness.

A major threat to racial advancement, in the opinion of Black leaders, male and female, was the figure of the loose woman—insatiable, promiscuous, and vulgar—a stereotype that was a product of racist mythology. Wells invokes the stereotype, indirectly, when she commends a White newspaper editor who "declared it was not now as it had been that colored women were harlots." "Respectable" women like Wells define themselves, in opposition to the loose woman, as genteel, cultured, and refined. The figure of the "refined lady" owes much to the ideology of puritanical Victorianism, instilled in students by the missionary teachers at Rust University, which Wells attended from age two to fifteen. Inspired by evangelical Methodism, the teachers viewed their work as a Christian civilizing mission. They enforced an ethic of self-discipline, self-help, and service, believing that "the adornment of young women [should] be that of character and intelligence" (Houghton, n.d., 16). This model of feminine womanhood deeply impressed Wells, who uses the metaphors of romantic poetry and the language of sentimental novels to describe one of these missionary teachers: "Was introduced to Miss Atkinson the music teacher, who seemed so fair and pure, so divinely good, whose motions were grace &

poetry personified." Her diary, then, serves as a kind of notebook in which she analyzes, through words and images, various representations of womanhood—the lady, missionary, harlot, and heroine—in order to construct a different mode of being.

Her search for self-identity is apparent in the incessant activities that characterize her daily life—the constant visits, walks, meetings, excursions, and travels—and in the kinetic images with which she describes her movements: "My wavering footsteps"; "I am drifting along"; "I got about briskly"; and "I have gone about constantly." She seldom depicts herself inside the house, washing, ironing, or cooking; she portrays herself most often outside the domestic sphere and in motion: visiting friends, going to church, horseback riding, walking to school through a snowfall of fourteen inches, and moving, every few months or so, from one rundown boardinghouse to another. This restlessness is an expression of her energy, drive, and ambition, for she is an adventurous woman, determined to shape an active life for herself. Inventive and creative, she has an eye for economic opportunities: she speaks of writing short stories and a novel and of starting a chicken farm with her brother; and, later, we know that she bought an interest in the *Free Speech* and the *Chicago Conservator* newspapers. Instead of locating the subject of her narrative within a closed domestic space, she places her in open, public spaces, where Black males engage in political and philosophical discourse. Wells portrays herself, for example, in the classroom, "I am this day seated in a room of the Rust University building," or in the lecture hall, "I listened to the speeches and saw the earnestness of the men present." The woman in the text is an independent thinker and intellectual who struggles against the constricting female roles of sister, niece, and teacher. She is a woman in conflict, torn between duty and desire, between pressure to conform and the impulse to achieve in unconventional ways.

She expresses this internal conflict in metaphysical language, using words like *exorcise* and *demon* to underscore the moral, ethical, and religious dimensions of her struggle for autonomy. Her religiosity takes many forms: she has an ecumenical bent, prays constantly (even on the written page), visits several churches in a single day, attends White churches and Jewish synagogues on occasion, and leads a Sunday school class. She seems to have transcended some of the fundamentalist preachings of the Black church, although she often evokes traditional Christian figures and rituals.

In the pages of her diary, she introduces members of Memphis's Black middle class—the ministers, teachers, doctors, lawyers, shop owners, housewives, and boardinghouse operators with whom she associated. With an education from Rust University and a coveted teaching position, Wells moves comfortably among this group, making frequent, frank, and sometimes humorous references to them in her diary; she describes the Honorable J. Pennoyer Jones, for example, as "a gas bag if not worse" and the Reverend R. C. O. Benjamin as "a very slender, puerile-looking, small specimen of humanity." Although her position as a public school teacher situates her in the middle class, and although she participates in the rituals of Black Memphis society—the endless round of socials, picnics, church fairs, receptions, surprise parties, moonlight walks, and "entertainments for young ladies"—she frequently feels herself outside that "gentle, confined world." She often feels lonely and isolated because she has difficulty making and keeping friends, particularly women friends. She writes on one occasion, "I have not kept the friends I have won, but will try from this on."

Wells seems to disdain traditional women, the "young ladies" with whom she works and housewives like Mrs. Theodore W. Lott, whom she describes, patronizingly, as "good & kind and soft as a mouse," before adding, tartly, "I like her immensely but can't say the feeling's returned." The only woman she openly admires is Mary "Mollie" Church, a graduate of Oberlin College and the daughter of Robert R. Church, the Memphis businessman who was shot in the 1866 Riot. She admires Mollie, perhaps, because she, too, is an independent, accomplished, and ambitious young woman, who chooses a teaching career over the stringent objections of her patrician and patriarchal father. Wells writes, "Her ambitions seem so in consonance with mine. . . . [S]he is the first woman of my age I've met who is similarly inspired with the same desires hopes & ambitions." The two Memphians, however, never became friends, although they had similar interests and were both involved in the women's club movement.

Aware of her social "difference," Wells struggles against prevailing definitions of Black womanhood at great peril to herself, as she realizes. In spite of her apparent feminist leanings, she is, at least in her early years, a very male-identified woman, one who moves confidently and comfortably in men's domains: lecture rooms, convention halls, and newspaper offices. Margaret Hennig (Hennig and Jardin 1977, 76) characterizes the achieving woman as first-born, closely connected to her father, involved with him in masculine activities, influenced by a male mentor, and determined to avoid the female destiny of her mother. Ida B. Wells fits the pattern in many ways. The oldest of eight children, she was very attached to her father, who encouraged her intellectual aspirations: "My earliest recollections are of reading the newspaper to my father and an admiring group of his friends" (Duster 1970, 9). Jim Wells was a leader in Holly Springs's Black community. A carpenter by trade, he was active in politics, a master Mason, and a trustee of Rust University; he made coffins for yellow fever victims, whom he tended during the epidemic of 1878. It is possible that he belonged to the Loyal League, a Black voting rights organization, and even attended a meeting that was raided by the Ku Klux Klan (Hamilton 1984, 43). His eldest daughter writes, "He was interested in politics and I heard the words Ku Klux Klan long before I knew what they meant" (Duster 1970, 9). Although Ida learned important lessons on religion, discipline, morality, and housework at home from her mother, she received her political and civic training from her father and other Black Holly Springs men like Bob Miller and James Hall. She chose to emulate her father, not her mother.

In the 1880s, Memphis, like Holly Springs, was a patriarchal community, where most of the Black leaders, including Edward Shaw, a former Shelby County commissioner and member of the Memphis City Council, and B. A. Imes, pastor of the Second Congregational Church, were males. After attending a meeting of the Negro Mutual Protective Association, where she heard Shaw and Imes speak, Wells writes ecstatically about the "patriarchal demeanor" of the two speakers, who demonstrate that "the men of the race . . . are endeavoring to put their thoughts in action." These dynamic men of ideas and action are the heroic models—the only models—of who an ambitious, intelligent, and racially committed Black woman might become, for Black Memphis women at that time occupied neither the pulpit nor the podium.

Twenty-four and unmarried, Wells socializes extensively with males: younger men who are her escorts and companions, older men who function as mentors, and newspapermen who encourage her journalism, although it was at that time a male-dominated profession. She writes in great detail about her correspondence with journalists such as T. Thomas Fortune, editor of the *New York Age*, William J. Simmons of the *American Baptist*, and J. A. Arneaux of the *New York Enterprise*, all of whom she meets during this two-year period as she establishes a national network to support her writing. One of her most interesting friendships is with Alfred Froman, an older, prominent Memphian, who once printed the *Memphis Weekly Planet* but owned a harness and saddle shop when Wells knew him. As her mentor, he helps her with her brothers, advises her to return to Memphis from Visalia, requests a loan of Robert R. Church for her, and handles her legal fees; on occasion, he escorts her to parties or the theater and even gives her flowers after a successful program. Like other Black Memphians—businessman Robert R. Church, teacher Green P. Hamilton, Attorney Benjamin F. Booth, and barber M. W. Dogan—Froman was probably a native of Holly Springs and an old family friend.

Wells privileges other men in her diary. She writes often about her brothers, Jim and George, who have a "passion for gaming," but less frequently about her sisters, Annie and Lily. (In 1930, she also writes about her son Herman but seldom mentions daughters Alfreda and Ida, even though the latter is still living at home.) She organizes a Sunday school class at the Collins Chapel C.M.E. Church in Memphis solely for young men, as, later, she would found the Negro Fellowship League for Black male migrants in Chicago. Ironically, it is the men in nineteenth-century Memphis who create models of bourgeois respectability, establishing and enforcing codes of "proper" womanly behavior. Once, when a male friend reports that other men—community leaders—criticized her for attending the theater, Wells vows to serve as a better example to her students. Males often monitor her behavior: her elocution teacher accuses her of flirting with men, and her landlord, a married attorney, warns that she is "playing with edged tools." Wells does not object to such criticism because she admires strong, intelligent men of good character. She explains to a friend, "I told him I had no objection to cultivating the acquaintance of cultured and thinking men of the race." Likewise, she abhors "weak, deceitful creatures" and "miserable excuses for men," like the two men who were discourteous to her during her visit to Kansas City, Missouri.

Her relationships with her "gentlemen callers" constitute one of the most revealing and fascinating topics of Wells's diary because she describes in great detail the courtship rituals that prevailed among the Black middle class during the Victorian period. Young men escort her to church, socials, and concerts; they visit her in the evening to talk or play checkers or Parcheesi; and they exchange letters, cards, and photographs. With a group of men and women friends, Wells attends baseball games, goes horseback riding, visits friends in neighboring towns, takes one-day excursions to Raleigh, and travels to conventions. Her two-year diary describes in some detail her relationships with three men: Charles S. Morris, a Louisville journalist and aspiring novelist with whom she corresponds; Louis M. Brown, a former Memphian who returns often to the city; and I. J. Graham, a teacher, who marries another woman unexpectedly in October 1886. Both Morris and Brown live in other cities, so they carry on a long-distance courtship with Wells through letters and occasional visits, but Graham, who sees Wells every day at the school where they teach, has frequent and often intense encounters with his lady friend.

Nineteenth-century diarists rarely reveal the intimate details of their secret, inner lives, particularly details about their sexual feelings and experiences. Ida B. Wells is no exception to the rule, so one must read between the lines and in the margins of her text(s) to decode what she hides or merely hints at. In her mid-twenties, she is an attractive, sensitive, and passionate young woman, who has been financially and emotionally independent for nine years. She is desirable and desiring, as she discovers in an amorous pas de deux with Graham. On February 14, 1886 (Valentine's Day), after quarreling with him, she writes, "I blush to think I allowed him to caress me, that he would dare take such liberties and yet not make a declaration." But Wells has too much at stake—her independence, reputation, teaching career, and writing profession—to risk committing an indiscretion. Besides, unreliable methods of birth control forced even the most adventurous Victorian maidens to repress their sexual desires. Evidence of Wells's sexual inexperience is her lack of knowledge about birth control: exactly nine months after her wedding at age thirty-three—very late for women of that period—she gave birth to her first baby. She confesses, "[I was glad] that I had not been swayed by advice given me on the night of my marriage which had for its object to teach me how to keep from having a baby" (Duster 1970, 252).

As a single young woman in Memphis, however, Wells paid a high price—isolation, criticism, and calumny—for her ambition and independence and for her rejection of woman's "maternal destiny." Her refusal to play the feminine game exposes her to the charge that she is a silly flirt and a heartless coquette who toys with men's affections. She becomes the subject of vicious rumors: that, as a girl of sixteen, she was sexually involved with a White man in Holly Springs, that she and a male teacher have been dismissed for "immoral conduct," and that her sister Lily is really her daughter. Sometimes she responds angrily to such rumors, lashing out furiously at her detractor: "I grow wild almost & determine to pay him back." At other times, she casts herself in the role of martyr or helpless victim. Her relationships with men are often problematic and short lived because she has exacting standards and is sometimes critical of others. She writes of her "pity and contempt" for B. F. Poole, a journalist and former suitor; she calls William Calvin Chase, a Washington newspaper editor, "contemptible and juvenile"; and she describes I. J. Graham as "narrow and suspicious." Although noted for her sharp tongue, she probably confines such barbed language to the pages of her diary because it would have been unladylike to be so open and expressive. Her diary, then, becomes an emotional safety valve, where she can vent anger and hostility toward others. Her criticism of males may be a defense mechanism because she is all too aware of her vulnerability as an unprotected single woman. Looking back on that period of her life, she explains, "[M]y good name was all that I had in the world, [because] I had no [older] brother or father to protect it for me" (Duster 1970, 44).

THE Memphis diary functions as a writing notebook in which Wells records topics for future articles, plans for writing a novel, lists of articles written and published, and correspondence with editors. Wells experiments with various forms of writing, such as fiction, journalism, and personal narratives, often blurring the boundaries between genres. Along with her personal letters and newspaper articles, her diary serves as a form of literary apprenticeship in which she consciously experiments with language (particularly that of romantic narratives and sentimental novels), rhetorical strategies, and narrative structures as well as with the concepts and modes of expression found in coterminous Black newspapers. Indeed, her writing in the 1880s reveals many of the characteristics that mark her later, more deliberately fashioned works: a direct, plain, and down-to-earth style; wit, irony, and wordplay; concrete details in descriptive passages; fictive devices, such as plot, denouement, and dramatic tension in her expository writing; and the repetition of formulaic details (letters written and received, money earned and spent, visits paid and received). Most significant, Wells is aware of herself as a beginning writer, intent on acquiring the critical skills of her craft.

As we know, Charlotte Forten's journal and Alice Dunbar-Nelson's diary are the only other published diaries of early African American women writers. Dorothy Sterling's (1984) publication of excerpts from the manuscript diaries of four nineteenth-century Black women—Frances Anne Rollin, Mary Virginia Montgomery, Laura Hamilton, and Ida B. Wells—suggests that diary writing may have been more common among early writers than we suspect. Although few journals by White women writers were published in the nineteenth century, Wells might have been introduced to the genre by teachers at Rust University because it was not unusual for missionary teachers to keep diaries to record their experiences and to assuage the loneliness of their exile in the South. It is clear that Wells is familiar with the genre, its form and structure as well as its terminology, for she writes knowingly about the "entries" in her "diary."

What is so remarkable about Ida B. Wells's work is that she wrote not one but four first-person narratives at different stages of her life: the 1885–87 diary, an 1893 travel journal, an autobiography, which she began in 1928, and a 1930 diary. Readers are most familiar with *Crusade for Justice: The Autobiography of Ida B. Wells*, edited and published posthumously in 1970 by Wells's daughter, Alfreda M. Duster. Written late in life, when her achievements in civil rights and women's suffrage had been neglected by historians and almost forgotten by the larger community, her autobiography depicts the public Ida B. Wells who is concerned about preserving race history. She explains: "It is therefore for the young people who have so little of our race's history recorded that I am for the first time in my life writing about myself. I am all the more constrained to do this because there is such a lack of authentic race history of Reconstruction times written by the Negro himself" (Duster 1970, 4). In her 1930 diary, Wells–Barnett suggests another reason that might have motivated her to write her life history: the need to validate her "years of toil and labor." On Monday, January 13, she writes, "Ida & I attended meeting of local Negro History club. Reading from Carter Woodson's Book . . . in which is no mention of my anti-lynching contribution."

Beneath the surface of this objective statement the reader can sense the disappointment that Wells, a proud and confident woman, must have felt at being slighted by the foremost African American historian of the period. She is more expansive about her feelings in the final pages of *Crusade for Justice*, when, after recovering from an illness, she confesses, "I did more serious thinking from a personal point of view than ever before in my life. All at once the realization came to me that I had nothing to show for all those years of toil and labor" (Duster 1970, 414). Significantly, she wrote these passages in her diary and in her autobiography at about the same time: the winter of 1930. The January 9 entry reveals that she was completing her autobiography: "Tried to get on to the last chapter of my book." The diary ends with the May 19 entry, and, ten months later, Wells–Barnett died unexpectedly after a brief illness.

Although not as familiar to readers as *Crusade for Justice*, the three diaries, written at different stages in her life, complement the autobiography, filling in gaps in her life story and revealing personal details about a very complex, complicated, and sometimes controversial woman. In *Crusade*, the private person is obscured by the public persona, a serious and committed militant, who shapes and controls, retrospectively, the narrative of her life, always conscious of her audience and confident about her place in history. Occasionally, the autobiographer reveals her private thoughts and feelings, but she does so only to explain past actions or to justify her social views. In "A Divided Duty," for example, Wells confesses her lack of maternal feelings—"I had not entered into the bonds of matrimony with the same longing for children that so many other women have" (Duster 1970, 251)—because feminists like Susan B. Anthony had criticized her for abandoning public life to raise children.

It is possible, then, to read these two different forms of self-writing against each other. Wells's diaries are periodic records of events and observations that construct her life in progress, while her autobiography reconstructs her life from a fixed point in time, giving shape and meaning to past experience. Wells is unique among Black women writers in having completed an autobiography as well as three diaries—personal narratives that are both similar and different. Each of the diaries was written during a time of growth, change, or movement. She began the first during a very challenging but unsettling period of her life: she was twenty-five years old, looking back on a "butterfly existence," while also wondering "what kind of creature [she would] become."

Six years later, when she began her travel journal, she was again on the move, anticipating an exciting and productive tour of England and Scotland, where she would lecture and organize international support for her antilynching campaign. This lively journal, now lost except for the fragment published in her autobiography and reprinted here, is a provocative self-narrative. She offers an amusing self-portrait of a seasick woman with all her defenses down as the preface to this journal. The autobiographer seldom reveals such physical weaknesses, but the diarist writes about frequent illness, depression, loneliness, and rage.

Still an active and spirited woman at sixty-eight, Wells begins her last diary at another significant time in her life, a month before initiating her last major campaign: a race for the Illinois State Senate. She is in constant motion, going to meetings, giving speeches, attending lectures, soliciting funds, and calling on politicians and ministers. Although brief—three-line entries crowded onto small pages—this diary is similar in form, content, and style to the first two. Wells is still busily engaged in writing: diary entries, reports, personal and business letters, and her autobiography. She hints at money problems and describes at length her despair over her son: "Have been thro hell over revelations of Herman's actions." As usual, her family is relegated to the background of her text, while the spotlight focuses on the protagonist: the diarist herself.

The three diaries, written when she was twenty-four, thirty-one, and sixty-eight years old, are remarkably similar. They have the same short entries, which conform to space limitations; the same conversational language and informal tone; and the same cryptic style, characterized by abbreviations, omission of subject pronouns, repetition of past participles, and a preponderance of short sentences. The existence of these diaries suggests that periodic life writing was continuous throughout Wells's life. The impulse that informs her last diary—the need to order and control the circumstances of her life by recording events and activities—is the same that impelled her writing forty-five years earlier.

The Memphis diary establishes the pattern of the later narratives: the cumulative and cyclic structure of the entries and the rhythm of the periodic writing with its repetitious recounting of events and activities. Throughout that two-year period, Wells wrote five to six entries per month on various days of the week with the regularity of clockwork. Generally, she wrote at night before retiring, completing an entry in one sitting. In Louisville, however, she once resumed writing after a break: "Must stop & prepare a toilet to go out. Later: Had a dozen photographs ordered today." Apparently, she seldom reread entries because she did not correct glaring errors ("Went went to look at the proof.") and repeated or forgot information already recorded. She once admitted, "I've not remembered where I left off."

She seems to have written quickly, jotting down names, numbers, and places, sometimes in abbreviated form, as she scribbled across the page, racing to keep up with her thoughts and crossing out mistakes as she went. She wrote for herself alone: publication of her narrative would have been unthinkable; she locked her diary in a portable "writing desk" away from prying eyes; and she was open and unguarded in her personal revelations, unaware of and unconcerned about readers who might be looking over her shoulder. A fast writer with an agile mind, she jumped swiftly from topic to topic with sometimes disconcerting shifts in subject and tone. For example, after bemoaning the massacre of thirteen Blacks, she continued: "Like my boarding place splendidly; Mr. & Mrs. S[ettle] . . . seem to be congenial spirits." Wells frequently interrupted the flow of her narrative to introduce newspaper stories, travel accounts, critiques of plays, books, and sermons, essays on various subjects, and character sketches. This fragmented and disconnected form of self-writing is, according to one critic, "analogous to the fragmented, interrupted, and formless nature of [women's] lives" (Jelinek 1980, 19). During her mid-twenties, Wells was indeed in a constant state of emotional, physical, and intellectual flux, and that disequilibrium is apparent in the form and shape of her fragmented narrative.

Her entries of July 1886 are particularly interesting because they reveal the diversity of her interests and the regularity of her writing even under the pressure of travel. On July 4, she wrote from Memphis, where she was preparing for a trip to a national convention; on July 8, she recorded the "sayings & doings of the people" in Kansas City; in Topeka, on July 13, she added details about her visit to Kansas City; on July 20, she described her tour of the West; and she recounted her visit to San Francisco on July 29. At times she did not write for several weeks. On December 21, 1886, for example, she complained, "Over two weeks since I wrote! I do not like to be so long as I am sure to forget something, but it seems I cannot help it." Ordinarily, her entries averaged three to five pages in length, but she wrote longer, more introspective entries after emotional experiences, such as her return to Holly Springs in December 1885 and June 1886. She did not write at all or wrote half-page entries during difficult periods such as the fall of 1886, when she encountered problems in Visalia, Kansas City, and Memphis as well as rumors about her conduct and the sudden marriage of I. J. Graham. When Wells was troubled, her writing—the careless script, crossed-out lines, and intermittent dashes—reflected her emotional turmoil. Generally, however, her clear script and regular entries suggest that Ida B. Wells was a disciplined, deliberate, and well-organized woman of exacting standards, one who took pride in her writing.

Through the act of committing her life to paper, Ida Bell Wells suggests that she is a special person whose life is unique and valuable. She must have known that she was destined for greatness because throughout her life she carefully kept, in one form or another, a detailed record of her achievements, preserving for posterity the many articles, letters, speeches, pamphlets, photographs, and newspaper clippings by and about her. In a cruel twist of fate, however, most of her personal and professional papers were destroyed by two fires in her Chicago home. Fortunately, among the items that escaped the flames was the diary that Wells began in Memphis in 1885.

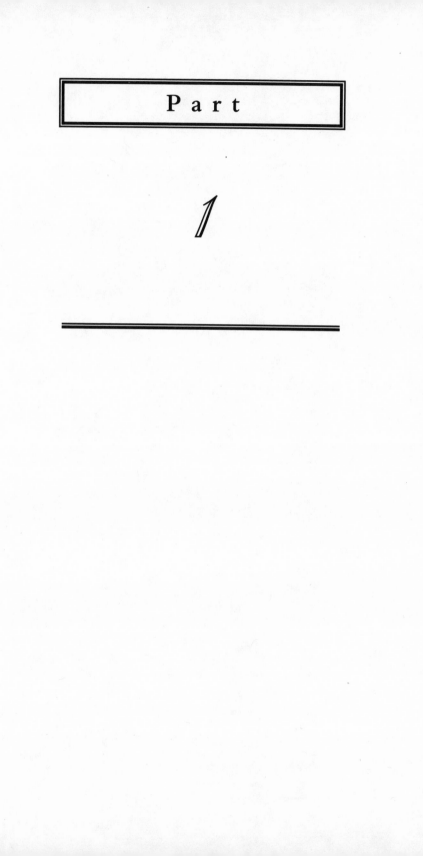

Part

1

From a Butterfly Schoolgirl to a Genuine Woman

December 29, 1885–May 23, 1886

*T*WENTY-THREE years old and caught between the unrealized dreams of the schoolgirl and the unsatisfied yearnings of the schoolteacher, Ida B. Wells struggles in the "winter of her discontent" to earn a living, improve herself intellectually, and assert herself as an independent young woman. Years ago, she had abandoned a small-town frame house and a one-room schoolhouse in rural Mississippi to seek greater opportunities in Memphis, a large urban center. Significantly, she begins her diary in the place of her birth, the little town of Holly Springs, where, in a conscious act of catharsis, she evokes the dark shadows of her past life with its unseasonable deaths and ruptured relationships. Now, she buries those memories in a Mississippi graveyard and once again boards the train to Memphis, determined not to look back.

It is December 1885, and Wells looks optimistically toward the future. According to a newspaperman, she dreams of becoming "a full fledged journalist, a physician, or an actress" (Penn 1891, 409). An accomplished woman of intelligence, confidence, determination, strong moral values, and deep religious faith, she has the easy grace and gentle refinement of a young lady educated in missionary schools. In the five-month period between December 29 and May 23, Wells records, in weekly entries, her day-to-day struggle to survive in the tenuous post–Reconstruction period, when most Black women in Memphis worked as domestics or laundresses for as little as $4.00 a week. She describes her continuing efforts to find housing, pay rent, and balance her budget. Sometimes sick or cold or tired, she pays bills, mounts debts, and fights slander, all the while battling the internal demons—a quick temper and sharp tongue—that bring on occasional bouts of loneliness and feelings of alienation from others. She describes herself, at such times, as just "drifting along."

She has been working for seven years, beginning at age sixteen, when she taught in rural Mississippi for a year and then for four years in Shelby County. This is her second year in Memphis, and she considers herself fortunate to be one of only twenty or so Black public school teachers, but the work is difficult: classes are overcrowded, students are often unruly, and pay is irregular. Teaching is also monotonous and confining. Although she has a reputation as a conscientious and experienced teacher, Wells confesses in her autobiography, "I never cared for teaching" (Duster 1970, 31). She reiterates this theme throughout the first part of her diary: "Friday was a trying day in school"; "A day's worry with these children has brought my temper to the surface." Her antipathy to teaching is, perhaps, even more apparent in what she does *not* write in her diary: names of students, descriptions of activities, reports of teachers' meetings—the details of a rewarding and pleasurable vocation. By contrast, Charlotte L. Forten, a teacher "called and chosen," records in her journal the accomplishments of her students: "I gave [Harry] his first lesson in writing to-night, and his progress was wonderful. He held the pen almost perfectly right the first time" (Billington 1953, 150).

Wells reveals the conflict between her *need* to make a living as a teacher and her *desire* to express herself, creatively, through the writing of personal letters (as many as seven a day!), editorials for religious weeklies, and articles for Afro-American newspapers throughout the country. Many years later, she realizes the significance of that yearning for personal fulfillment, but, in 1886, she has not yet found an outlet for self-expression and she cannot imagine a career in journalism. As far as she knows, there are no Black women in the field, and most friends, Black newspapermen like Robert N. Countee of Memphis and William J. Simmons of Louisville, work primarily as teachers or ministers. Consequently, her diary and letters, which she describes in detail, become vehicles for expressing her emotions: joy at receiving callers, hope of coauthoring a novel, contempt for weak men, pride in dressing well, and frustration over financial problems. In her diary, she vividly outlines the contours of her personal life: wedding receptions and evenings at the theater, visits to churches, baseball games and horseback riding, checkers or Parcheesi with gentlemen callers, and elocution lessons from experienced teachers. She is also actively involved in community work, organizing lectures, giving dramatic readings, and attending meetings of the literary society at LeMoyne Normal Institute.

She seldom writes about her painful past: the deaths of her brother Eddie of spinal meningitis, of her parents and baby brother Stanley in the yellow fever epidemic of 1878, and, later, of her crippled sister Eugenia; the abrupt termination of her education; the difficulty of making a living while caring for her younger siblings after their parents' deaths; and the rumors about her "asking white men for money" (Duster 1970, 17). After a visit to Rust University, she describes, in the diary's first entry, the emotional trauma of reliving the past. Something happened in Holly Springs that Wells does not disclose, but she writes that her "hateful words" created "enemies." Here, the reader encounters one of the most intriguing silences of the text.

When Wells does write about that period of her life, she evokes the image of the "butterfly school girl" with all its connotations: innocence, purity, and vulnerability. In chapter 2, "Hard Beginnings," of her autobiography, the sixty-something matron characterizes herself during that early period with these phrases: "a happy, light-hearted schoolgirl," "a butterfly fourteen-year-old schoolgirl," "a young, inexperienced girl," and "a green girl in my teens" (Duster, 1970, 16, 17, 22). Interestingly, the twenty-three-year-old diarist retreats behind this same youthful, feminine mask when under attack. On January 30, for example, she writes that the young men, who accuse her of high-handedness in her courtships, "have formed themselves in a league against a defenseless girl."

Her diary reveals Wells's increasing interest in racial problems—lynching and other atrocities, the segregation of public facilities, unjust laws and unfair sentences—which intensified in the 1880s.

By this time, she is personally involved in the struggle and writes about her suit against the Chesapeake, Ohio and Southwestern Railroad, but she is more concerned about racial conditions in general. On February 8, she complains about "caste distinction" in White churches, and, ten days later, she criticizes the unfair sentencing of a Black girl.

In the first pages of her diary, then, Wells introduces the topics that will increasingly preoccupy her throughout the 1880s, the years before she begins her crusade against lynching.

IN her first entry, Wells describes a visit to Rust University, where a new building, E. L. Rust Hall, had been completed in 1884. There, she visited friends and former teachers, including Professor W. W. Hooper, president of the institution between 1876 and 1885. She also located the grave of her father, Jim Wells (1840–78), who was probably buried with other victims of the 1878 yellow fever epidemic in Hillcrest Cemetery, located three blocks south of the town square and within walking distance of Rust.

Wells also records her journalistic activities and association with newspapermen, such as Charles S. Morris of Kentucky, Louis M. Brown, a Memphian living in Washington, and a Mr. Fulton. About 1884, she began writing for two Black Memphis periodicals, including a religious weekly, the Living Way; *these articles were reprinted in newspapers such as the* Little Rock Sun *and the* Washington Bee. *She began corresponding with T. Thomas Fortune (1856–1928), editor of the* New York Freeman *(later the* New York Age), *who published her article "Woman's Mission" (see "Selected Articles"). When Wells was forced to leave Memphis in 1892, Fortune hired her to write for the* Age.

In Holly Springs, she met students, such as Anderson and Howard, talked with a former teacher, Professor W. W. Hooper, and visited family friends. Bob Miller and James Hall, friends of Jim Wells's, were appointed guardians of the Wells children after their parents' death. As Masons, they had to care for the families of deceased members.

On her return to Memphis, Wells had calls from gentlemen friends, including Fred Savage, Jr., and her mentor, Alfred Froman. She recited passages from Shakespeare's Macbeth *for her second elocution lesson and, later, read a historical novel,* Ivanhoe *by Sir Walter Scott (1771–*

1832), and a sentimental novel, Vashti, or Until Death Do Us Part
by Augusta Jane Evans Wilson.

I   8   8   5

Holly Springs, Mississippi
Tuesday, December 29

I am this day seated in a room of the Rust University building; in
the land of my birth, the home of my nativity. How strange everything seems! Nearly 4 years ago since I last set foot here and then
there was only the foundation of this magnificent 4 story building
they call Rust University. I could not get to K[ansas] C[ity] so
started here Sunday but got left. Yesterday morning started from
home to the depot; met Mr. Fulton the manager of the Little Rock
Sun, who promised to send me his papers. Received a letter from
Mr. M[orris] in which he excuses his delay in writing by saying he
had lost my letter, but receiving The Bee that I asked L[ouis] M.
B[rown] to mail him he wrote again in care of the Living Way office. The letter had been there a week when I got there. He mentioned that a copy of the Times was sent me with the letter in which
was a description of himself, from which I could judge of his
makeup, but it was not there & I have not received it. The tone of
his letter is good but a recollection of his motto is eminently necessary in deciphering his hyeroglyphics: "Read what you can &
guess at the rest." Have read it twice & yet there are somethings to
guess at. Will wait til I go home at any rate, before I answer, then
possibly until I receive the paper. Mr. Fortune sent me 10 copies of
the paper with my article entitled "Woman's Mission" in it; characterizing it: "a beautiful essay." Sold two copies & will sell the others too. It reads very well, but a little disconnected. Left a list of
personals at the office; heard from Miss King that Mr. Davis was
married; if so, and to the woman they say, I pity him from the
depths of my heart. Left on the 4 o'clock train & arrived here at
night about 8; came on to the college building where Mr. & Mrs.
Hall greeted me. Today have been all over the building, inspected
everything with the eager eyes of curiosity. Mr. Miller came to see
me & we had a long talk. Then we all went out for a walk; strolled

around town, meeting many I knew in the days of "auld lang syne," greeting some pleasantly, passing others indifferently, unconcernedly; and making the acquaintance of many who were children when I was here but are grown up now and almost out of knowledge. Visited the cemetery & found my father's and possibly my mother's grave, and was present at a burying. Came home very tired. Matt D. came down to see me; he looks something like a man & more like Howard every day. Gave him a paper & a slight sketch of myself for spite's sake. Caught two glimpses of Prof. H[ooper] but have not spoken to him. Went up stairs to a social this evening and spent a very pleasant time. Met two gentlemen who are students here that I liked very much: Messrs Anderson & Howard. The day has been a trying one to me; seeing old enemies, visiting old scenes, recalling the most painful memories of my life, talking them over with those who were prominent actors during my darkest days. They counsel me to forget, to cast the dark shadows out and exorcise the spirit that haunts me, but I—forgetting the vows that I had taken on myself *to* forget, and the assurances I have made that I was glad because my Father saw fit to send these trials & to fit me for His kingdom—clenched my hands darkly and proudly declared I would never forget! O My Father, forgive me, forgive me & take away the remembrance of those hateful words, uttered for the satisfaction of self. Humble the pride exhibited and make me Thy child. My position seems to be so favorably considered here that I shall certainly look twice before I jump anywhere, Father. I pray that . . . and went to bid him goodby. There was no reference to the past but he inquired solicitously concerning our welfare. Saw that Mr. B. of "The Little Rock Sun" at the depot the morning I came away, but as Mr. Hall did not come to the train with me I did not get an introduction to him; he is a phlegmatic-looking individual, with little to recommend him to the casual observer. Found not a single letter when I got home from any source, and of course was annoyed & disappointed at this proof of my friends remembrance. I fully expected a missive from L[ouis] M. B[rown] anyhow. He has no right to affect dignified anger or silence as my reply was forced by his request to state the offensive part of his letter. Curiosity as to the tone he would adopt was what animated me as much as any other. Received a letter from Miss F[ord] of N[ashville] who informs me she had but recently received my Sept. letter. Took my second lesson of Lady M[acbeth] yesterday. My interval of the day was filled up with reading Walter Scott's "Ivanhoe." It is the second of his novels I have read and the simple language yet strong portraiture of the characters, invest them with a peculiar charm in my eyesight. Borrowed "Vashti" of Mrs. T[hompson] & have been reading it all day. It is another of Miss Evans' pedantic novels, that have—in spite of their being a printed advertisement of her acquaintance with lore & skill in literature, ancient as well as modern, poetic & historical, mythological & biblical—in spite of which they have a peculiar charm to me. I had not read this one in so long—it seemed like a new story to me altogether. The authoress has skillfully grouped her characters, there are different addenda, different surroundings to all, but she loves to deal with the weird, the—I had almost said inhuman & the same principal elements run thro & compose all her creations—inflexible sternness, haughtiness, independence, unyielding pride, indomitable steadfastness of purpose throughout all trials, sacrifice of self; and there has in all her books to be found a doubting, scoffing, jeering, sneering, infidel devil, sometimes man, sometimes woman, so much so that it has almost grown monotonous. Her different characters change sex in different books. And the women have an exorbitant ambition that they feed, & trample every thing & every body under their feet— to accomplish. I especially admire her novels tho' for the beautiful, if labored finish of every thing; the description of the least minutae of person, surroundings, nature pictures are beautiful word-pictures garnished by analogies & similes that are chaste, beautiful but many times unmeaning to an ordinary reader. Her references, quotations, and general language and especially her dialogue—are all elegant, the language chaste and the thought pure & elevating, the dialogue cutting, witty, masterpieces. From reading the books I should like to know something of the authoress. I should judge her to be an exquisitely refined creature, passionately devoted to music, art, literature, flowers with all the useless panoply & luxury money can provide—added. She could hardly be otherwise than pure who writes so purely & she must be possessed of a mighty intellect. I am disappointed in "Vashti." The idea that Ulpian Grey could *never* love Salome Owen and yet be with her constantly

makes him more of a god than a natural human being with heart &
soul, to me; and I cannot fathom that nature that could willingly
leave such a creature, knowing she loved him dearly, and go thro'
life without one spark of affection for her, ever—and yet retaining
its sweetness without having ties to call it forth. And the idea of her
never marrying because of her hopeless love seems unnatural.

Messrs Savage & Hodges called this afternoon in the rain &
stayed a short while. They painted the reception in such glowing
colors I am a little sorry I did not go. Mr. F[roman] was up last evening & loaned me the $3 I asked. M[enken] sent in a bill of $78 and
I've no money to pay it. Looking back at my debts I am thankful I
could not accomplish my purpose & borrow money to get away—
I would have been more deeply in debt and I am very sorry I did
not resist the impulse to buy that cloak; I would have been $15
richer. Paid Mrs. P[owell] $3 according to promise on her rent yes-
terday. She wishes to raise my board but I cannot do it. George
came at 10 this evening but I did not admit him. Am sorry I was so
hasty.

*DURING her first years as a teacher in Memphis, Wells moved fre-
quently from one boardinghouse to another. She rented rooms for
$10.00–$15.00 a month from landladies like Mrs. Hill, Mrs. Powell,
and Mrs. Spillman, who lived at 15 Wright Avenue (the wife of William L. Spillman, blacksmith, of 17 Wright Avenue). When Wells was
unable to pay her rent on time, Mrs. Powell was forced to "hire [herself]
out" or go into domestic service.*

*Wells details her relationships with prominent young Memphis
professional men. Fred Savage, Jr., was a railroad supervisor, and
Granville Marcus, Jr., who boarded at 352 Washington, taught at the
Monroe Street School. Her most frequent escort was I. J. Graham,
whom she identifies as G., Mr. G., I.J.G., or Mr. Graham. A graduate of Atlanta University, he began teaching in the Memphis public
schools in 1884 and eventually became principal of the Virginia Avenue
School. Considered "a marvel of industry, economy and thrift," he became, according to G. P. Hamilton, the "wealthiest school teacher in the
state of Tennessee" (1908, 263). Wells was aware of his "affluence,"
because she asked him for a loan at 10 percent interest.*

She wrote this entry at 8:00 P.M., just before retiring for the night.

I 8 8 6

Tuesday, January 5

School reassembled yesterday all right—I now have 3 classes. No letters or papers yesterday and no papers today. Perhaps the editors are taking a holiday. The Living Way came out Saturday with half my letter in it; don't know if they print the other next week or no. Mr. Marcus came out last night for the first time. His talk did not altogether suit me but I could not resent it as I wished—this being his first time here. I guess he finds I'm not so silly as I seemed. Taught today, feeling worse than I have for some time; my chest & head have been in an uproar all day & I feel very badly tonight. The winter of my discontent is made more so by Mrs. P[owell]'s determination to hire out at the end of the week. I ought to have the money to pay her for my board & she would not have to go. I am so sorry I bought that sacque when I could have done without it. I asked a loan of Mr. G[raham] today; don't know what his answer will be. I hated very badly to do it—but was compelled. I want to pay her even if I go. I will hate to go as the weather is very cold just now & I feel like I am going to be sick. I promised to pay him 10 per cent interest. Wrote to Miss Ford last night and tonight to Messrs Morris, Hall, Avant. The last, asking for his picture & autograph & renewing our acquaintance. Found a letter from Mr. F[ulton] of "Little Rock Sun" offering me a scheme to have a branch of his paper published here & I get my pay by selling the papers. He wishes me to assume editorial control, & compliments me as a "powfull writer." Shall not accept as I could not make it pay. It is only 8 o'clock but I go to bed early to see if it will not help me to feel better in the morning.

ISHAM F. NORRIS *operated a wood and coal company, I. F. Norris and Co. In 1885, he opened a grocery store on the corner of Calhoun and Hernando streets, where he also sold medicine; a year later, he was joined by T. J. Turner and Taylor Nightingale, grocers, at 155 Beale; and, in 1887, he placed a half-page ad in the city directory, advertising "I. F. Norris, Dealer in Staple and Fancy Groceries at 141 Beale Street." Norris represented Shelby County in the Tennessee General Assembly for two terms, 1881–83 and 1891–93.*

In the city elections on January 7, 1886, two Blacks were defeated in their campaigns for election as "School Visitors" (board members): Frederick Savage (1835–1910) (the father of Ida's friend Fred Savage, Jr.), who was a shoemaker with Zellner and Company and who had been elected to the Board of Education in the 1880s; and Taylor Nightingale, pastor of the First (Beale Street Baptist) Church at 169 Beale. The Memphis Daily Appeal *reported that Nightingale intended to contest the election on the grounds of fraud. Wells believed that Nightingale (who later invited her to join the* Free Speech and Headlight*) was a racial accommodationist at a time when "colored schools" were separate but substantially unequal. Only a third of Black school-age children attended school, buildings were inadequate, classes were overcrowded, and the salaries of Black teachers and principals were lower than those of Whites. In 1891, Wells wrote, without Nightingale's signature, an editorial protesting conditions in minority schools; the School Board retaliated by refusing to reappoint her.*

Wells writes frequently about her brothers, Jim, age nineteen, a laborer who lived at 16 Alabama Street, and George, sixteen, who also lived in Memphis. Following the deaths of their parents, the two boys were apprenticed as carpenters, but Ida worried about them: their drinking and gambling, employment problems, and association with persons of questionable reputation. She often depended on her older friend and mentor Alfred Froman, whom she calls "Dad" or "Pap," for help with her brothers. Froman lived at 289 Hernando Street, where he sold harnesses and saddles.

Wednesday, January 13

Have been very sick since I last wrote, but kept at school, I am thankful to say & because I was not able to receive visitors I had them in abundance all last week. Was reduced to such direful extremity that I wrote a note to G[raham] to lend me some money at 10 per cent int[erest], but he came by last Wednesday afternoon after school to say he had it not. He expressed his agreeable surprise at receiving the set & we would have "made it up" if I had been willing to answer a question he asked—but I thought it was conceding too much, considering he had never told me anything & would not. I would like to be friends but shall do nothing more to make us so, nor will I submit to "conditions" in order to compass it. Mr.

N[orris] sent me some medicine by G[raham] which I took that night. Mr. M[arcus] came shortly after dark the same afternoon & stayed till 10 o'clock! I was so worried & sick & thought he would never go.

Thursday was city election day; I was not interested in anything but the School Board & both colored men were beaten; we now have an entirely white Board. As Mr. S[avage] could not be elected I was heartily glad the other one could not be, for I believe him to be a toady and could unknowingly be used by the white men. Then he boasted so and conducted himself generally in such an obnoxious manner that it completely disgusted me with him. Mr. West came up to see me & stayed quite awhile tho' I was very sick while he was here. Jim came to the school to see me the same day and wanted money, of course. He has gotten into trouble & can't go back where he was. I have no money & told him so, but gave him a note to Mr. F[roman] who, I knew, would help him if he could & told him to come back that night & tell me the result but he came not and sick as I was, I waited up for him till ten o'clock. During the night, it turned bitterly cold & I was very much surprised on opening the blinds next morning to find snow. It was very cold all day but I went with George to see Mr. F[roman] that afternoon about J[im]. He had given him a note & sent him to a friend of his & the prospects were that everything would be all right only he did not like the idea of J[im]'s companion (of whom I knew nothing). Did nothing all day Saturday but sit by the fire & try to keep warm; it was the coldest day I've experienced. I could not keep warm Saturday & Friday nights but did a little better Sunday. Went down to church but got there too late Sunday morning. Came back home & thought I would answer my letters as I had received them from Eddie, Mr. Anderson of H[olly] S[prings], and L[ouis] M. B[rown], but it was late before I got at it and then only wrote to L[ouis]. He sent me a letter in answer to mine of before Christmas, early in the week, in which, while he did not beg pardon he requested a cessation of hostilities [and] is assured we can become the dear friends he addresses me as & closes by asking me to be his little sister. I told him I would have respected him more if he had owned up his sins & begged pardon honestly instead of beating the bush & trying to excuse his ungentlemanly letter behind my sins. He deeply insulted me by assuming it necessary to tell me he was capable of a feeling no higher than friendship, and expects me to forget the enormity of his crime without even an apology. He is one who never likes to acknowledge himself in the wrong & wishes to smooth things over without such humiliation.

Mrs. Powell adhered to her determination to move & altho I had paid her $4 on what I owed her & gave her a bill on Menken's for $2.50, she went, and I was forced to hunt another place. Went to carry some books home Monday & found her gone when I came. Went to F[annie]'s & stayed all night and last night too. Wrote to C[harles] S. M[orris] over a week ago & received an early reply on Monday. He is pleased to receive a letter from a "genuine woman" as he has hitherto been overflooded with schoolgirl notes. I think I scent a faint odor of patronage pervading his tone but I will not be so suspicious as to let it be known unless it develops itself more strongly. I answered that night before I went to F[annie]'s. Received a letter from Miss Ford yesterday & one from Aunt F[annie] & Annie today. Will go to Mrs. Herman's tonight as my things were sent there today & stay till I can find some place more convenient. Mr. W[est] was to visit the schools today.

In 1886, Wells carried on a long-distance courtship with two journalist associates, Charles S. Morris and Louis M. Brown. Her women friends included Fannie J. Thompson, 58 Mill Street, who taught with her at the Saffarans School, and Fannie J. Bradshaw, a teacher at the Kortrecht Grammar School, but her relationships with women were often problematic. She had several older, married friends such as Mrs. Majors, Mrs. Herman, Mrs. Hill, who often invited her to dinner or to spend the night, and Mrs. Thompson, from whom she took elocution lessons. Thursday night, she and Fannie went to the Lurrie Theater to see Oliver Byron in his new play, Inside Track.

Her correspondence with Nashvilleans such as Miss Ford and Sam C. suggests that she might have attended Fisk University, as her daughter claims, although there is no other internal evidence to support this claim. Among the five letters that she received on Thursday was one from Preston Taylor, a Nashville minister, undertaker, and businessman.

Besides Ida, Mrs. Hill kept at least two other boarders, a young woman named Ella and a male teenager named Boots. Often, students

*or laborers from rural areas boarded with older women or couples when
they moved to towns or cities to study or work. Generational conflicts
over "proper behavior" created tensions that could erupt into violence.
Here, Wells intervenes in the dispute, but she, too, frequently had conflicts with landladies.*

Thursday, January 21

Went out to Mrs Hill's Wednesday night as Mr. H[ill] had decided
after promising to take me, that he could not and I went out there
thoroughly disheartened. Said nothing to her about staying there
for I wished to get nearer to school, if possible.

Thursday night I went out to Mrs. Majors & stayed and Friday
night at Miss T[hompson]'s again. Every afternoon I went to a
number of places to find board but did not succeed until finally I
grew desperate and went to see Mrs. H[ill] Saturday morning.
Made arrangements with her immediately and went up town to
have my things moved. Got to Miss T[hompson]'s as she was going
to theatre & went. The play was "The Inside Track," and a very
good one of its kind. Mr. Nevils came home with us. Did not go
to Mrs. T[hompson]'s as I did not know the piece and was
bothered.

Sunday I went to S[unday] S[chool] & church at the Cong-
[regational Church]. Mrs. B[radshaw] came home with Mrs. Hill
to dinner & remained all the evening. I have discovered the keynote
to her actions, I think. That she would have, is most desirous of,
she labors to appear indifferent to but her real aim is to secure her
ends without seeming to put forth effort. Her studied indifference
to "me royal highness" has piqued me & I am determined that she
shall not succeed in making me show interest in her without a corresponding show on her side.

Was late to school monday but have been on time ever since. Received letters from Mr. Carr, Avant, Mosely, Morris, & Taylor.
Mr. Morris writes a very interesting letter & sends me his picture.
I told him I liked the face but it is the face of a mere boy; whereas I
had been led, from his writings to suppose him a man. I sent him
a picture, that I request him to return as it is borrowed—but promise him one for his own when I have my cabinets taken. He is a good
critic & takes me to task for one of my expressions regarding Lady

M[acbeth]: he thinks I could have found one less objectionable than the one I used. I described myself according to promise only withholding my age till I know his, as I wish to make the unpleasant discovery that I am his senior—first. If a boy, he certainly has a naive head and a man's thoughts in that head. He is sarcastic on the lack of our women to make their homes beautiful, clean, and homes in the best sense of the term. My other letters were not of much interest as I have not yet received L[ouis] M. B[rown]'s letter. I wrote and mailed 7 letters yesterday to Messrs Mosely, Carr, Anderson, Fulton, Morris, Taylor and Jones. Some of them I've owed since way before Christmas. I have yet to answer Cornelia's and Mr. Avant's letter & Mrs. Hall's. Mr. A[vant] promises me a picture at "some future day." Sent Mr. Mosely a bundle of papers as he requested.

Things have been running along very smoothly at my boarding place till last night. Mrs. H[ill] is very quarrelsome & picayunish and she started after E[lla] last night and E[lla] got up & went out doors and she had the door locked on her; this morning about 1 o'clock she came to bed as cold as ice almost & told me she had been out doors all night! Mrs H[ill] tried to force her to eat her breakfast and she would not; whereupon a scuffle ensued & blows were passed. B[oots] stood it till she began beating E[lla] with a stick of wood when he pitched in and I interfered between them to keep her from bruising him. I left with them still fussing & E[lla] declaring she would go to her mother, Mrs. H[ill] saying she should not & B[oots] standing by to see what was going to become of "sister." It is a sad sad thing and an unhappy household because the mistress of it does not know how to control her temper or manage the children. I earnestly pray for light to help bring peace out of this confusion. Came by Mr. T. Lott's on my way home from school to borrow a number of the A.M.E. Church Review that I saw there. It has Mr. Fortune's article "Civil Rights & Social Privileges" in it & I was anxious to read it. He let me have it and I remained some time. He is very fond of teasing and as he firmly believes that he is teasing me I let him delude himself with the idea as he seems to take so much pleasure in it. His wife is an easy sweet tempered, sweet minded mortal. Mr. Carr came tonight & brought a present for Mrs. H[ill] from H. P. H[uyette]. He had received my letter only this evening.

WELLS *comments frequently about her unsatisfactory working conditions. Public school teachers worked for eight months, but pay was irregular, and teachers had to be reappointed each year. Frequently, appointments were not made until late, as Wells notes on August 2, 1886: "The election of teachers has not taken place yet in Memphis & all are undecided & I know not whether I'm on the list or not." According to the city directories of 1885 and 1886, Wells was a teacher at the Saffarans School for one year and then at the Grant School, where teachers earned a salary of $60.00 per month. On October 2, 1886, she wrote, "Was at the teachers meeting next day & assigned to Clay st. building." Of the five schools for Blacks, the Kortrecht Grammar School (the former Clay Street School) was the most desirable. According to the July 13, 1886,* Daily Appeal, *it was "a two-story brick building, exterior dimensions 75 × 62 feet; four rooms on a floor. Average attendance 650 [students, taught by nine teachers]. Water connection with sewers. An excellent building, but much overcrowded." The other schools for colored were one-story, two-room frame buildings. Working conditions at Kortrecht, however, were difficult for even the most dedicated teacher. Wells complained on October 2, 1886, that she had been "at work all the week with 70 pupils."*

Wells mentions other public school teachers, including I. J. Graham, Fannie J. Thompson, and A. W. Brown. Mrs. Dr. Phillips is the wife of the Reverend C. H. Phillips, a graduate of Central Tennessee College. Wells and other young teachers joined the Lyceum, a literary club that met at LeMoyne Normal Institute every Friday evening. She describes their activities in her autobiography: "The literary exercises consisted of recitations, essays, and debates interspersed with music. The exercises always closed with the reading of the Evening Star—*a spicy journal prepared and read by the editor" (Duster 1970, 23).*

Sunday, January 24

The month is rapidly drawing to a close; I am truly thankful I am spared to keep up so well this far, but my system is not in good order and I cannot consult a physician till I get some money. If I once get out of debt I hope this lesson will be remembered and profited by: to think I am in debt more than one month's salary & if anything should happen I have not more than enough money coming to me to cancel my expenses. I earnestly pray the Board will pay for two

months when next they meet. Friday it rained and was very dis-
agreeable; in the afternoon a pipe had broken & it was very muddy
coming home but I. J. G[raham] & Mr. B[rown] piloted me safely
thro the mud. F[annie] J. T[hompson] remained with some of her
children. She has been singularly uncommunicative this week & I
have not sought to woo her from her silence. She brought me a
message from Mrs. Dr. P[hillips] to the effect that she had something to tell me: must go over when I can find a pilot. Went to the
Literary meeting at LeMoyne Friday night to see Macbeth played
but they read it thro. It was exceedingly dull & tiresome & some of
the pronunciation was execrable in the extreme. Took my 3rd lesson of the season from Mrs. T[hompson] yesterday. The weather
was miserably cold as the second "blizzard" came sometime Friday
night after we got home, but I went as I realize I am losing valuable
time by not going. Did not know it thoroughly but got along very
well. She told me Mrs. O[usley] was the one who had engaged to
take lessons with her—but as she had violated the contract between
them, she, Mrs. T[hompson], did not feel herself bound to obey
her injunction—to "not tell Miss Wells." She questioned me minutely about her but I evaded her as much as possible because I don't
wish her to discard her for anything I may say. Came home &
ironed my clothes that Mrs. G[raham] brought home in the morning & charged me 40 cts. for. It is very cold today & so I have not
been out of the house today. Later: went out to Mrs. Ragland's &
returned about dark. No visitors except George.

*R. C. O. BENJAMIN (b. 1855), although not a native Memphian,
completed a legal internship under a Memphis lawyer in 1880. A
teacher and writer as well, he edited the* Colored Citizen *in Pittsburgh,
the* Chronicle *in Evansville, and the* Negro American *in Birming-
ham. Wells expresses surprise that he is also a "preacher," and she writes
a scathing critique of his "talk" in her entry for February 1.*

*She describes in considerable detail her relationships with Louis M.
Brown and Charles S. Morris, with whom she planned to write a novel.
Brown was probably the former editor of the* Evening Star, *whom
Wells portrays in her autobiography. In 1886, Brown was associated
with the* Washington Bee, *edited by W. Calvin Chase, and might have
written the following portrait of Wells, published in the* Bee *and re-*

printed in the Freeman *on December 11, 1885: "She is about four and half feet high, tolerably well proportioned, about twenty Summers, and of ready address. Her ambition is not found in most girls, or women either, and it points in a triangular fashion: that is, she is ambitious to become a full fledged journalist, a physician, or an actress." Perhaps Brown wanted to make amends after W. Calvin Chase had attacked Wells, calling her the "star-eyed goddess" in a derisive and sarcastic article.*

    Two other correspondents included J. D. Bowser, editor of the Gate City Press *in Kansas City, and B. F. Poole, with whom she was at one time romantically linked.*

Thursday, January 28

No letters Monday nor papers. All of the latter have gradually come in since then but "The Freeman." Letters from Messrs Morris, Mosely, & Jones Tuesday. Answered C[harlie] S. M[orris] that night also wrote to H. H. A[vant]. Mr. M[orris] returned my picture & repeated the word "boy" so often I fear it nettled him a little altho' he declares it does not bother him. He urges me to write the book I spoke of; to make it classical, representative and standard and I shall make myself loved, honored & respected. He speaks so authoritatively about things and I could accept his calm reproof, superior criticism & logic if he were not my junior; he is what I have long wished for as a correspondent, an interested, intellectual being who could lead & direct my wavering footsteps in intellectual paths. His youth, tho, prevents my asking & seeking information of him as I would one who was my superior in age as well as intellectuality. I may overcome the feeling tho' as there is not any pleasure without its alloy. He denominates my nose as my weakest feature but says it denotes war—petty war, perhaps. He phrenologizes my features minutely and unerringly, as well as amusingly. He writes a good letter & I feel my sceptre departing from me, before him as before no other & it is somewhat humiliating. He is progressing, his path is onward and upward while I—am drifting along with no visible improvement. Yet it is not altogether procrastination, I don't know what books to read that will do the most good & know not where I am to obtain the knowledge. The stupendous idea of writing a work of fiction causes me to smile in de-

rision of myself at daring to dream of such a thing—but his enthusiasm is catching. Yesterday found a card from Mr. T[alley]
saying a Mr. Benjamin would preach for us Sunday. I have read
some of Mr. B[enjamin]'s literary productions and had gathered
that he was a lawyer, & am surprised to learn he is a preacher. Shall
go to hear him with some curiosity. A second letter was from Mr.
Bowser who is evidently disposed to favorably regard my asking
for pay & asks me to state my price—which is an embarrassing
thing to do. I have no idea of its worth & shall tell him so when I
answer. The last letter I received in yesterday's mail was from—Mr.
P[oole] who thanks me earnestly for the picture and begs me to assure him I respect him as the assurance that I did *not*—rankles in his
breast night & day. I don't know what to say to him as I still have
the feeling of pity & contempt for the man, who is not strong
enough to rise superior to circumstances—that I had when I first
wrote. I could not withhold a grain of comfort for revenge's sake—
but can I truthfully say I respect him? He said not one word about
his unreturned letters; he is far nobler than I in that he trusts me
more.

L[ouis] M. B[rown] sent me a copy of "The Bee" in which there
is a marked article from the pen of his very incapable editor, I suppose. The article in question speaks of "the star-eyed goddess" as
not knowing what she is talking about, (as everybody is accused
who differs from the Bee), essays to be sarcastic and volunteers the
information that the A.M.E. Church Review would pay me for my
articles if I "*really wrote*" anything. He is contemptible & juvenile
in the extreme and knows as much about what constitutes journalism as—as—Louis Brown! I would not write for him for great pay
& I will write something some day that will make him wince.
Chase (the editor) marries—why tonight is the time / yes, he takes
unto himself a bride this evening. I think he has good ideas about
most things but he has no tact or ingenuity about *how* to express
them in a way to gain attention or give weight to his words; he is
either a fanatic or talks like one. I will outline my heroine; character
in my next entry.

*WELLS's circle of friends included several Black professionals: teachers,
physicians, and businessmen. Dr. C. H. Phillips was pastor of the Col-*

lins Chapel Colored Methodist Episcopal Church. Theodore W. Lott was a teacher in the Memphis public schools, whom G. P. Hamilton described as "the brilliant, ambitious, irrepressible, and inimitable Prof. T. W. Lott" (Hamilton 1927, 10). His wife, whom Wells regarded as "an easy sweet tempered, sweet minded mortal," taught at the Kortrecht School.

Saturday, January 30

Friday was a trying day in school. I know not what method to use to get my children to become more interested in their lessons. Had a talk with G[raham] who informed me that some one had reported me as saying any young man I went with ought to feel honored because of the "privilege" & that whenever any one was with me all the young men in town knew it & said of him that he was highly honored. He did not add (altho' I knew it must be so) that they hasted to tell such an one of the rumor & thus maliciously have been setting all the young men against me & by their cock & bull stories have kept them away, for a silly speech of mine—if, indeed—I really said it (of which I have not the slightest remembrance). This bit of information opens my eyes to some things, which while I did not understand them I attributed them to pique on his part; I now learn them to be premeditated and deliberate insults & my blood boils at the tame submission to them. I simply and calmly told him I had been misrepresented as I had too often been and betook myself off to think. I went in my room & wrote & asked him if he was in earnest when he asked me if I would try to love him; he replied that he was, indeed, I then said alright. I know it is unchristian-like to burn for revenge as I do, but a demon is tempting me to lead him on & fool him at last. When I think of how I could & can fool him and of his weak imaginings to the contrary, petty evidences of spite work, that he has been safe hitherto because I would not stoop to deceit—I grow wild almost & determine to pay him back. But I cannot do that; I will do the right as I know it—because it *is* right and not as for pay. I have never stooped to underhand measures to accomplish any end and I will not begin at this late day by doing that that my soul abhors; sugaring men, weak, deceitful creatures, with flattery to retain them as escorts or to gratify a revenge, & I earnestly pray My Father to show me the right & give me the strength to do it because it is right, despite temptations. I shall pray for Mr. G[raham] & all the others who have formed themselves in a league against a defenseless girl, that they may see the light & the injustice done me and that I may bear it meekly, patiently. If I ever get a chance I shall speak to him about his soul as I have intended to do since Mr. P. died—otherwise I shall treat him as dignifiedly and courteously as any other acquaintance. I will not thrust myself on him and give the opportunities for rough treatment that I have. Received letters from Mrs. Rice, Mrs. Sprague & a card from Mr. Neal giving subscription for Freeman. Have become negligent about correspondence, because I am out of stationery & money, too I suppose, & have answered only Mr. M[orris]'s letter. Did not go to the surprise party tendered Dr. P[hillips] last evening altho Mr. W[est] came & sat awhile. Went to Mrs. T[hompson]'s & took my 4th lesson today & $2.00 is due here therefor. Went from there to call on Mrs. Neal, who is very bright complexioned, with fair skin & black hair, and rather pretty—was more so, before she married. The inevitable baby is there with the habits peculiar to all baby-hood. From there I went to Mrs. T[heodore] W. L[ott]'s expecting some fun with her mischievous spouse but he was not present. She is as good & kind and soft as a mouse. I like her immensely but can't say the feeling's returned. Came home feeling very, very badly but at this writing am some better.

ALTHOUGH Wells was a very religious woman, the daughter of devout parents and the product of a missionary education, she was critical of ill-prepared, corrupt, or insincere clergymen, who did not make "practical talks" or give people "guidance in everyday life." In a letter written November 30, 1890, to Booker T. Washington, for example, she applauded him for his "manly criticism of our corrupt and ignorant ministry" (Harlan 1975, vol. 3). Her critique of Benjamin's style and delivery, as well as of the form and content of his "talk," indicates that she was an independent and critical thinker, unintimidated by the power and prestige of Black male leaders.

Monday, February 1

Went to service yesterday morning & found a very slender, puerile-looking, small specimen of humanity occupying the pulpit. His "talk" was premature somewhat, and yet applicable; his peculiarities & oddities certainly have the spice of novelty and daring which surprises too much for demur and carries one by storm almost against the judgment. He was presented to me at the close of the meeting but said little; the predominant feeling then was that he had great enthusiasm for the work & that faculty alone would cover a multitude of defects & help resurrect the church. I went back last night to hear him *preach* in order to come to a decision and came away doubtful as to his holy zeal & fitness for the work. A constant arraignment of the Negro as compared to the whites, a burlesque of Negro worship, a repetition of what he did not believe in, and the telling of jokes together with a reiteration of his text "ye must be born again" made up his "sermon." It was in style so closely allied to his "talk" of the morning that I detected little difference between the two. If I were to judge I should say he lacks some of the essential elements that compose a preacher; he *seems* to be wanting in stability, and there seems also, to my mind, to be a lack of reverence in touching & dealing with holy things; a disregard of the Father's command to "take of [*sic*] thy shoes; for the ground on which thou standest is holy." Was troubled with neuralgia most of yesterday. Mr. Mosely came to see me yesterday afternoon & remained a short while; made an engagement to go with him to Dr. P[hillip]'s tonight. Went & spent an enjoyable evening. Received two letters this afternoon & my Freeman. Sam C. writes from N[ashville], & Mr. A[nderson] of Rust University of H[olly] S[prings].

*THIS is the first time in the diary that Wells refers to herself as "Iola,"
a name that she adopted, according to her autobiography, when she began
submitting articles or "weekly letters" to the* Living Way.
Her "Louisville correspondent" is Charles S. Morris.

Tuesday, February 2

A snowstorm set in this morning & has raged all day. Have been very blue all day & G[raham] was in trying to comfort me but he makes a mess of it always. Found a letter from my Louisville correspondent who thinks I said more than I intended when I spoke of the fact of my being his senior as "unpleasant," and objects to being patronized as the expression, "my youthful friend" seems to imply. L[ouis] M. B[rown] excuses his long silence in the fact that he has assisted in launching Mr. Chase on the matrimonial seas, and seems to gloat over the fact of fighting back against "Iola" with a vengeance. I don't know whether it is worth my while to try and make him understand my reasons for refraining an answer to "The Bee's" squib. Must answer Mr. Bowser's letter tonight ere I sleep; I don't seem very anxious for pay seeing my backwardness in ans[wering].

On Friday night, February 5, 1886, Wells attended a play at the Memphis Theater. The day before, the Memphis Daily Appeal *announced, "Mr. Reed and company will arrive from Little Rock to-day and will appear in Humbug at the theater to-night." On February 8, she returned to the theater, where the Ford English Comic Opera Company began a week-long run of the* Mikado, *starring "the brilliant contralto Miss Ray Samuels." Wells's passion for the theater continued throughout her life. Her daughter, Alfreda Duster, recounted that Mrs. Wells-Barnett "liked classical music and plays, and helped budding actors" (Duster 1976). She frequently organized theater parties, including a graduation party for her daughter.*

The Avery Chapel African Methodist Episcopal Church was founded by Black Union soldiers during the Civil War. In 1867, the congregation moved into a $10,000 building on the corner of Hernando and DeSoto. Wells frequently visited the church, where she taught a Sunday school class for young men. Here, she describes visits to Avery Chapel and Cumberland Presbyterian, a White church located on Court Street, to hear evangelists Dwight L. Moody and Ira D. Sankey. Although they spoke at both Black and White churches, they conformed to Southern "caste arrangements" by addressing segregated audiences. Consequently, Wells had to sit in the gallery at the Cumberland Presbyterian Church. Mr. Payne, an old friend with whom Wells probably boarded when she taught in the county, came from Woodstock to attend the service at Cumberland.

Monday, February 8

Last Wednesday morning was the most trying of my school-life here; the snow (which fell all of Tuesday night) was from 10 to 14

inches deep & as there was no locomotion of any kind I had to foot
it to school, all around by Main street as there was most travel &
the likelihood was greater of the snow being tramped down, on that
street—and I got to school about 10 o'clock utterly exhausted with
wading thro' the snow. On account of the storm the week slipped
by & was gone ere we were aware. This is my 4th week here & no
letter from aunt F[annie] yet. If G[eorge] had not received one from
Eddie saying all were well I should be uneasy. No other letters of
consequence & my papers ended my week's mail. I have answered
none of the letters but C[harles] S. M[orris]. I think of his as he tells
me in one received today that he does of mine & hasten to answer
them. I certainly enjoy them because there is always something interesting and couched in such chaste and apt language I am instructed entertained and amused. L[ouis] M. B[rown] is older, has
a more varied experience, considers himself a blase man of the
world with no new worlds to conquer or nothing fresh or new to
be, for him, learned under the sun—but if I decided to end either,
it should be his—for he revels so in small things and is—a petty
warrior. With all his accomplishments and advantages there seems
to be no depth to him; but I forget—comparisons are odious. I have
not answered L[ouis] M. B[rown]'s letter yet, but will when I get
time. Friday night I went to the theatre with Ella & Boots, to see
"Humbug" & humbug it was. Mr. G[raham] assured me during
the day that it was "fire" and I went; yielded more to persuasion
tho' than any desire of my own & was fully repaid for it—for I was
completely worn out & used up when I got home. Received the
"Free Lance" & a note from Mr. Benjamin & have not had the time
to read the one nor the grace to answer the other. I had hoped to
have received a call from him ere this & returned my thanks, made
my apologies in person—but he comes not. Went nowhere Saturday, not even to take a lesson—as I did't know it, but took a bath
in the afternoon & patched the rest of the day. H. P. H[uyette] came
from Kansas City & stayed quite a while that night. I had intended
retiring early in order to rise soon enough to attend the Moody &
Sankey meeting Sunday morning. We came very near being late but
got a front seat in the gallery. The singing was grand, but had we
not gone to Avery Chapel to hear him also, I should have been disappointed because I could not hear very well from where we were
in the Cumberland Presbyterian Church. His style is so simple,

plain and natural. He told the old, old story in an easy conversational way that charms the listener ere he is aware and the secret of his success is, I think—that he does not preach a far-away God—a hard to be reconciled Saviour but uses a natural earnest tone and tells in a natural way without any long drawn doctrine or finely spun theology or rhetoric the simple truth that Christ Jesus came on earth to seek & save that which was lost. Mr. Sankey's singing is a sermon in itself. Mr. Payne was there & I brought him home to dinner with me; he, Huyette & Mr. West took up all the afternoon & I had no opportunity to make an entry or write a letter either. Truly "there is no pleasure without alloy." I intended writing Mr. Moody a letter asking him why ministers never touched on that phase of sin—the caste distinction—practised even in the churches and among christianity(?) but rather, tacitly conniving at it by assenting to their caste arrangements, and accepting it as a matter of course, instead of rectifying it—but I had no chance, & he left the city yesterday; so I know not where to address him. The weather has moderated and the snow is—under the very warm rays of the Sun god—melting fast away. He has unlocked Jack Frost's fingers & loosened old Jack's grasp on the face of mother Earth; for which kindness she is now weeping tears of joy as she smiles & basks in the warmth of his presence. That which Old Boreas used to harden and freeze her with—The Sun God turns to tears of joy at her release and eventually will dry *them* all away. (But it's *awfully* muddy & sloppy for all that.) Was to school this morning by 8:00 and felt peculiarly pleasant and—good. A day's worry with these children has brought my temper to the surface. Found a letter from Mr. C[harles] S. M[orris] on my arrival home this afternoon instead of tomorrow as I expected. He understands & sympathizes with my position of almost complete isolation from my fellow being on account of lack of congeniality—and I think he does so the more fully because his *own* experience coincides with mine. His fine humor & sarcasm are very refreshing & I believe I can say at last I have found a thoroughly congenial correspondent, and I sincerely hope it (the correspondence) may not die the death of the others but may be the earnest and foundation of a lasting friendship increasing with the years, such as I read about, often, see very rarely and have experienced—never! F[annie] J. B[radshaw] was here when I came from school but as she came ostensibly to see Mrs. Hill I made no effort to deprive her of the visit. H[uyette] went with Ella to the theatre & Mrs. H[ill] had to go too & as there was no one to stay with me, I went too—not that I wished so much to go, for I had seen "The Mikado" before. It is a delightful jumble of ridiculous and laughable; a comic combination of songs, speeches, and actions, and dress; for everything is represented as Japanese. It is very bright and sparkling, with no suggestion of the coarse or vulgar; the character of Ko-Ko is inimitable & it was acted to perfection. Yum-Yum is also a delightful, silly little creature. Lost my veil up there & came home wishing I had stayed when here.

MR. IMES *was pastor of the Second (Congregational) Church, and Mr. Williams owned a stationery shop, N. Williams and Company, at 270½ Main Street, where Wells bought writing supplies.*

Louise Cage was the daughter of Frank Cage, a letter carrier with the post office (a prestigious occupation for Blacks at the time), who lived at 19 Tate. The occupant of 22 Tate was William Hill, driver, who was apparently the husband of Wells's landlady. When Wells writes that "we are just across the street from them," the "we" probably included her cousin Stella because the directory lists "Stella Butler, seamstress, r[esidence] 22 Tate."

In November 1885, Wells wrote a letter to the Freeman, *which appeared on November 7 and which the editor headlined "Freedom of Political Action: A Woman's Magnificent Definition of the Political Situation," to which she refers in this entry. After stating that she had no allegiance to Republicans or Democrats, she concluded, "Let a man be Democrat, Republican or Independent as the judgement dictates, if he is obeying honest and intelligent convictions. It is the spirit of intolerance and narrow mindedness among colored men of intelligence that is censured and detested." A "Miss Gaines of State Normal School" took issue with "Iola" for her controversial political views, given the fact that most Blacks supported the party of Abraham Lincoln. The State Normal School shared the campus of Shaw/Rust University until 1872, when the state school was relocated and renamed Mississippi Industrial College. It is interesting that Wells did not defend herself after Chase attacked her credibility but that she did respond to Gaines.*

No letters last week and few papers, except from aunt F[annie] who is well. Answered C[harles] S. M[orris]'s letter and explained fully my position. I hate the barren formality of our address to each other. I want to say "my dear Charlie" but I hesitate about breaking the ice, tho' I know the advance ought and must come from me. Mr. G[raham] & I had a bout last week; he took my hat and walked off with it in the rain & I had to come home bare headed. I took that all in good part till I saw my hat next morning & then I became very angry for it was utterly ruined by being held in the rain. I would not speak to him for two days when he wrote to ask for his umbrella & suggested that we stop playing as we could not do so without getting angry. I acquiesced & told him to come for his umbrella that evening. He did so and stood around like a mummy a long while but finally offered a dictated apology. He renewed his question of a former occasion as if I would tell him I "cared for him" without a like assertion on his part. He seems to think I ought to encourage him to speak by speaking first—but that I'll never do. It's conceding *too* much and I don't think I need buy any man's love. I blush to think I allowed him to caress me, that he would dare take such liberties and yet not make a declaration. He seems to not have confidence in my actions and were he to plead with me on his knees now, for no consideration would I consider his proposition. He had his opportunity and lost it thro' fear of being deceived and other timidity and it shall not occur again. He is too narrow and suspicious. Right here comes my temptation to flirt with him; to make him declare himself and forget all others, but I cannot—I *will* not consider it. I have preached and I must practice under *all* circumstances. I could not respect myself and do so & I will not exert any influence over him tho' he richly deserves to be punished. Heard a sermon from Mr. Imes this morning. Little Louise Cage is very ill with scarlet fever and we are just across the street from them. Did not get any money as I expected yesterday and went nowhere—not even to take a lesson. Got 90 cts. worth of stationery Friday from Mr. Williams on credit. Saw an article from some Miss Gaines of State Normal School of Miss[issippi] in "The Little Rock Sun" & took it upon myself to answer her erroneous views on "Women in Politics," partly because she seemed striking at me about "telling whether she is a Democrat or Republican" because I did such a thing in my article to the Freeman. Also wrote a comparatively short letter to L[ouis] M. B[rown] in which I gave him my candid opinion of his petty mode of warfare, and asked him to procure me Guttmann's Aesthetic Physical Self-Culture & I would pay him for it.

WELLS corresponded with J. A. Arneaux, who was born in Georgia in 1855 to parents of French descent. An actor and a journalist, he edited the New York Enterprise.

On Tuesday, February 16, she went to the Leubrie Theater to attend a New York company's performance of Silver King, *starring Frank C. Bangs.*

She notes the death of Louise Cage in a short, unsentimental sentence, unlike the florid obituary that she wrote for the Living Way *on October 5, 1855: "The death Angel has flapped his black wings and among the number who went at his summons the past week was Mrs. Fred. R. Hunt." (The husband of the deceased was recorder of deeds in the city during the 1880s.)*

This entry reveals that Wells occasionally used her diary as a mnemonic device to record anecdotes that she planned to use in other writing. She explains that she will "jot down" the details of a racial incident involving two girls. The cataloging of incidents is the same process that she uses to make a case against lynching in Southern Horrors *(1892),* A Red Record *(1895), and* Mob Rule in New Orleans *(1900) (see Wells 1969). At this early stage in her journalism, she uses her diary to record some of these incidents for further reference.*

Mary Burton is not listed in the city directory.

Thursday, February 18

Some of my good friends remembered me extensively in the burlesque valentine line as I have received this time no less than half a dozen, some by hand, some by post, and some from the schoolchildren. Wrote to Aunt Fannie & Mr. Arneaux of N.Y. Monday evening—also a letter to the Gate City Press. Found a letter from "Charlie," who is as bright, enthusiastic, and witty as usual. Went to the theatre but it was crowded Monday evening and so we went

Tuesday night to see "The Silver King." Answered C[harles] S. M[orris]'s letter yesterday and sent him two different pictures to look at—so he might not forget me, but they are to be returned and last night answered the nearly a month old letter of B. F. P[oole]'s, that I have. I told him respect did not come at the bidding but was called forth by action. Louise died yesterday. There are 3 stamps missing as I cannot remember but 7 letters I've written & have only 5 stamps left. Mr. B[rown] has told me an incident of Judge Greer's court that for fear I will not remember it when I write my "novel" I will jot down now. It seems that a white and colored girl had been in the habit of passing and repassing, morning and evening, on a narrow path in the woods up the country, and there had never been manifested on the part of the white girl any desire to give half of the walk. One day they passed while the white girl's brother was with her and he pushed the girl from the path and abused her. The next day they met again when each were alone and the white girl attempted to imitate the example of her brother of the day previous and they fought; the colored girl getting the best of the fight, and she was reported, a complaint lodged against her and in the trial the jury brought in a verdict of guilty but fixed no penalty & the judge carried it to the utmost of his power by giving her 11 months 29 days & a half in the workhouse! one half day more would have been a penitentiary offence & those are fixed by the jury.

I read of a case, or heard tell of one, where a white man could not get a license to marry a colored girl and he cut open her three fingers & sucked her blood & then told them he had Negro blood in his veins & therewith procured a license; the facts were brought out in his subsequent trial as his friends knew him to be of caucasian birth & parentage, & proved it.

George B. of this city and Mary Burton lived together 9 years then when they procured a license thro' a white friend they had to steal away like culprits to be married & then they tried to send them to penitentiary for legally doing what had been illegally suffered and nothing said or done about it. They had several children and he wished to legitimize his union & their parentage.

IN her essay "A Story of 1900," Wells recounts the moral lessons of a young Black teacher who exhorted her students "to lay a foundation for a noble character that would convince the world that worth and not color made the man" (see "Selected Articles"). After completing and mailing her essay, she attended the theater Friday night, where she saw the three-act comic vaudeville play M'lle Nitouche.

Wells frequented two Main Street department stores: Menken's Palatial Emporium, located in a five-story brick building at 371–79 Main Street, which advertised "Thirty Stores Under One Roof"; and B. Lowenstein and Brothers, at 247–49 Main Street, who were "Importers and Dealers in Dry Goods, Notions, [and] Hosiery." Curiously, the city directory of 1884 lists "Miss Ida Wells" as a clerk at Menken Brothers. In their fictional biography of Julia Hooks, Selma S. Lewis and Marjean G. Kremer (1986), believe that this is a reference to the native of Holly Springs. This Miss Wells could not, however, be Jim Wells's daughter because (1) Ida always gave her name as Ida B. Wells, (2) the compilers of the directory did not confer titles on Black women, (3) there is no (c) following the name to indicate that she is "colored," and (4) Black women were not hired as clerks in Memphis businesses during that period.

On Sundays, she attended several churches in the Beale Street area, the center of the Black community, south of downtown Memphis. The Second Congregational Church, located at 283 Orleans, was founded by the American Missionary Association in 1868. The Tabernacle Missionary Baptist Church, located at Turley and Beale, was organized by the Reverend Robert N. Countee after he was forced to resign the pastorate of the Beale Street Baptist Church because of an alleged extramarital affair with a parishioner. It is surprising that Wells attended Countee's church after such a scandal because she frequently attacked, sometimes by name, corrupt and immoral "race leaders." The Collins Chapel Colored Methodist Episcopal Church, founded in 1859, was located at 350 Washington, to the north of Beale Street.

Tuesday, February 23

Friday I finished and sent off the article I've been preparing for the Fisk Herald, entitled "A story of 1900." Went to see Lotta in "Mlle Nitouche" with Ella and Huyette that night. She is a bundle of fun, nonsense and comicalities. The play affords her numberless opportunities for kicking up her heels and otherwise exhibiting her marvelous freshness and apparent juvenility. She is near forty but for all the world looks precisely like a girl of 10, full of gaiety, innocence, and of wonderfully small stature. Mrs. Hill is sick; has been ever since Saturday. The Board paid us for Dec., only Saturday & as a consequence mine is gone already and no money to send Aunt F[annie] yet. Paid Menken $20, Mrs. H[ill] $22.25, Mrs. Powell $7.00; have reserved $6.75 (after deducting 95 cts. to Williams, the bookstore man) for street car fare & incidentals. Still owe Menken's $61, Mrs. Majors $4.00, Mrs. Thompson $2. We hope to get some more in about two weeks & then I shall send Aunt F[annie] some. Went to Cong[regational] S[unday] S[chool], to Countee's church for morning service, to see Mrs. Graham in the afternoon, and to Collins Chapel at night—is the manner in which my sabbath was spent. Mr. Carr came out in the afternoon & he escorted me. H[uyette] left yesterday—so he told us that night—and I am not sorry, for I got tired playing second fiddle & running around with them. Mrs. H[ill] wouldn't let them go alone and they honored me by preferring me as chaperone. Yesterday was Washington's birthday and we had a holiday in consequence, but I profited little by it. I went up town and made a small bill at Lowenstein's—about $4.00, for some things I really needed, came back & went to see Mrs. Turner & Mrs. Graham again—darned some socks for myself—and came home about dusk. Mr. G[raham] came out and sat like a mummy for some time & left with little benefit from his visit. Received all the papers & a letter from Sam. George was here last night and went to sleep, then I told him to go home. He went off, telling me he was going away from M[emphis]. Tonight he came here with Mrs. Ragland but hardly spoke to me & refused to tell me goodby. I think he is carrying his "miff" to a great extent.

Thursday, February 25

Mrs. Hill is still sick in bed; I wish she was able to be up. Received letters from H. H. Avant & Mr. Arneaux and both requested a picture of myself. Mr. A[rneaux] of N.Y. requests me to read up Emilia in "Othello" as he "may need me" in that part. Began to study again last night, and learned almost a page more of "Lady M[acbeth]." He sent me several copies of "The Enterprise," also received "The Bee," but no letter from L[ouis] M. B[rown] or C[harles] S. M[orris] yet. I wonder what the matter can be?

WELLS occasionally wrote letters to the Memphis Appeal, *the* Memphis Avalanche, *and the* Memphis Daily Scimitar, *three of the city's White newspapers.*

In 1886, George Wells was listed in the directory as a hostler with Lacey Brothers. He was apparently laid off because he moved that year to Woodstock, where he lived with Mr. Payne, Wells's friend. C. H. Collier, a White man, was superintendent of Memphis Public Schools, and A. W. Brown, a Black man, was the "head teacher" at the Saffarans School.

Monday, March 1

"Charlie's" letter was here when I came home Thursday afternoon; he did not send the pictures but promised to in his next. He did send me Blanton Duncan's notorious letter against the Negro & his own answer which is magnificent and comprehensive in its scope. I answered & returned Mr. D[uncan]'s letter and sent him Miss Gaines' article, my answer and The Fisk Herald article to read. I sent it (his speech) to The Appeal because I wish it published broadcast, but I don't know whether they will do it. I have been perusing the exchanges today & I see not a single mention of it in one of them. Got a letter from L[ouis] M. B[rown], Saturday & he as usual is on the warpath; he tells me again about his affections, and makes use of the following ambiguous statement: "I could understand you better in another way." I don't know what construction to put on it and lest I should be charged with the wrong one I make none. I answered his letter Sunday and told him I would certainly cease correspondence if he ever again considered it necessary to let me know the state of his affections were not inclining toward myself. He did not send the picture. Went nowhere all Saturday or Sunday. Had intended going to Mrs. Thompson's the first day, as I paid her what I owed her the day before, but it rained & sleeted all the morning and I did not go out. Found my papers and a letter from Paul Jones Esq. this afternoon when I got home. I am somewhat embarrassed by it as there seems to be a tone of constraint about the few lines he did write, as he says, at the suggestion of Mr. Huyette. I have in mind to give H[uyette] a good scolding for I had no dreams he was in earnest when I bantered him about Mr. J[ones]. I started first not to answer it & then thought if I did—I would apologize for the divulgence by H[uyette] of any of my silly tales. But I reflected that it would be best to answer in the ordinary tone and a dignified way; which I did, with no personal allusion whatever. I also wrote to Mr. A[rneaux] to acknowledge the receipt of the handsome picture of himself which happened last week. The day I got it, George came in from the country and says Mr. A. came with him & promised to call on me, but he has not done so, so I wrote thinking perhaps he had gone back. I also mailed a letter to Mr. Fulton yesterday endeavoring to seek employment as a representative of his paper to Washington to the Press Convention. George has gone out to Mr. Payne's to work as he could get nothing to do here. I hope he will do well. Mrs. Hill told me this morning she would have to move soon and as she goes farther out I, of course, will have to get another boarding place. It seems as if the old prophecy is coming true in my case: I was traveling New Year's day & I have moved twice already since then.

I have found out that some one tattles to Collier everything I do, & I have expressed myself pretty freely to Mr. B[rown] this morning about it & he affects ignorance of it all. Yet I do not fear; God is over all & He will, so long as I am in the right, fight my battles, and give me what is my right. He tried to show me the folly of fighting against the tide & told me what I already know of the enmity of the men in societies against me for expressing my honest convictions. God help me to be on the watch and do the right; to harm no man but do my duty ever!

MRS. RICE, *a friend of Wells's Aunt Fannie and a resident of Visalia, California, wrote suggesting that Wells apply to the Visalia School Board for a teaching position. Although Wells was ambitious for professional advancement, she was keenly aware of the gaps in her educational training. She was forced to leave Rust University before completing the secondary school degree, and she points out in this entry that she cannot "stand examination in algebra, natural philosophy, etc." Like many institutions of the period, Rust had two academic programs: a classical curriculum for students expected to pursue advanced degrees and a teacher-training curriculum. An 1892 Rust catalog lists courses in algebra, Latin, and Greek in the "College Preparatory: Classical" curriculum. Like most of the other 250 students enrolled at Rust during the early years, Wells took the more general, less rigorous curriculum, but she notes in her autobiography (Duster 1970, 22) that she "had had no normal training" (i.e., no preparation for teaching).* She continued, however, to learn, reading books like Bricks without Straw *by Albion Winegar Tourgee (1838–1905), and taking lessons from Mrs. Thompson and Mr. Theodore W. Lott. As a part of her training in public speaking, she gave dramatic readings—the soliloquy of Lady Macbeth, for example—at literary society meetings at LeMoyne Normal Institute.*

Wells continued to correspond with T. Thomas Fortune, the editor of the New York Age, *whose photograph—with his long hair and spectacles—disappointed her. When they finally met, in Indianapolis, in 1888, Fortune wrote, "I met 'Iola' at the conference. She has become famous as one of the few women who handles a goose quill with diamond point as handily as any of us men in newspaper work. Her name is Ida B. Wells. She teaches school in Memphis. She is rather girlish looking in physique, with sharp regular features, penetrating eyes, firm set thin lips and a sweet voice. . . . [S]he is as smart as a steel trap, and she has no sympathy with humbug" (*New York Age, *August 11, 1888).*

The diarist does not elaborate on what she calls the persecution that she is "undergoing concerning societies." In the 1880s, secret societies such as the Masons, the Sons of Ham, the Odd Fellows, the Knights of Pythias, and the Knights of Labor became the subject of considerable controversy. The Reverend R. N. Countee openly criticized them in the pages of the Living Way, *and it is likely that Wells joined the fray, incurring the wrath of society members.*

M. W. Dogan washed and shampooed her hair, and Mrs. Talley lived with her husband, the Reverend Robert Talley, at 425 Manassas.

Thursday, March 11

I have let one thing and another delay me so I've not remembered where I left off. I received a letter from Huyette and one from Mr. Paul Jones of his city: I cogitated some time before I answered the latter because it was so stiff, and he plainly stated that it was the suggestion of H[uyette] that caused him to do so. I told him I had no objection to cultivating the acquaintance of cultured and thinking men of the race, and in my letter to H[uyette] scolded him roundly for his evident blundering. Received answers to both letters yesterday. Mr J[ones]'s is a long homily on the requirements of the race and H[uyette]'s is an explanation of what I did not understand. He professes to like the name I gave him "silly boy." Answered Mrs. Rice's long-delayed letter also last week but never thought of sending in my application for the school, until I received aunt F[annie]'s letter the same day I mailed it—when I answered aunt F[annie]'s tho' I sent the application thro' her. Received C[harles] S. M[orris]'s letter the day I made the last entry but found no time to answer it till Friday, and mailed it Saturday with my aunt's. Took the first lesson of a new month of Mrs. T[hompson] Saturday and read all day, after going home, "Bricks without Straw" by Judge Tourgee. It deals with the Reconstruction era of Negro freedom and American history, and I like it somewhat. The writer is actuated by a noble purpose and tells some startling truths. Mrs. Hill decided Sunday night to move next day and she did so. I bought a pair of shoes on credit of Menken's costing $3.97 & endeavored to wear them to school but they hurt me so I had to go home at 12 o'clock & change them. Received a letter from Fortune notifying me of the end of my subscription for the Freeman and an invitation from Brother T. to a tea-party in Nashville. Mr. F[ortune] might afford to send me his paper, I think as I've sent him several subscribers. I'll not renew because I expect to leave shortly. His picture adorned the paper last week. My curiosity is satisfied but I am disappointed in him. With his long hair, curling about his forehead and his spectacles he looks more like the dude of the period than the strong, sensible, brainy man I have pictured him. But then, as I told Charlie M[orris], one should not judge a person by the cut or rather uncut of his hair any more than by his clothes. The Sun unhesitatingly accepts my offer to go to Washington as its representative but remains pointedly mum about the money question. I answered immediately to say I could not go without them paying my way but nothing has resulted but a silence blank and discreet. Tuesday I came in with Mr. H[ill] on the wagon, early and stayed to F[annie] J. T[hompson]'s house till time to go to school. Received cards from L[ouis] M. B[rown] & C[harles] S. M[orris]. The former has received the "grand bounce" & will be home in about a month. I wrote him immediately, saying I would be glad to see him. C[harlie]'s card reminded me that I was in his debt one letter & intimated that if it was the fault of our very faulty School board that he would supply the deficiency in his next. Did not answer that for I knew he had received my letter; and sent an answer to that this morning. It is a good letter and I feel so refreshed after reading it. He is indignant at what I told him about the persecution I am undergoing concerning societies. He is a good writer and a good boy I believe. He understands how to steer his epistolary bark clear of the shoals and quicksands. He picks his way so deftly and skillfully out of the complicated labyrinth of woman's various moods & petty fancies. He wishes to know if I can stand examination in algebra, natural philosophy etc. and I must confess my inability. I guess he means to do what he can for me there. I now begin to think of the golden moments wasted, the precious hours I should have treasured and used to store up knowledge for future use. It seems so hard to get at it (study) and I've made so many resolutions I am ashamed to make any more. Went to see Mrs. Settle, Mrs. Bradshaw, Mrs. Graham and Mrs. Love Tuesday evening where I stayed that night and think I will board. Mr. J. stays there and he will help me study, if I go. Went yesterday to see Mrs. Dogan; met Mr. M[arcus] as I came out Madison st. and he went with me to Mrs. Tally's, but I don't think I should like to stay there. Received a letter from "The Plaindealer Co," who wish to know what I will charge for 2 letters per month to their paper. Answered today and stated that I would do as he wished for $2. per article. Don't know what they will say. Sent the article I have been writing on for sometime to Mr. Arneaux today, entitled "Our Name." Mr M[orris] says for me to write the plot of my novel & for us to write one in partnership.

MRS. HILL evidently moved from her Tate Street residence to a place outside of the city, which Wells characterizes as "away out there," for she is not listed in the city directory after 1886. Frequently, Wells went out to visit her, and then rode back into town with William Hill, who drove a wagon.

Monday, March 15

No letters since last week. Wrote to "Charlie" & mailed it on Saturday. Had some pictures taken then & broke my $5. to pay for them. I would have remained at Mrs. H[ill]'s but she told me she could not board me for less than $15. and I could not stand that away out there, so came to see Mrs. S[ettle] who agreed to take me; as this is nearer than Mrs. L[ove]'s I decided to come at once. So I moved this morning & so far like it much. Will begin taking lessons of Mr. L[ott].

THE incident in Carrollton County, Mississippi, which Wells records in the following entry, was described in a letter of April 10, 1886, to the Freeman. *According to the newspaper account, a Black man, who killed a White in self-defense, was brought to trial: "On the day of the preliminary examination a crowd of 20 colored men were in attendance at the trial, all unarmed, when like a Texas cyclone a gang of 50 cutthroats with Winchester rifles, rode into town, surrounded the courthouse and opened fire on all the colored men, killing 10 outright, wounding mortally 3, and severely wounding six. Only one was able to escape the massacre."*

Changing the subject abruptly, Wells expresses satisfaction with her new "boarding place," the home of Mr. and Mrs. Settle at 378 Lauderdale. Other prominent Black families, including the Robert R. Churches and the Charles F. Hookses, also lived on Lauderdale Street. Josiah T. Settle (1850–1915), a graduate of Oberlin College and Howard University, was elected to the Mississippi legislature in 1883 and moved to Memphis in 1885. In 1886, he practiced law with Humbert, Griggs, Settle and Matthews at 32 Poplar, and, in 1887, he was appointed assistant attorney general of the Criminal Court. "Joe" married Theresa T. Vogelsang of Annapolis, Maryland, around 1875. Both Ida B. Wells and William J. Simmons describe Mrs. Settle as an elegant and cultured lady. The teacher in her twenties and the matron in her thirties became friends: they attended church, concerts, and literary society meetings together. Wells dutifully wrote her from Kansas, Colorado, and California that summer. Yet, in conformity to the social code of the Victorian period, Wells always addressed her as "Mrs. Settle," never "Theresa."

Thursday, March 18

The daily papers bring notice this morning that 13 colored men were shot down in cold blood yesterday in Miss[issippi]—Carroll co[unty], I think. O, God when will these massacres cease—it was only because they had attempted to assassinate a white man (and for just cause I suppose). Colored men rarely attempt to wreak vengance [*sic*] on a white one unless he has provoked it unduly. Like my boarding place splendidly; Mr. & Mrs. S[ettle] seem to be congenial spirits. She is the sweetest, quietest and most lady like little creature it has been my good fortune to meet. Mr. H[uyette] is back in Memphis & came to see me last night but he never did tell me why he came back so soon: he remained late. Have taken 3 lessons from Mr. L[ott] & find it hard to rouse my sluggish nature to study. Letters from Charlie & The P[laindealer] Co. The latter are not able to come to my figures, so they say—will write them the article requested & send tomorrow if possible. Answered C[harlie]'s] letter tonight & will get a picture to send him tomorrow as they will all be done.

THE *plan that she discussed with Mr. Froman, her "Dad," was that she move to Visalia and take a teaching position there.*

Tuesday, March 23

Made small progress in books last week & hoped to have done better this week but I seem to find such little time to do anything in. Got my pictures and like them somewhat but the more I look at them the less I like them. Sent one to Charlie and one to Mrs. Hall of H[olly] S[prings]. Mrs. H[ill] came by where I was Friday & took one of them. I have not been for it yet but will go soon. Took the second lesson of the series in elocution Sat. but still have not learned all of Lady M[acbeth]'s soli[loquy]. Letter from L[ouis] M. B[rown] yesterday & he is still hunting for his place. George came in Saturday from Mr. P[ayne]'s & brought me a dollar; he stayed all night and went back on the cars Sunday, I giving him 30 cts. to do so. Received an invitation this morning to the marriage of Mrs. Booth. I was greatly surprised for I've never had any faith in it, but the ticket says "Thursday March 25th., 1886." Will go down if possible. Had a long talk with "Dad" this evening who thinks my plan a faulty one and suggests for me to go to Louisville until the election is over.

GEORGE DARDIS, JR., *was a musician who lived with his parents at*
432 Calhoun. His father pastored the Avery Chapel C.M.E. Church.

Tuesday, March 30

Received a long genial letter from C[harles] S. M[orris] last
Wednesday and answered that night & sent him a copy of "The Enterprise." Mr. M[arcus] came that evening & we went to Avery
Chapel to hear Asbury preach. Received a letter from Mr. J[ones]
of K[ansas] C[ity] by same mail. He uses chaste language but his
letters have not the easy and natural grace of a personal letter, rather
has more of the essay in its makeup. Answered it only Sunday &
my answer was almost equally dry. I knew absolutely nothing to
say. Went to the marriage & wedding & had a very nice time. Mr.
D[ardis] was my company. Gave the bride a glass butter-dish &
pepper-boxes costing $1.04. No lessons of any-kind were covered
Saturday or sewing done, the biggest job undertaken & finished
was—a bath. Sunday remained home to finish a labor-article for
The Detroit Plaindealer but doubt if it will get in for this issue. A
card from Mr. Bowser for an article combating "Aunt Peggy's" assertion & my papers were all my mail yesterday. Letters from Nathan Lewis & George this day. Answered them & wrote to Mr.
Ousley tonight.

HERE, *Wells writes about her case against the Chesapeake, Ohio and*
Southwestern Railroad. In May 1884, a conductor dragged her from the
first-class section of the train after she refused to move to the smoking car.
Wells engaged a Black Memphis attorney, Thomas F. Cassels, who had
represented Memphis and Shelby County in the Tennessee General As-
sembly from 1881 to 1883, to sue the railroad. Suspecting that he had
been bought off, she observed that "white men choose men of the race to
accomplish the ruin of any young girl." She then hired James M. Greer,
a former Union officer affiliated with Greer and Adams at 56 Court, to
defend her. When she won her case in December 1884, the Memphis
Daily Appeal *ran a headline:* A DARKY DAMSEL OBTAINS A VERDICT
FOR DAMAGES AGAINST THE CHESAPEAKE & OHIO RAILROAD. *The*
railroad, however, appealed to the Supreme Court of Tennessee, and it
is that litigation to which Wells refers in this entry.

Although her experience with T. F. Cassels was unfortunate, Wells always supported Black professionals. She later hired Benjamin F. Booth, a young, activist lawyer, who began practicing law in Memphis in 1888. Six years younger than Wells, he graduated from Mississippi Industrial College in Holly Springs. In 1905, Booth and Settle challenged the state Jim Crow law mandating segregation on the streetcars.

Saturday, April 3

Nothing of importance to record for the past week. No letter from C[harles] S. M[orris] yet. Sent him a postal card today in which I reminded him that he owed me a letter. Received an answer from Mr. J[ones] which was shorter and more personal than the preceding ones. Also a card from Mr. Bowser asking for an article combating some of Aunt Peggy's statements. I did not comply with his request. Answered Mr. J[ones]'s letter last night. The Board paid us for Jan. today and it's very uncertain when we will get any more. Guess I'd better hold on to this, or what's left since I paid my debts; Paid Menken $20. Mrs. Settle $7.00. Bought a pair of gloves for 20 cts. and gave Mr. Froman $10. to pay Judge Greer for me. The case will come up in the Supreme Court some time this month and a tried friend of mine has unfolded a conspiracy to me that is on foot to quash the case. I will wait and watch and fear not. Judge G[reer] charges that as traveling expenses. It is a painful fact that white men choose men of the race to accomplish the ruin of any young girl but that one would deliberately ask a man of reputation to encompass the ruin of one's reputation for the sake of gain is a startling commentary on the estimation in which our race is held. A younger man would have violently resented the imputation but the older blood is wiser as well as cooler and thus will use the knowledge gained to circumvent plots. Have bundled all Mr. P[oole]'s letters up to send home but have not done it yet. Will get them off some time next week. Have seen or heard nothing of L[ouis] M. B[rown] for some time. He will be home soon I suppose. Was out to Mrs. Love's to supper one evening last week & Mr. J. came home with me. We had a fine time debating. Am getting along nicely in my studies. Hope I'll have perseverance to continue. I'll not pay Mrs. H[ill] what I owe her until I get some more money. Took the third elocution lesson of the month this morning & am thro' Lady Macbeth.

MOSES H. BARKER, *evidently a member of the Congregational Church, was a letter carrier with the post office, and the Reverend James Lott (as distinguished from Theodore W. Lott) was editor of a religious weekly, the* Memphis Watchman. *Sara Lanier Love, with whom Wells boarded briefly, and her husband, John, a brick mason and contractor, lived on St. John Street.*

Among the churches that Wells attended regularly was the Immanuel Episcopal Church at 256 Third, pastored in the mid-1880s by the Reverent I. E. Black, and attended by such prominent Memphians as Dr. A. S. J. Burchett and Mr. and Mrs. Robert Church.

Money was a problem for Wells, partly because of family obligations: $10.00 a month support for her two sisters, Annie and Lily, who lived in California with their Aunt Fannie; and occasional assistance to her brothers, Jim and George. Wells used her diary as an account book, in which she meticulously recorded expenditures for rent, carfare, clothing, and lessons. Her diary of 1930 reveals the same concern for expenses: "Bought dress for self $15.00 & a marked down jersey for Ida [her daughter] for $3.00." Her one extravagance was clothes. She spent, for example, $23.00—almost half a month's salary—on one dress, paying $15.80 for materials and $7.60 for labor. Like diarist Alice Dunbar-Nelson, Wells was determined to dress well, no matter what the cost.

In spite of her flair for fashion, Wells was painfully aware of her difference. Her status as a public school teacher gained her access to the Black middle class, and she participated in the bourgeois rituals of the Black Memphis elite—the continual round of visits, teas, parties, and entertainments. In February 1889, for example, she joined Mr. and Mrs. I. F. Norris, Mr. and Mrs. J. T. Settle, the Honorable S. A. McElwee, Mr. and Mrs. R. R. Church, and other "aristocrats of color" at a banquet given by the Live Oak Club. The Memphis Watchman *reported that it was "the most successful social occasion that Memphis has witnessed in Colored society. The event was held at the Natatorium Hall. The reception began at 8 PM, dancing at 9, and refreshments were served at 11 PM. Elegant cards of invitation tied in satin ribbon were issued, and the menu consisted of turkey, ham, oysters, salads, ice cream, fruits and wines" (Church and Walter 1987, 127). The ladies in attendance included "Miss Ida B. Wells [in a] blue surrah lace over-dress." Wells, however, frequently felt herself outside that "gentle, confined world," away from the centers of power, and excluded from the cultural patterns that bound her community. She had difficulty making and keeping friends, especially women friends; she was often the subject of gossip; and she was frequently misrepresented by others. In the entry below, she expresses feelings of loneliness, estrangement, and isolation.*

Sunday, April 11

Paid a dollar to Mr. Barker for the Cong[regational] church, & 50 cts to Mr. Dogan for trimming & shampooing my hair Friday evening, 20 cts. for repairing my shoes. Went to Episcopal church last Sabbath; Mr. W[est] called in the afternoon & took me over to see the bride. Nothing of interest transpired the first of the week. Messrs Mosely & Phillips called Tuesday afternoon but I was not at home. Messrs Marcus & Settle called that night and we played checkers. Mr. L[ott] took my peanuts Monday when I was there & I did not go back to recite the whole of the week. Made arrangements to take up the whole of my May salary at Menken's & gave them an order on the Secretary for it. I bought enough silk to finish my dress with, and buttons, thread, linings etc. amounting to $15.80 & yet have no parasol, or other things I would like to have. My expenses are transcending my income; I must stop. Have not paid Lowenstein, Mrs. Majors, Mrs. Love or Mrs. Hill. It seems as if I should never be out of debt. George came today and gave me $1.00. I now have 1.70 of his money. Received letters from Messrs Bowser, Jones & on Friday came the long-looked for missive from C[harles] S. M[orris]. He has moved hence the delay. I answered his letter today; have been nearly all day at it, & wrote ten pages; so much indeed that I grew tired of it myself. Also answered Mr. Jones' letter today and in both of them I discussed marriage. L[ouis] M. B[rown] arrived on the scene last week & came to see me yesterday afternoon. He looks as well as ever, and I was real glad to see him. Had no visitors today. I am in as correspondingly low spirits tonight as I was cheerful this morning. I don't know what's the matter with me, I feel so dissatisfied with my life, so isolated from all my kind. I cannot or do not make friends & these fits of loneliness will come & I tire of everything. My life seems awry, the machinery out of gear & I feel there is something wrong. Will take it to my father. Have concluded not to take part in the entertainment being gotten up by the young ladies.

Wednesday, April 14

Monday afternoon L[ouis] M. B[rown] came out to the school-house just as school was dismissing and walked home with me & spent the afternoon. He then went out walking with me and we had a very pleasant walk. Missed my lesson that evening. Went to recite yesterday afternoon and gave Mr. Lott a dollar to buy me a philosphy with and I began the study of it today. I hope I may not grow weary in well doing and I shall earnestly pray for strength to continue. Mr. E.W.M. called last evening and remained very late; he brought me a fine cabinet photograph of himself and of course procured one of mine in return. Went to try on my dress today. It will cost me more than I can afford but as I am in for it, I shall be compelled to finish it up nicely. I need a parasol, fan and I ought to have a hat & pair of gloves but will not be able to purchase only those I really need.

Tuesday, April 20

Thursday evening Mr. L[ouis] M. B[rown] came out and we had an interesting game of checkers, in which I beat—of course surprising him greatly. Mr. West called too but left very soon. Went no where Saturday but remained home & attended to my patching. Friday evening I went to service with Mrs. Settle, from thence we came to the Church fair at LeMoyne school & spent a very enjoyable evening indeed. Took no lesson last Saturday as my book had not come. Sunday went to Cong[regational] S[unday] S[chool] & went to see Annie from there & brought her home with me to stay the remainder of the day. Endeavored to read "Fool's Errand" but made poor success. Received Mr. Jones' letter but have not answered it yet. L[ouis] M. B[rown] came by on his way to Mrs. B[radshaw]'s and promised to return the next evening. No other callers. He did come & we took a long walk out as far as Mrs. Milburn's, & when we returned the moon was shining so clear, calm and bright that we sat in the moonlight and enjoyed the scene. It was delightful. The din, dust and smoke seemed left far behind; all was peaceful calm and still; the mellow moonlight air was beautiful and the landscape spread out before us. Took lessons Tuesday and tried on my dress this evening.

J. T. TURNER was associate editor of the Memphis Watchman *and a teacher at the Winchester School. Mrs. Page was a laundress. Wells had acquired some domestic skills; she writes occasionally of sewing (making a dress for Lily or her Aunt Fannie), patching, and cooking (when Mrs. Settle was ill, e.g.). These are, however, "chores" that she did not enjoy, so she paid others for such services when she could afford it. Her aversion to housework was lifelong. (See Dorothy Sterling's interview with Alfreda Duster in the "Afterword.")*

Sunday, April 25

Easter Sunday! the day on which our Lord arose from the grave. I fear I have not spent it as consecratedly as I should have done, but I have attended service all day; at S[unday] S[chool] this morning, remained to church. Went to Avery Chapel this afternoon & Mr. B[rown] came home with me, and again at church tonight with Mrs. S[ettle]. I am thoroughly tired and worn out. Wore my new dress & hat as they were finished up & like the dress very much. Paid the woman $7.60 for making it and altogether it cost a good deal. Paid Mr. Lott $2. Thursday, 22nd, & sent Mr. P[oole] his letters yesterday, which cost me 24 cts. L[ouis] M. B[rown] came and remained late last night & I don't like it, that he came Saturday evening. Received a letter from Mr. M[arcus] who will be out tomorrow sometime. Had a holiday Friday & spent it in visiting and sewing—Went to see Mrs. Page & gave her 25 cts. Also saw Messrs Turner & Ashford a little while. Only finished one garment for the whole number of days. Letter from C[harles] S. M[orris], Friday, who as usual, had misplaced my letter & could not answer relative thereto, in addition also begged an excuse for allowing 6 days to intervene between the receipt of his & answer to it. I have not hastened to give him a repetition of that excuse, for his letter is still unanswered. Have answered none of my letters tho' for lack of time. A letter yesterday from Mrs. Rice who anticipates a pleasant time in my society and hopes in me to find a friend. I wonder if her hopes will be blasted? Owe Mr. Jones a letter of over a week's date. Received one from H. H. A[vant], relative to the school; he had only just seen the writing I had done in the back of the book & had answered accordingly to find out all about it. He made no mention of the letter he owed me, nor did I, in my reply. I find tho, that I have erred somewhat in my representation of facts to him and will have to write again soon as I find out some things I wish to know. L[ouis] M. B[rown] was out again last Thursday night and we went walking again; went to Mrs. Hill's that time but she was not at home, only Mr. H[ill]. Mrs. Ragland has professed religion. Will endeavor to study this week and sew some, too, as I am very much behind hand with both. George was in today and had some pictures taken.

GEORGE MCNEAL, *a musician, boarded at 86 Monroe.*

J. M. Keating, like other former Union officers, continued to use his military title. On April 29, 1886, the Memphis Daily Appeal *reported, "The inauguration of the training school for manual labor occurred at LeMoyne Institute last evening. There was a crowd of colored people present and a number of whites. Addresses were delivered by Col. J. M. Keating and others." Among the "others" was Rabbi Max Samfield, who headed the Jewish synagogue, Congregation Children Israel, on Poplar Street.*

Green Polonius Hamilton (1867–1932) was one of Memphis's most distinguished early educators. Only eighteen when Wells wrote of him, he taught at the Kortrecht Grammar School, of which he was appointed principal in 1892, and published three books: Beacon Lights of the Race *(1911),* The Bright Side of Memphis *(1908), and* Booker T. Washington High School: Retrospective Prospective *(1927).*

Thursday, April 29

Monday no letters or papers arrived and I was kept so busy receiving visitors at school that I had no time at recess for anything. LeMoyne had a holiday that day & her students came over in great numbers. Messrs Mosely & McNeal called to see me Monday eve-

ning & we had a pleasant visit. While they were here Mr. Lawson
came to the door and handed me a note. Little thinking of the contents I toyed carelessly with it—but on my utter surprise when
opening it, I found it to be a notification that I had circulated the
report that he wearied me with his attentions! He wrote to beg pardon for the one offence of having asked my company once assuring
me it would not happen again. I was very angry and shocked; I
racked my brain trying to remember anything I might have said
that could be so construed but could not—and wrote & told him so
& repeated what I *had* said. I desired to know who of my friends (?)
had told him any such thing so requested him to call the next afternoon. He did so but would not tell me his author, but promised to
do so at some future day. I can't conceive any one trying to injure
me maliciously but some one has and is continually doing so. I may
be doing I. J. G[raham] an injustice but I believe it was he. I hope
not, but the mere thought has incensed me so against him that I cannot bear him. Letter from Mrs. Rice Tuesday telling me I would
have to be there in June to stand examination when I am not sure
school will be closed here. It is impossible for me to be the[re] at the
time set. I wrote immediately and told her so & received one from
aunt F[annie] yesterday imparting the same information. So, I
know not whether to go or not. I shall have to be guided by circumstances. Wrote to Mr. J[ones] but C[harles] S. M[orris]'s letter
is still unanswered. I had hoped I was entirely out of the party the
girls intend giving but it seems that is not to be for Fan[nie] Thompson gave my name to Mrs. B[radshaw] & she has issued invitations
to company for me. I am vexed and perplexed. I know not what to
do. In consideration of Aunt F[annie]'s letter & the small amount
of money I've sent her I am not able and feel it to be doing her an
injustice to spend money in frolic when she is bearing all the load.
I was not able to buy that dress but did so & now I am to be drawn
into something else expensive & profitless against my will. I trust
to time & fortune to extricate myself. On the other hand owing to
the peculiar position in which I am placed before the young men of
the place, if it were known that I rejected him on that score, it
would only serve to intensify the feeling against me. Went to hear
an address from Col. Keating on the opening of the school of manual training, and was agreeably surprised by a rare treat from Rabbi
Samfield. It's the first time I ever heard a Jewish intellectual dis-

course. Started an article on it last night but did not finish it. Went
to take a lesson yesterday and found Mr. Hamilton there. In a subsequent conversation Mr. Lott made me very angry by declaring I
only was amiable to men in order to repulse them and attributing
every thing to me that is associated with a heartless flirt. It made me
very angry and I left; I am strongly in doubt whether to ever go
again. I have been so long misrepresented that I begin to rebel. I
should not have allowed it [to] go so far without rebuke. No "Freeman," "Enterprise," have made an appearance this week.

*WELLS's assessment for the "entertainment" was $1.50, which she paid
to Fannie J. Bradshaw, a sister teacher, whom she did not particularly
like and always addressed formally as "Mrs. B." In spite of her reluc-
tance, she went to the party and "enjoyed [herself] hugely." She participated in a group dance, which she calls a "set," for the first time.*

Thursday, May 6

I had no choice but to pay my assessment and go to the entertainment last week, so tried to sell my encyclopedia to raise the money
without breaking my $10. but I could not. So I bought two pairs
of drawers (90 cts.), paid Mrs. B[radshaw] 1.50 & Mrs. Settle $6.00
for half the month of April lacking one dollar. Borrowed Mrs. F's
diamonds(?) for the occasion and wore my black silk. Enjoyed myself hugely and Mr. G[raham] handed me a verse declaring he knew
I loved him & he longed to sip the nectar from my curling lip. I received it in silence, but intended keeping it. Mr. M[arcus] attempted familiarity that I quickly resented. Was on the floor in a set
for the first time in my life and got through better than I expected.
Mr. Dardis asked me to read a piece for his concert next week and
altho' it is such short notice I shall do something because I wish to
be present at his concert but am not able to pay anything & have
long ceased expecting company. Went over to see Mrs. Thompson
& we did not decide on anything. I like Lady Mac[beth]'s soliloquy
& sleepwalking scene but it is almost impossible to arrange it. I will
give that or "Le Marriage de Convenience" or "The Doom of
Claudius & Cynthia." Came home & slept till 3 o'clock when

Misses Hamilton & Barnes calling—Mrs. S[ettle] awoke me. Saw Mr. Humphries of Miss[issippi] who will call soon he says. To church Sunday & Episcopal in the afternoon—home & bed sunday evening early. George was in Saturday afternoon & gave me $1.15 to add to his $1.70. His pile grows slowly. His pictures are very good indeed. No letter Monday or papers. Tuesday a letter from Mr. P[oole] in answer to the note I sent with his letters over a week ago. He calls me the twin mate of his soul and I know not that he is not telling the truth, and asks me to write again and let him know I received his letter which was sent to a new address. Had a talk with G[raham] that day and requested that we be more civil in our treatment of each other especially in the presence of strangers. I told him I desired always to do right but failed sometimes, and I think I convinced him of my sincerity. He called that evening and remained till after Mr. S[ettle] had gone. He asked me to kiss him, but I gently but firmly refused. Another lost opportunity of his, for springing the question that evidently seems uppermost in his mind. I believe he loves me, but he is certainly very enigmatical in his behavior. Have seen nothing of L[ouis] M. B[rown] for nearly two weeks; shall not ask him why he did not come when he arrives. Mr. West was here Monday night and we played checkers for some time. No callers last night but a letter yesterday from Mr. Jones. No letters today and as there was a rainstorm this afternoon, I settled myself for a good long evening of study but alas for the perpetuity of human hopes! I had 4 callers tonight who came in simultaneously and remained the same length of time except H[umphries], who left on business. They were Messrs. Lawson & Humphries, Messrs Huyette and McGee from Kansas City; the latter brought a letter of introduction from Mr. Jones. We four spent a pleasant agreeable evening. Shall write to Mr. J[ones] tonight.

SAMUEL ALLEN MCELWEE was a member of the Tennessee State Legislature, and, in 1887, he made an impassioned speech underscoring the "wrong and outrage perpetrated upon the Negroes by mob violence" (Simmons [1887] 1968, 97). Holmes Cummins served as the attorney for the Chesapeake, Ohio and Southwestern Railroad in the Wells case.

Sunday, May 9

A letter from my aunt, Friday who wants me to decide what to do; she thinks I ought to be sure of something. Went to the literary Friday night. Went to recite Saturday but have made no choice of a piece yet. Went up town for my dress but it was not finished. Met Mr. McAlwee who walked up the street with me & spoke of coming to see me. George is thinking of going to California. Saw Mr. F[roman] who told me of the dirty method Mr. Cummins is attempting to quash my case. He ordered him to stop it. I honor & respect "my dad" highly. A letter from C[harles] S. M[orris] that was lengthy, bright, and witty in the extreme; also a card from Mr. Mosely that I am undecided about answering. Answered "Charlie's" letter today & called him by his christian name. Don't know how he will take it. Wrote no other letters and remained indoors all day. Went nowhere & had no callers.

WELLS *probably attended the game in the new facility for professional baseball that was built on Orleans just south of Vance.*

Ida Atkins was a teacher at the Winchester School, located on Front Street.

Tuesday, May 19

No callers last week and only a letter from Mr. Jones, who wishes to know what I mean by "man of the world." The schoolboard paid two months Sat. and I paid all outstanding debts except Menken's, Mrs. Thompson, Mr. Lott; paid my board up to June 1st, sent aunt F[annie] $10, and today deposited $50. in bank. Bought Mrs. G[raham] a parasol for $2. nearly and have $15. with which to pay all others. I thank God for that. Saturday evening I went to the baseball park & saw a professional game for the first time, but lost my temper & acted in an unladylike way toward those in whose company I was & hardly noticed L[ouis] M. B[rown]. Went in the afternoon to pay Fannie H[amilton] a call, but she was not there, from there went to Ida's to see Miss Harvey, whom I liked very much. Received a letter from Cal[ifornia] & the children's pictures which are splendid.

WELLS probably went horseback riding at Hernando Trotting Park, located two miles away from the center of town on the old Hernando Road. She would have taken the Hernando streetcar (a mule-driven vehicle), which ran within a quarter mile of the park.

Sunday, May 23

I had a terrible fall from a horse yesterday afternoon. Started out riding a strange horse who, I was told, was afraid of the streetcars, & the first one I met, he ran up on the mules & began rearing and plunging. I was terribly frightened but kept my seat until we got a little to one side, when the horse's leg became entangled in the traces & that threw him and I went over his back, & fell on my back; the small of my back is swollen & painful yet, where I struck. I was very uneasy for fear some of my bones were broken or my spine injured some way & I do not know yet if such is not the case. I think of my escape with a solemn thankfulness. Received letters from Mr. M[cGee] and Mr. Jones. No letter from "Charlie" yet. Mr. L[ouis] M. B[rown] came by and tarried quite a while last night. Answered the two first of my number & wrote to G[ate] C[ity] P[ress]. Received a telegram from my aunt today saying the examination would be held June 15th and telling me to come immediately. I don't know what to do, my business is not arranged to leave on such short notice.

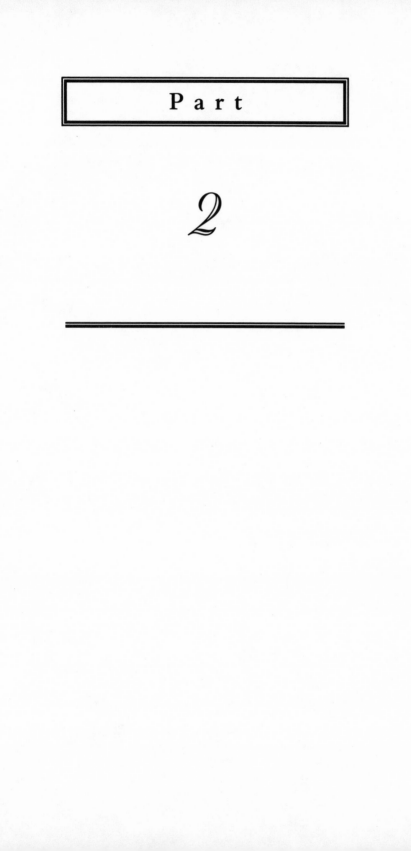

Part

2

Exorcising the Demon of Unrest and Dissatisfaction

June 3–September 14, 1886

*T*HE summer of 1886 is an exciting time of change and of experimentation for Ida B. Wells: the butterfly is clearly spreading her wings. She takes a long trip out West, traveling by train through Missouri, Kansas, Colorado, Utah, and California. She writes a short story, outlines a novel, and describes her travels in articles to the *Watchman*, the *Gate City Press*, and the *A.M.E. Church Review*. She meets prominent Blacks, including a school principal from Indiana, the state auditor of Kansas, a candidate for the Colorado State Legislature, and the editor of San Francisco's major Black newspaper. She is wined and dined by editors and clubwomen, by teachers and doctors in Kansas City, Topeka, and San Francisco; she goes on carriage rides with handsome gentlemen, visits fancy hotels and resorts, and attends dinners and receptions. Wells is constantly on the move, a restless and adventurous young woman of twenty-four, torn between duty to her family and desire for deeper, more fulfilling experiences: travel, education, writing, a professional career, and a loving relationship with a man.

She begins the summer with great expectations. It is June, the schools are closed, and she has a full calendar of social activities: picnics, concerts, and a party with members of the Golden Star Club. In the hectic weeks following the end of the term, she is busy washing, ironing, sewing, shopping, visiting friends in Woodstock, and packing for her first major trip—to a national convention in Topeka, Kansas. On July 4, 1886, she and several other teachers leave Memphis for a brief stay in Kansas City, Missouri, before going on to a meeting of the National Educational Association in Topeka. From there, she joins a GAR (Grand Army of the Republic) tour to San Francisco and continues to Visalia, California, where she spends a month and a half with her Aunt Fannie. She sells her return ticket to Memphis and begins teaching in Visalia's one-room school for Blacks to assist her aunt in raising her two younger sisters.

The summer of 1886 is also a time for reflection and deep introspection, a time for confronting, openly and honestly, the complex woman whom she has become. Although Wells writes enthusiastically about "enjoying existence," she often feels lonely and isolated from others, as she explains in the entries of June 12 and August 9. In the first, she describes her longing for the "might have been" (the education she did not complete), her feelings of inadequacy in comparison with a more "tractable" and "ladylike" young woman, and her recollection of pain on meeting a former lover, now married to another woman. In August, she laments her isolation in Visalia, a small, hot, dusty town, founded by former slaveowners. She is among the few Blacks—transplanted Southerners, for the most part—in that "dull" town, and she chafes at the hard work and restrictions in her aunt's home. As a consequence, Wells makes the only decision that she can make—to hold onto her hard-won freedom and independence by leaving Visalia.

Resolute in the face of opposition, and determined to have her way, she is often in conflict with other people: Aunt Fannie, who wants her to remain in Visalia; men, who accuse her of being a heartless flirt; and teachers, resentful of preferential treatment for an "outsider." Some of the conflicts are of her own making because she is, at times, indecisive, impulsive, and temperamental. In her entries of August and September, for example, it is interesting to watch her vacillate between staying in Visalia, taking a job in Kansas City, and returning to Memphis, all the while keeping her options open. It is even more fascinating to read her rationalizations: "[I]f I am re-elected will return . . . [B]ut it will be a better money plan [to remain in Visalia]. . . . But if I stay, I can save money. . . . I know not if I will ever have another chance." Incredibly, she manages to teach in three cities in one month, but finally chooses what is right for her, as opposed to what others consider her duty. Perceptive and insightful, Wells fully understands the roots of her restlessness and dissatisfaction—ambition for a fuller life. Her problem at this stage in her life is that she is not sure in what direction to channel her ambition: she does not like teaching, but needs the steady income; she enjoys writing for newspapers, but receives little money for writing; she wants the company of men, but has no interest in marriage.

An unconventional single woman leading an adventurous and experimental life, Wells is often at the center of controversy and always in the middle of some mess, as she confesses in her diary and autobiography. She has a run-in, for example, with Messieurs Jones and McGee of Kansas City—"miserable excuses for manhood"— whom she accuses of social improprieties. When she returns to Kansas City in September to teach, she encounters the hostility of local teachers, who consider her—an "imported" teacher—to be a "disturbing influence" (Duster 1970, 30) in the schools. Quietly and discreetly, in this case, she resigns her position and leaves Kansas City.

In both incidents, Wells is misrepresented and misunderstood. Although she often complains about such misrepresentation, she also accepts responsibility for her "tempestuous, rebellious, hard headed willfulness" and her "disposition to question . . . authority." Ironically, it is the very qualities that problematize her personal relationships—her tenacity, rebelliousness, and disputatiousness— that will impel her to undertake, six years later, a courageous crusade against lynching.

THE exhibition that she describes in the following entry was a part of the school closing exercises of the public schools, and the picnic was an occasion for students and teachers to celebrate the end of the term.

In 1874, David Whittier Washington (1852–1930) was the first Black appointed as a letter carrier in Memphis. An astute businessman, he acquired extensive real estate holdings in the city.

Wells writes about a former beau, identified here only as Mr. C. (James B. Combs), whom she meets unexpectedly on a visit to Holly Springs. (See her entry for June 12.) Apparently, they were sweethearts when they attended Rust University; now, however, the gentleman is married and has a family.

I 8 8 6

Thursday, June 3

School is out & the exhibition attempted but it was a complete farce. The house was jammed & crowded & so noisy, we could hear nothing; so half the exercises were omitted. Am tired out—as we have been on the pad, night & day for nearly two weeks. Messrs Lee & Washington called Sunday and I received Charlie's long-looked-for letter Tuesday before going to school. He offers as consolation for the delay in his writing the thought that he has thought of me. Also wishes to know if I can come to Louisville this summer. I would like very much to go but fear I can't spell able. Won't answer his letter soon. Got one from Mr. Jones this morning & his letters assume a deeper love. I hardly know what to do.

Tuesday Mr. G[raham] came home with me & told me of his love for me & I reciprocated. I told him I was not conscious of an absorbing feeling for him but I thought it would grow. I feel so lonely and isolated and the temptation of a lover is irresistible. I should not like to go thro' another winter as wearily as heretofore. But its all so new and strange. The only thing I regret is I did not tell him the exact truth for he asked if I had loved any one since the rupture between myself & Mr. C[ombs] & I said no—I must rectify that mistake. I could not live under false colors. We went to the picnic next day and he was unvaryingly kind & attentive. Paid a woman 50 cts. to do my washing & ironed yesterday myself. Went to call on Misses Barnes & Hamilton in the afternoon. I shall patiently wait to see what the future shall bring forth. Mr. B[rown] was out last evening & we went walking; he had a debt to settle with me about Tuesday night's escapade & he talked in such a lofty strain & gave me withal some such good advice—enacted the real friend he professes to be—that I was agreeably surprised and delighted with him, when he soared above personal pique & forgot self in my behalf. He gave me a higher opinion of himself than I've had & I now begin to think of him as a friend to be kept. I have not kept the friends I have won, but will try from this on.

AFTER *leaving the post office on the corner of Second and Main streets and making a purchase, Wells went to the railroad station, where she met her cousin Stella and two friends. All the young women were natives of Holly Springs and/or graduates of Rust University, as were many other Blacks, like Robert R. Church, Benjamin F. Booth, and Green P. Hamilton, who moved to Memphis in search of greater opportunities. On the way to Holly Springs, the women prevailed against an attempt to move them out of the first-class coach.*

In Holly Springs, Ida stayed with Mrs. Rachel Rather, identified by the census of 1880 as a sixty-year-old widow, a servant from Virginia, who could neither read nor write. Many Blacks in Holly Springs—Ida's mother, Elizabeth "Lizzie" Warrenton Wells; Lizzie's two sisters; and the Wells's close friends, Mr. and Mrs. James Hall (guardians of the Wells children after their parents' death) and Mrs. Rachel Rather—reported in the census that they were originally from Virginia. Mr. and Mrs. Hall were James Hall, twenty-four in 1870, a mulatto laborer, and his wife Tilla. Rachel Rather is undoubtedly the friend who kept the Wells children after Ida's grandmother had a stroke. According to Wells, "I then found a woman who had been an old friend of my mother's to stay at the house with the children while I went out to my country school to teach" (Duster 1970, 17). Mrs. Rather was probably a surrogate mother to Lizzie Wells because, in 1870, she was fifty years old, to the younger woman's twenty-six.

Wells most likely attended the Asbury Methodist Church, where the Shaw University (now Rust University) was first located. The church was co-founded by the Reverend Albert Collier McDonald of the Freedmen's Aid Society, and the Reverend Moses Adams, a friend of Jim Wells's. The church is located near Court House Square, just a few blocks from Rust.

Holly Springs, Mississippi
Monday, June 7

Didn't decide until 12 o'clock Saturday to come to H[olly] S[prings] but after making my waist Friday, I went out walking. Received a letter from Mr. Jones Thursday & answered it & Charlie's & Mr. Mosely's & sent Charlie one of the pictures of my school. Went up town to mail my letters & got a wagon to bring me to the depot for 50 cts. Bought a waist for $1.25 and hurried to the depot where I found Fannie H[amilton], Susie B[arnes] and Stella B[utler] all bent on the same excursion as myself. Of course we had the usual trouble about the first-class coach but we conquered. Am stopping at Mrs. Rather's and having a very pleasant time. Went to church 4 times yesterday and spent a very pleasant time; met many old friends & acquaintances among whom were Willis S, Henry A[nderson], Annie T, Lucy Mc, Victor T, and spent a very pleasant time; the first two came home & spent the afternoon. Henry A[nderson] went to church with me & Mrs. L. S. Rust talked last night. Wrote a letter to L[ouis] M. B[rown] & a card to I. J. G[raham]. Went to Rust today & spent the time in the recitation rooms. Gave H[enry] A. my picture.

THE *following entry is one of the most interesting of Wells's diary because she examines her past life, repents former misdeeds, admits character flaws, and depicts two models of womanhood.*

Unlike diarist Alice Dunbar-Nelson, Ida B. Wells reveals very little color consciousness, one of the preoccupations of nineteenth-century Blacks. In her description of Annie, a former classmate, she raises the question of color for the first and last time. Her daughter Alfreda noted in an interview that the Wells children, descendants of White and Black grandparents, varied in color: "Annie looked white; Ida and Lily [were] mulatto; and George and Jim [were] lighter than Ida or Lily" (Duster 1976).

Wells's portrait of her classmate Annie synthesizes the archetypal mulatta and the Victorian lady. Professor Hooper, a White teacher at Rust, privileges the Black "lady," but Wells recognizes that it is not Annie's color or intelligence that he esteems but her "obedient disposition." Here, Wells suggests a connection between race and gender, but it will be several years before she explores, theoretically and systematically, the sexualization of racism.

Her characterization of Miss Atkinson owes much to the ideology of puritanical Victorianism, propagated by White missionary teachers at Rust University. Inspired by evangelical Methodism, and viewing their work as a Christian civilizing mission, these teachers enforced an ethic of self-discipline, self-help, and service, maintaining that "the adornment of young women [should] be that of character and intelligence" (Houghton, n.d., 6). This model of feminine womanhood deeply im-

pressed Wells, who uses the metaphors of romantic poetry and the language of sentimental novels in describing Miss Atkinson.

Frank Epps, twenty years old, was the son of Prince and Sarah Epps, and his sisters were teachers. In the 1880 census, John Hibbler was identified as a "mulatto, male, 20, boarder, at school." The census describes James B. Combs, Wells's former boyfriend, as a "mulatto, 26, boarder, from Georgia." Like other out-of-town students attending Rust, he boarded with Holly Springs families while attending school. Wells does not identify, here or elsewhere, her "cousin L." Perhaps she is a sister (or brother) of Stella Butler's.

Memphis
Saturday, June 12

Left Holly Springs on Thursday as the crowd came that day and am here. I spent a very pleasant time at home, better than ever before. Monday night we went to the college in a bus to witness the literary exercises, Frank Epps going with me. We had a jolly good time and enjoyed it immensely. Tuesday was commencement day and after those exercises came the alumni exercises which, tho' long were interesting. As I witnessed the triumph of the graduates and thought of my lost opportunity a great sob arose in my throat and I yearned with unutterable longing for the "might have been." When Will said to me afterward: "Ida, you ought to come back here and graduate," I could not restrain my tears at the sense of injustice I felt, and begged him not to ask me why I said "I could not." I quickly conquered that feeling and as heartily wished the graduates joy as tho' no bitterness had mingled with my pleasure. I had heard it asserted before I got to H[olly] S[prings] that Will & Annie would be married but the time was near at hand and I had met no one who could tell me positively that it would happen, or that had received an invitation, but an idea prevailed that it would be at the "students reunion" so all went & assembled themselves in the chapel and waited. Their waiting was not in vain, for they walked in after a while and were married as unpretentiously as possible; the ceremony, pronounced by Prof. H[ooper] was solemnly & impressively beautiful. He has watched over and shielded Annie ever since he has been there, and it was but fitting that he should be proud of the successful termination of his care. When thinking over it the

next day & endeavoring to find an adequate reason for his particular
interest & care for her, I decided that it was not—as I used to think
in my childish rage & jealousy at his evident preference for her—
because of her color (for there have been others who were brighter
in color and withal prettier than she and yet who won not his favor);
it was not her high intellectual powers (for many I know were more
brilliant, Florence especially was more intellectual yet he interested
himself not in their behalf as in Annie's) and so I've come to the
conclusion that it was her obedient disposition, her extreme tract-
ableness and therefore easily controlled and her evident ladylike refinement and where I think of my tempestuous, rebellious, hard
headed wilfulness, the trouble I gave, the disposition to question his
authority—I remember that Mr. H[ooper] is but human and I no
longer cherish feelings of resentment, nor blame him that my scho-
lastic career was cut short; my own experience as a teacher enables
me to see more clearly and I know that I was to blame. I congratulated them both heartily and was cordially received. Was introduced to Miss Atkinson the music teacher, who seemed so fair and
pure, so divinely good, whose motions were grace & poetry personified—she seemed to me, one of the few women that I have met
who come near justifying the ravings of poets and proving their
metaphors not inspired alone by the imagination. She seems so
thoroughly pleasant, so bubbling over with an effervescence of
youth, health, high spirits, cheerfulness and withal such an exu-
berance of vitality in every look or motion that every one is
charmed without knowing why. She is quite young—just from college and when she is toned down somewhat, will be a truly noble-
minded woman. Was introduced to Messrs Forbes & Hibbler—the
former went home with me, the latter called next day but I was not
at home; both seem to be thoughtful entertaining gentlemen.
Wednesday had several callers & in the afternoon when it cleared
up, went to see Aunt Rachel R[ather]; from there I came to cousin
L's to dinner and we had a splendid one! Ate so much and stayed so
long is why I missed Mr. H[ibbler]. The boys gave a sociable(?) to
the visiting girls that evening and sent Mr. Combs after us! I was
speechless with surprise when he presented himself with all his old
time sang froid and announced that he was our escort! We went but
I kept him at a respectful distance that did not allow a nearer ap-
proach, he did not attempt to go over it. His wife greeted me with

cordiality and as I manifested a desire to see the babies took me in & we had a chat. Left next morning and as my ticket was through mistake purchased for Illinois C[entral] R[ail] R[oad] I had to come that way with the crowd. George with his usual improvidence, went there with only enough money to carry him, depending on me to bring his money—as I did not, I had to leave him there. We were all day coming, as we stayed at the junction til 8 o'clock. Found letters from Preston T.—T. T[homas] Fortune and Mr. J[ones] who informed me he would leave for here the 14th, inst[ead]. I answered & mailed him a reply yesterday which I hope he will get before he leaves. I am very eager to see him and hope I'll not be disappointed. I am glad I'll not have to wait till I go to K[ansas] C[ity] to see him. Went to see Dr. Sinclair about my ear, & am to go again to day. Mr. I. J. G[raham] came out last night and I spent an agreeable evening in his society. He is very thin, poor fellow.

In the next two entries, Wells analyzes her relationships with men, including three Memphians and two correspondents. She confesses the contradiction in her desire to have male company without, however, entering into marriage and confesses that she is an anomaly even to herself. Although many of her friends, like Theresa Settle and Fannie Bradshaw, are married, she also has a circle of unmarried friends: the Misses Thompson, Barnes, and Hamilton.

Sallie Rather is one of eight children of Mr. and Mrs. Daniel Rather of Holly Springs, who was, perhaps, related to Mrs. Rachel Rather.

The A.M.E. Church Review, an organ of the African Methodist Episcopal Church, was one of the most important Black periodicals of the nineteenth century. The editor, the Reverend L. J. Coppin, was married to Fannie Jackson Coppin, an outstanding educator, and he encouraged Black women to write for the Review.

Tuesday, June 15

Mr. B[rown] and I took a long walk Saturday evening and he told me some things that surprised me a little—especially about his loving me. He said he'd carefully guarded against such as I was just the kind of girl of whom he would become infatuated. I begged him not to spoil all by any such course; whereupon he said, as many others have, that he did not believe I had any heart or could love anyone. I did not endeavor to change his belief. He furthermore said; that he thought Mr. G[raham] idolized me; I neither affirmed nor denied the statement. Sunday I went to the doctor and then to Collins Chapel to afternoon service. Mr. Mosely preached. It was fearfully warm and as we were coming home a heavy rainstorm came up. Luckily we were on the cars. He came home with me and remained all the afternoon. He also, thinks I have no heart. Mr. B[rown] came that night and we spent a cozy evening together despite the rain. He told me all about his engagement with Miss C. of Ga. He is the embodiment of frankness. With me, my affairs are always at one extreme or the other. I either have an abundance of company or none at all. Just now there are three in the city who, with the least encouragement, would make love to me; I have two correspondents in the same predicament—but past experience will serve to keep me from driving them from me. I am enjoying existence very much just now; I don't wonder longer, but will enjoy life as it comes. I am an anomaly to my self as well as to others. I do not wish to be married but I do wish for the society of the gentlemen. Received a letter from Charlie yesterday and answered immediately. He is bubbling over with fun & nonsense and wishes to know how "that sister" looks. Wrote to Sallie R[ather] also, asking her to come up on the 28th. Am assured that I will be re-elected to my position but am afraid to leave until I know it as a certainty. Will write to Mrs. Bowser today also answer Messrs Taylor's & Fortune's letter. No message or letter from Mr. Jones yet. Would have washed yesterday but it rained all day & is raining now. My railroad case will not come up in the supreme court this term. Gave Henrietta F. a note to Mr. Payne today as she is in search of a school, and she seemed to take it as her due. Of course I don't wish any one to bow down and worship me but I would like them to express gratitude for an attempted favor.

Preserve me from narrowness & bigotry, I sincerely pray. Received a copy of the A.M.E. Church Review this morning and a letter from the editor asking an article from my brilliant (?) pen. I have not decided on accepting as yet. Also received C[harles] S. M[orris]'s "Journal"; it is very good as a beginning but rather abrupt.

DR. ALEXANDER G. SINCLAIR *was a White eye, ear, and throat specialist with offices in the Masonic Temple. Moses Strickland owned a secondhand furniture store at 235 Second Street.*

Throughout her diary, Wells relied heavily on two older men for advice and support. Businessman Alfred Froman shared her interest in journalism; in 1872, he was a successful printer and business manager of the Memphis Weekly Planet. *A family friend, he escorted Wells to the theater and took her home from a party. Louis Payne, a Woodstock teacher or principal, gave jobs to her brothers, visited her in Memphis, and invited her to his home in Shelby County. Other men like J. T. Settle, her landlord, tried to monitor her personal behavior, particularly her relationships with men.*

Wells describes the courtship patterns of middle-class Black Southerners in the late nineteenth century, when girls adhered to a rigorous code of behavior, taught by women and enforced by men.

Monday, June 28

It rained every day of the week in which I made my last entry and I did not get to washing until Friday. Going to the Dr. every day about my ear bothered me somewhat. Earnest C. came to see me one evening, and Mr. M[osely] another. Received a letter from Mr. Jones Friday morning explaining why he did not come. Mrs. S[ettle], Mrs. B[radshaw] and myself went to confirmation Thursday evening and L[ouis] M. B[rown] came after we returned and stayed some time. Mrs. B[radshaw] stayed all night and we had a long confab & came nearer being acquainted than ever before.

Went up town to get our salary from the Board Friday morning and I also went to the Dr. again. Hurried home & went to Mrs. Turner's to washing and Mr. Graham came while I was away, and did not return that night. He left me without a farewell & I thought he would return but he did not. I don't know how to take him. He is either afraid to trust me, or does not care for me one. I am too proud to beg but I must be loved with more warmth than that. Saturday morning I went with Mrs. Graham to the Dr. and paid him $3.00 for myself. Put her on the cars to go home and went to see Mr. Strickland about that furniture, but he was not in. Went to Menken's & paid him $69.—my whole indebtedness to him & thank God it shall be my last. Put $40. in the bank which makes $90

to my account. Received a letter from aunt F[annie] who is very angry and disappointed because I did not come to California. Answered and tried to pacify her as much as I could. Intended to go
and iron on Saturday but Mr. Payne came for me & I went home
with him and stayed a week. Just returned day before yesterday.
Endeavored to make some entries while there but had no ink and
very little time for this as I was pretty busy all the time. Wrote to
L[ouis] M. B[rown]—P[aul] J[ones]—and a card to Mrs. Turner on
Sunday and took a walk in the afternoon with George. Sewed all
the week very near and made four garments. Washed and ironed
also and my clothes are so pretty & white. Received a letter from
L[ouis] M. B[rown] while there, in which he told me about dread-
ing my influence as he was afraid he was falling in love with me,
also that he was going to Washington. I answered and told him not
to do either, and assured him I would in response to his pleadings
be in on Saturday, also told him I believed him incapable of love in
its strongest, best sense. I came in early Saturday and found letters
from Messrs Taylor, Fortune, Jones, Mosely, McGee, and cards
from I. J. G[raham] and Mrs. M. I wrote immediately to Messrs
Taylor & Mc[Gee], telling the former what to give me as a birthday
present and asking the latter to write and tell me immediately what
he means by his warning regarding a stopping place. Have answered none of the others as yet. Went up town Saturday eve. and
visited several places. Mr. B[rown] came out and persuaded me to
go walking with him & he forced me to our trysting place. I weakly
yielded to his importunities to be seated and then he too told me a
tale of love and asked me directly if I were pledged to any one. I
could not say yea, and I did say nay. For with all the encouragement
I've given G[raham] he has not sought to bind me to him & seems
so utterly indifferent that I don't and can't feel that I belong to him.
I told Mr. B[rown] I did not love him, but I was sorry that would
cause a cessation of his visits. He talked sometime longer and then
begged so hard for the right to pay his addresses to me to hope, that
I could not satisfactorily give. But he kissed me—twice—& it
seems even now as if they blistered my lips. I feel so humiliated in
my own estimation at the thought that I cannot look any one
straight in the face. I feel somehow as if I were defrauded of something since then. I came home and lay thinking of the awkward predicament I am in and the remark made by Mr. Settle the other

morning at the breakfast-table recurred to me, "you are playing with edged tools" and I feel that I have degraded myself in that I had not the courage to repulse the one or the other. I know not which of the two I prefer—One has qualities the other does not possess & I cannot choose between them. I don't think I want either for a husband but I would miss them sadly as friends—and of course that would be an intermission of friendship if I said nay. But God helping me, I will free myself from this predicament, some-how and I pray for tact and judgment so to do wisely but firmly. It seems I can establish no middle ground between me and my visi-tors—it is either love or nothing. Went to church yesterday morn-ing and saw Fan[nie] Thompson, who tells me they will have berths & all the ladies will take the sleeper. I am unable and unwilling to do so, especially the round about trip they will take on the C[hesapeake] O[hio] & S[outh]W[estern] R[ail]R[oad] and think I'll take the regular K[ansas] C[ity] route. Slept all the afternoon and rose & dressed just about time Mr. B[rown] made his appearance on the scene. I scarcely spoke to him directly and Mrs. S[ettle] came in and helped to entertain him. He made an engagement for Tues-day evening. Went with Mrs. S[ettle] to the guild and from there went to do some shopping. Met Will. S., Matt. D. and Henry A[nderson] on my way home and the last named came home with me and remained to supper. L[ouis] M. B[rown] came in and was introduced. We played logamachy and they stayed till late. H[enry] seems backward and constrained in the presence of strangers.

SEVERAL *Memphis teachers, including Wells, planned to travel to a meeting of the National Educational Association in Topeka, Kansas, in July with a stop in Kansas City, Missouri. Paul Jones and Mr. McGee of Kansas City, with whom she had corresponded for several months, offered to make room reservations for Wells, but she questioned the pro-priety of permitting them to make such arrangements. The delegation left Memphis at 4:00 P.M., July 4, on the Kansas City, Springfield and Memphis Railroad, traveling 488 miles to Kansas City, where they spent several days, before continuing to Topeka.*

Julia Britton Hooks (1852–1942), dubbed the "Angel of Beale Street," was born in Frankfort, Kentucky, and attended Berea College. An accomplished musician, she moved to Memphis in 1876, taught in

the public schools, and founded the Hooks Cottage School. Wells prob-
ably attended a concert of classical music sponsored by the Liszt-Mullard
Club, a musical group active in the 1880s. Mrs. Turner was the wife of
J. T. Turner, a teacher, and Mrs. Mosby was the wife of Cash Mosby,
who organized railroad excursions between Memphis and other South-
ern cities.

Sunday, July 4

We have definitely concluded to go on the excursion which leaves
this afternoon for the west. Am all in a turmoil as to what I shall do
and how get out of the predicament in which I am placed. Received
another letter from Mr. Mc[Gee] Tuesday in which he was more
explicit and yet made no specifications. I carried the letter to
F[annie] J. B[radshaw] and she said it was not worth attention and
for us to adhere to our original decision. I immediately sent him
word that we would come and stop where we had originally intended as we had a cordial invitation to do so & were not disposed
to throw over old friends without cause. Went to Mrs. H[ooks]'s
concert & recited "The Letter Reading" & Sleep-walking scenes
from "Lady McBeth." The first was loudly applauded the last,
given in my Mother Hubbard was not so effective as I could have
wished. Mr. B[rown] seemed very cold & contrary that night and
I wondered where the glamour of his presence was. Wednesday I
washed & ironed at Mrs. Turner's but did not finish in time to attend Mrs. Mosby's funeral. Expected Mr. G[raham] out but he
came not and as I needed rest, I retired early. Ironed some Thursday
and sewed the rest of the day. Thursday eve L[ouis] M. B[rown]
came to pay his farewell respects. Or at least we started walking up
street, but I was afraid he wished me to go to our usual resort and
I affected to be very tired. Friday we went to Mrs. Hill's and stayed
all day and had a delightful dinner. We came home in the cool of
the evening and found letters awaiting us. One from Mr. P[aul]
J[ones] requesting the same as Mr. McGee about our stopping-
place and informing me he had procured a place for us. Had he not
spoken so positively and concluded by affirming that the Rector of
one of the churches here had endorsed his motives and gone with
him to procure us a place & if we would telegraph when we started
would have a carriage in waiting. I submitted this letter to Mrs. Set-

tle's judgment & she advised that we stop not at all. That was the best thing I saw to do and I wrote him to say we would not come at all and the same to Mrs. Bowser. Fan[nie] B[radshaw] objected to my ruling and insisted that I send him a telegram and I did so, stating that we would be there and for him to look for us. Went to a social of the Golden Star club Friday evening and enjoyed myself hugely. Mr. Robert Lee accompanied me. Recited "Widder Budd" for their amusement. Mr. G[raham] came before we went tho' and informed me he had been there twice before. Dr. Smith of Murfreesboro was to see me Tuesday & very indignant over his bad treatment by the deacons of the church as he was not employed as he was led to believe. I could offer nothing in extenuation because I knew he spoke truly. Mr. Mosely was in a few minutes Wednesday evening on his way to church & promised to come again later in the week to bid me goodby. Saturday morning first thing I went to town to get my jewelry as a letter & card from Mr. T[aylor] informed me was for me at the express office. It was his birthday gift & I could not wait to get home before I opened the box. They are just lovely. As my keys have been lost all of last week, I took my writing desk to town to have it filed open & when I returned found my keys where I had hidden them over a week before. Drew $85. all the money I have in the world from the bank and then came home. The rest of the day was spent in packing. As the convention was held on same day I expected & received no callers. Today I've been nowhere as I wished to keep my clothes all clean. We start about four this afternoon. I sincerely hope we'll have a pleasant trip and every thing turn out all right.

AMONG the Memphians attending the conference were Wells's friends *Fannie J. Bradshaw, Fannie Thompson, I. J. Graham, A. Love, A. Sidney J. Burchett, a physician, and B. K. Sampson, principal of the Kortrecht Grammar School.*

They went, first, to Kansas City, a grain market, industrial complex, and cattle-trading center, located on the bluffs of the Missouri River. The Black population (8,100 in 1880) was scattered from West Bottoms to Quality Hill, where a small middle class of doctors, dentists, and businessmen had homes. Those who entertained Wells included Bowser, editor of the Gate City Press, *and teachers Yates and Coles.*

Apparently angry over the housing arrangements that Jones and McGee had made for her, she stayed with the Bowsers.

Kansas City, Missouri
Thursday, July 8

Have been in the city four days and this is the first opportunity I've had to record the sayings & doings of the people whom I've met & the impressions of the country I've received. We had the most pleasant trip as we took a sleeper with a chair compartment attached and we stayed in that most of the time. The gentlemen were attentive and kind, and my first experience with a sleeper was by no means unpleasant. Until we got to St. Louis all went merry as a marriage bell but at that place they put us in a dingy old car that was very unpleasant, but thanks to Dr. Burchett we at last secured a very pleasant place in a chair car & the rest of the ride was comparatively pleasant. When we reached this place no one presented himself as Mr. Jones so we moved aimlessly about until Mr. & Mrs. Bowser came up and insisted on our going to supper if we returned to leave on the 10 o'clock train. We decided to stay till Wednesday & as Mr. G[raham] got left he stayed till next day. The next morning or rather that evening we went down to the church to an entertainment and were introduced to hundreds of folks—remembering their names no longer than they were spoken. I saw Mr. McGee & had a long talk with him. I explained our peculiar position & the embarrassment I felt in accepting the hospitality of people who, he had assured me, bore a bad reputation. My constraint was natural & I felt indignant that their statements had caused me to act so aimlessly and disconnectedly. He was sorry he had written and etc. I found there had been a personal altercation between Mr. J[ones] & this family & Mr. Mc[Gee] is a spy or proxy for him as he does not come here. Mr. M[arcus] came again the next day trying to plaster up for him but I treated him coldly and intimated that I thought it strange he could accept the hospitality of folks he still contends are not socially correct nor morally pure. We met a great many at an informal entertainment Mrs. Bowser had that evening, and enjoyed ourselves hugely. But have not laid eyes on Mr. J[ones] yet. He sent an invitation to go carriage riding yesterday for Fan[nie] T[hompson] and myself, but I was advised not to accept it *ith other convention delegates, she signed up for a half-fare GAR ...nd Army of the Republic) tour to San Francisco with stops in sev-...ities. The excursion gave her an opportunity to travel, write, and ...her family in California, as she notes: "As I had never done any ...ing, it would give me a chance to take advantage of these excursions ...see my aunt and get her consent to come back to Memphis. I went ...rote letters back to the Living Way describing Kansas City, To-...the Garden of the Gods, Denver, Salt Lake City, San Francisco, ...ch, all along the line" (Duster 1970, 24). After a day and a half ...Atchison, Topeka and Santa Fe Railroad, she reached Pueblo, ...ado, a center of iron and steel production, called the "Pittsburgh of ...est." The next stop was Colorado Springs, a "utopia of refinement ...upper class," built as a resort in 1871. It was called "Little Lon-...because of the British flavor of the shops, restaurants, and parks. ...spent the next day, Sunday, at Manitou Springs, the "Saratoga ...West," famous for its eight mineral springs. Once the land of the ...nd Comanches, the resort area was located in the Rocky Moun-...with Pike's Peak looming in the distance.*

...m there, she proceeded to Denver. Located on the Platte River, ...r had become a large distribution center with a population that ...rom 35,629 in 1880 to 106,713 in 1890. The city had saloons ...tels, warehouses and foundries, flour mills and stockyards, smelt-...l packing plants. Among its most impressive landmarks was the ...Grand Opera House, built by H. A. W. Tabor. In Denver, Wells ...ttorney James H. Stuart, a native of Tennessee, who set up his ...actice in Topeka in 1878.

Denver, Colorado
Tuesday, July 20

...e time in Topeka the three days I was there. Met many of ...ers from different parts. Prof. Sampson called on us as ...e heard of our being in T[opeka] & later on he brought ...Boyd, Cunningham & Vance to see us. Fan[nie] ...on] & I went out with the two latter to a speech making ...the colored churches but left before it was over. Spent the ...r of the time visiting the capitol building where I saw ...the present auditor of Kansas. He is a very polished

and I thought it a duty to my hostess to defer to her ruling as she is supposed to know people better than I. I did not, but requested my mail to be sent up to me & have written Mrs. S[ettle] to not send any if she has not done so. I guess I'll go from K[ansas] C[ity] as much of a stranger as I came here. For I hear he drinks & Mr. Fleming reported, as I forced him to do, verbatim the very rough conversation he held with him on my account and he has fallen steadily in my estimation. Have met Messrs Yates and Coles who have made themselves very agreeable. They are teachers in the schools. Have written to L[ouis] M. B[rown], Mrs. S[ettle], and must write to Mr. F[ortune] tonight—also a letter to The Watchman. Mrs. Bowser gave an informal reception to us Tuesday eve.

ALTHOUGH *the following entry was written in Topeka, much of it deals with people whom Wells had met and events that had transpired in Kansas City. On July 13, the Memphians reached Topeka, where racial tensions were exacerbated by the influx of Exodusters, Blacks from Missouri, Kentucky, and Tennessee who fled the South between 1869 and 1880. These migrants lived in neighborhoods like Tennesseetown, Redmonsville, and Up in the Sands, where they soon established churches, fraternal orders, lodge halls, schools, literary clubs, a YMCA, the Colored Women's Suffrage Association, and six newspapers, including the* Colored Citizen, *the* Tribune, *and the* Kansas State Ledger. Wells *celebrated her twenty-fourth birthday on July 16, 1886, with a tour of the city, but spent most of her time at meetings and receptions.*

The National Teachers Association was organized in Philadelphia, in 1857, and, although the name was changed in 1870 to the National Educational Association, Wells used the old name. Several thousand teachers, including about one hundred Blacks, attended sessions on such topics as "The Problem of Race Education in the United States." It was an integrated conference. Topekans on the committee for the reception on July 11 at Representative Hall included Edwin P. McCabe, a Black, elected state auditor on the Republican ticket in 1882. (McCabe and Paul Jones, the Kansas City "cur," were friends and native Chicagoans.)

Prominent Black Topekans, including attorneys James H. Guy and Wesley I. Jamison, hosted a reception for about "seventy-five teachers from abroad," according to the Topeka Daily Capital *(July 16, 1886).*

Topeka, Kansas
Tuesday, July 13

After a whole week of excitement and dissipation in Kansas City we left this morning for this place and are here. Met many very pleasant acquaintances while there among whom were Messrs Martin, Nash, Commodore, Perkins, Towsen, Edwards, Pettiford, Mr & Mrs Teeters, Mr & Mrs Blunk, Mr. and Mrs. Lucas, Mr & Mrs Andrews, Misses Jordan, Linwood, Warner, Moore, and Mrs. Sprague were among the most prominent we met besides Mrs. B. B. Brown, Mr. Fleming, Mr. Huyette and several others we knew before coming. Mr. Towsen took us the first ride thro' the city in a carriage, we also visited the cable line, engine house & the Coates Hotel that day besides a ride on the cable. Next day we went shopping & had our pictures taken. Thursday evening we went to Mrs. Andrews' to an entertainment, Mr. Coles accompanying me and we had a royal time. Received via Mr. Jones 3 forwarded letters from Aunt F[annie] telling me to come to California, from Charlie sending my pictures, from B. F. Tanner. Friday evening we went to the literary meeting & heard Messrs Coles, Bowser, and Yates debate; from there we went to an entertainment given by Mrs. Sprague and others at Mrs. Robinson's. Mr. C[ole] accompanied me and there I met Dr. B[urchette] & Mr. Love from our town. Was introduced to Mr. J[ones] the same evening; his physical appearance does not prepossess me, and I perfectly abhor him since later developments. Mr. M[cGee] made an engagement to go with us riding on Saturday but when he came he brought Mr. J[ones] & Fan[nie] would not go, & we excused ourselves. Sunday morning brought an insulting note from the cur accusing me for not accepting. I cared nothing for his denouncing our conduct as despicable, but when he accused me of [sic] went further to say he had heard bad things about me when he was running to Memphis but had believed none of them until now. I was so angry I foamed at the mouth, bit my lips & then realizing my impotence—ended in a fit of crying. Huyette went to church with me that morning to the Episcopal service and we saw both the miserable excuses for manhood. I answered his note declining further intercourse with either on the score of having discovered that neither were gentlemen. Met Prof. Vance of Indiana who was en route for Topeka. He is the

"Otto" about whom Nellie W. raved a ye[ar]
ing took us out on the most delightful driv[e]
Sunday evening and we returned to find t[he]
Went to church Sunday night with Mr. [ ]
ny's" and had a nice time. He is a perfec[t]
went calling first thing and visited a do[zen]
found the people all comfortably situate[d]
o'clock. and all lay down for a snooze. I [ ]
attempted to write but I've had so many i[ ]
only written the fewest number of lett[ers]
wrote to Mr. Mayo, Ella R., Charlie, [ ]
S[ettle]. Mr. Huyette took me riding ye[sterday]
a glorious time but I'm awfully sore fro[m]
went to Mrs. Lucas's entertainment. R[ ]
home, went to bed & rose this mornin[g]
goodby as he leaves for his work early. H[ ]
thoroughly modest man. I am charmed [ ]
unpretentiousness. I told them the w[ ]
Jones' scheming so they may know th[ ]
have done so had they not loosened th[ ]
honor bound. L[ouis] M. B[rown] sen[t]
someness & urging us to return. A num[ber]
of the place were down to see us off [ ]
much affected by their thoughtfulness. [ ]
P.M. and have a splendid boarding place [ ]
noon, to the headquarters of National [ ]
Capitol Building and while there called [ ]
auditor of the state of Kansas. He is a[n]
able gentleman and has held the positio[n]
called on us this afternoon and left e[ ]
some gentlemen later. He brought D[ ]
Mr. Cunningham of Indiana whom I [ ]
to the meetings at the opera house & t[ ]
we heard considerable spouting.

*BELOW, Wells repeats information t[ ]
gesting that she did not often reread en[ ]*

gentleman, and The Grand Opera house to hear the different papers on different subjects. Such crowds and crowds of people! I never saw so many teachers in my life, but none that I knew. I heard of Mr. Weaver but could not find him. About 30 are of our own race. Wrote "The Watchman" & L[ouis] M. B[rown] a letter about Kansas City also several cards. Went to a "so-called" reception the night before I left the place and met many people. Among whom were Mr. Keeling of Waco, Texas, who so wonderfully impressed me at a session of the N.E.A. by a spontaneous outburst on the subject of The Bible in Public Schools. I congratulated him on his speech and spent sometime in converse. He is a quiet modest man, hesitating but expressive in speech. Mr. Coles wanted to go home with me but as he only did so because Miss. C. had other company I refused him, & Prof. Vance took me home. Mr. Marcus took us driving through town Friday morning before we left; as that was my 24th birthday & the first time he had so honored me I took it as a birthday gift. We left Topeka at 1 o'clock that day and traveled all of the afternoon & night and landed in Pueblo, Col[orado] 9 o'clock Saturday morning & had to remain all day; at 6 we started again & got to Colorado Springs where I got my first glimpse of the mountains. Went to Manitou Springs Sunday and spent the day in the mountains drinking of the different springs. Did not undertake the ascent of the Peak, which is clearly visible from this point, as I had not my shoes or was sufficiently wrapped up. Went back to Colorado Springs that evening and went to bed early and had a good night's rest. Rose early next morning and wrote the Gate City Press a letter before leaving for this place where I arrived at one P.M. and found as much prejudice here as at Memphis almost. Mr. Y[ates] did not come with me as he stayed to go up The Peak but he followed later in the evening. Met Mr. Stewart a lawyer of Topeka, said to have the finest practice of any colored lawyer in the west. He is afflicted with asthma. He is a very entertaining talker tho', when well. A great many men I meet in this western country but so few ladies. A Mr. Caldwell was ready to propose on the spot almost. Wrote Mr. G[raham] along [*sic*] letter while on my way here. Denver has some fine public buildings; the finest and most complete opera-house I ever saw, The Tabor; a magnificent courthouse, over which we were carried by Mr. Hackley one of the finest young men it has been my good fortune to meet and the High School of the place. Mr. H[ackley] was out to call tonight but did not tarry long. He will call again tomorrow.

In the following entry, Wells completes the details of her four-day visit to Denver, where she enjoyed the attention of Edwin Hackley, a candidate for the Colorado State Legislature.

After a forty-one-hour ride, she reached Salt Lake City, lying at the foot of the Wasatch Mountains with the Great Salt Lake to the northwest and the Great Salt Lake Desert to the west. Founded in 1847 by Brigham Young, the city became the capital of the Mormon faith. After an uncomfortable night in a hotel sitting room, Wells took a brief tour of the city, during which she visited the Mormon Tabernacle, one of the most imposing monuments of the city. Later that afternoon, she boarded the train for San Francisco.

Before 1900, California had a relatively small Black population, primarily male, of seamen, gold miners, farmers, and servants; other African Americans migrated there in the 1880s to work as porters and redcaps on the railroads. Discrimination in employment, however, forced some San Franciscans to move to Los Angeles or across the Bay to Oakland. The Palace Hotel, for example, a luxury hotel that opened in 1875, hired hundreds of trained Black employees, but in the 1880s the number of such workers was greatly reduced.

The Chinese were also victims of discrimination. The racial slur, "Heathen Chinee," that Wells uses reflects prevailing attitudes toward that ethnic group.

The Elevator *(1865–89), edited by L. H. Douglass, was a militant Black weekly, founded by Phillip A. Bell.*

First constructed in 1863 and rebuilt in 1889 after an explosion, the Cliff House was a famous restaurant and saloon.

San Francisco
Thursday, July 29

Have been in this place two days and found people wearing jackets & overcoats and with good reason, for it has been as cold here in this one of our hottest months, as it is in December & March. The situation of the place accounts for that as it is directly on the beach or coast rather of the Pacific Ocean. I have not been to the coast yet and only caught a glimpse of the ocean thro' the Golden Gate as I passed across from Oakland on the ferry boat. As yet have only circulated around in the city looking at the shops and public buildings and going thro' Chinatown with its thousands of "Heathen Chinee" in all branches of industry. Went to the "Elevator" office yesterday and had quite a talk with the editor, who gave us flattering accounts of the negro, and claimed that there were several wealthy colored men here who drove expresses & blacked boots. Went to see Dr. Rutherford yesterday who gave me such a history of their trials since they emigrated to this state that I became despondent and have not been able to shake it off since. He paints Visalia and the colored inhabitants thereof in anything but glowing colors and makes me almost afraid to go there and I heartily regret having sold my ticket (which I did yesterday for $15). My heart is indeed heavy and I know not what to do.

I can only pray to the Father of all mercy for guidance and help. Yet if all he says is true, it's a mystery to one why Aunt F[annie] says she will not return home. Poor Aunt F[annie] she has had a burden to bear that was very heavy. I will not run and leave her alone. As I am so anxious to see her I will leave tomorrow for there. My journey to this place has been very interesting the scenery from Denver was beautiful in the extreme; there was something awful, majestic in the height of the mountains & solitary grandeur of the peaks. We climbed over the mountains at night and did not get the full benefit of our view. The remainder of my 4 days stay in Denver was made very pleasant indeed by Mr. H[ackley] who took me out twice, once on the cars & once in a buggy. The buggy ride was something to remember as he took me over the whole city consequently the ride lasted nearly 3 hours. Also gave me a picture of himself which is a very good likeness. I like him, better than any one I've known so short awhile. Met him also at the entertainment I attended the night before I left, & he was as kindly courteous as ever & when I bade him goodby he said he hated to see me leave & I can easily believe him, for I know I never hated so badly to bid a stranger goodby. I promised to write & really did leave him a note in Miss Julia's care, thanking him for his kindness to me & returning him some papers he left for my perusal. Travel without intermission after leaving Denver until Salt Lake City was reached 12 o'clock at night 41 hours later. We went to a hotel and I spent a fitful remainder of the night on a cot, without covering, in the sitting room of the place. Mr. Y[ates] found accommodation elsewhere. Strolled about the city next day especially to see the Mormons & visited their Tabernacle in the afternoon where I listened to a harangue from one of themselves. Was much impressed with what I saw and was sorry I had to leave before it was over. Left on the 4 o'clock train and came thro' without stopping elsewhere to this place, tho' I had intended stopping at Sacramento City. My money was fast giving out & I thought better of it. Had my picture taken yesterday. Don't know if I shall like it, but the negative is good. Visited the Palace Hotel, said to be the largest in the world and has 1780 rooms. Went out to the Cliff House and had a magnificent view of the ocean and sat for hours gazing out on the billows that "break, break, break, on the cold gray stones," and being fascinated with the white foam that looked like milk. The rocks in front of the house were lined with seals that looked like so many brown bags as they lay basking in the sunlight. Golden Gate Park, of more than a thousand acres, took up a considerable share of our time—with its broad smooth walks, beautiful parterres of flowers and conservatory with all manner of plants & flowers. Strolled home to find that I had had a caller but an unknown one, as he left no card and no one could tell who it was. Thoroughly tired out I shall retire as soon as possible. Sent a poem I found in a paper and consider peculiarly applicable to B. F. P[oole] to him without a line but he will know who it is from.

VISALIA is located about two hundred miles south of San Francisco and halfway between the Pacific Ocean and the Nevada border, on California's central plateau. Founded in 1852 by Nathaniel Vide of Kentucky, it was the home of many Confederate sympathizers and a pro-slavery newspaper. Very few Blacks lived in the area, and most of these had come as servants to former slaveowners who migrated there after the Civil War. Why, Wells must have wondered, would her aunt leave Memphis, a thriving industrial and distribution center, where vocational, educational, and cultural opportunities for Blacks were so much greater than in Visalia? The niece speculates that higher wages and a healthier climate might have prompted the move. She writes in her au-

tobiography that there "was good work and good wages for her, and bet-
ter health than back in Memphis, but no companionship" (Duster 1970,
25).

Fannie Butler named her daughter after Ida B. Wells.

Visalia, California
Monday, August 2

Left San Francisco Saturday after procuring my pictures for this
place & traveled all night. Arrived here at daybreak yesterday
morning & found all well and very glad to see me. The children
have all grown as tall and Annie & Ida are near my height and look
very much like women. I look at them in amazement and find the
little sisters of whom I spoke, shooting up into my own world and
ripening for similar experiences as my own. A letter was given me
from L[ouis] M. B[rown] that beat me here. In it he speaks very
tenderly and declares his intention of going out as far as Denver to
seek a competence and seductively seeks to know if he may return
for me some time in the future. I wrote to him hurriedly in order
to meet the morning's mail and did not enter on the question so
broadly as I might have done, but I commended his determination
and told him to do something that called forth admiration and respect and the rest would be easy. Wrote to Mr. Y[ates] also and, after consultation with aunt F[annie], told him not to buy the ticket.
Poor aunt F[annie]! she wants me to stay the year with her any how,
whether I get any work to do or not & I, seeing how careworn she
is with hard work and solicitude for the children—know she is right
& I should help her share the responsibility and God helping me I
will! It is not enough to take them and go right away if I could, but
I will stay with her a year. The election of teachers has not taken
place yet in Memphis & all are undecided & I know not whether I'm
on the list or not. It is very hot here during the day so different from
S[an] F[rancisco]. I could not make up my mind to stay there after
Dr. R[utherford]'s statement. I wished to come & see for myself.
Altho Mrs. R[utherford] offered to board me free until after the
grand parade on the 3rd. Also received a letter from Mr. G[raham]
who writes very disjointedly. I don't know what to think of him.
He says he always feels as if in a tight jacket when in my presence

and wishes to know if I love him & will live with him. I fear I don't but then I also fear I shall never love anybody.

MR. COLES *sent Wells an application for a teaching position in the schools of Kansas City, Missouri.*

Wednesday, August 4

Received 2 letters & ever so many papers yesterday. Mrs. Bowser sent the group picture and a very kind chatty letter—Mrs. Settle wrote a long interesting letter also that quite cheered my drooping spirits. Mr. Coles sent me a letter and the application for a school. I wrote to him sending it back filled out and a letter to Fan[nie] T[hompson] also one to Mr. Froman asking his advice about staying out here. Washed my clothes yesterday and a weary all day job it was. Rested today & wrote to Mrs. S[ettle], Mrs T[urner], and started an article for the A.M.E. Church Review but made little progress. Wrote a card to Mr. Y[ates] changing my mind about the articles in question. Lily brought me a letter from him when she came from the office & he was magnanimous enough to say he missed me more & more every day; also told me of two gentlemen calling to see me Sunday evening.

IT is clear that the heat, manual labor, and social isolation are taking their toll on Wells, who writes of her weariness, loneliness, and "drooping spirits." Visalia was a little country town that offered few diversions to a dynamic, young, single woman who was used to attending concerts, lectures, dramatic readings, and literary societies' meetings. In her autobiography, she described life in Visalia: "Not a dozen colored families lived there, and although there was plenty of work, it was very dull and lonely for my aunt and the five youngsters in the family." Furthermore, her freedom of movement was hampered by curious neighbors and a strict aunt, as she explains: "I told my aunt that it was even worse for me, a young woman, to have nothing to look forward to, as I was just beginning to live and had all my life before me" (Duster 1970, 25).

Tuesday, August 9

Worked very hard all last week and had the usual swelling of the hands & feet that always attends me after a hard day's manual labor. Received no more letters during the week but wrote to Mrs S[ettle] & Mrs Turner. Friday evening for the first time I went walking down the road with the children and was lying with my head in Lily's lap when Mr. Yates walked up. We spent the evening in animated conversation and it slipped away so quickly. He had a very pleasant time in S[an] F[rancisco] & enjoyed the parade. He met several of the people and of course enjoyed the chance of becoming better acquainted. He left next morning but not before coming down and bringing the things I told him to get & he did so before he received my card. I paid him for them & started down to the depot, but it was so hot & dusty & the people stared so, I gave it up & bade him goodby at the post office. He told me that if he wrote for me any time soon I might know he meant business, & to come right away. That assurance comforted me very much for I begin to feel lonely so far away from everything & everybody. Yesterday morning Mr. Hackley's letter was brought me & I eagerly devoured its contents. He writes in the easy, natural manner that he speaks and asks me to remember that "Iola" is my public name and not for private correspondence. I answered right away and told him many things. I also answered Mrs. Bowser's letter & sent her a picture of myself to exhibit alongside the group picture. Have not answered Mr. G[raham]'s letter yet, but will do so. Sewed a little today & will do more tomorrow. No mail from any source today. Took my first ride here, Saturday evening and enjoyed it immensely. School board at home elects teachers today & if I am re-elected will return & take Annie, if not both of the children with me; for I've no books, no companionship & even an embargo is laid on my riding out with the only one who can take me. Have not met Lutie yet. She called on me in S[an] F[rancisco].

THIS is the first time that Wells mentions Harry, a former beau whom she treated cruelly in spite of his gallantry in defending her from slander. The Reverend Robert N. Countee was business manager of the Living Way. *Wells sold her return ticket, from San Francisco to Topeka, as she*

explains: "When I got to the little town of Visalia, I was persuaded by
my aunt to sell my return ticket and accept the school offered to me there
by the superintendent." (Duster 1970, 24).

Wednesday, August 18

Have just received a letter from Fan[nie] in which she informs me
that Harry is dead. As I've not heard from him in some time I was
very much shocked. Poor Harry! I wonder if he was prepared to
go? I always felt that he had consumption, and was just thinking
about him only this week, for the first time in quite awhile, and my
heart smites me to think what a cruel letter I sent in answer to his
last declaration of love for me! A better boy, with kinder intentions
never breathed and when I think of the last time he came to see me
two years ago, and declared he was going away to work and that
he would come back for me I grieve that I did not treat him more
kindly. I wish I could have seen him before he died, for one short
hour. They brought him to Memphis a week before he died, and I
know he would like to have seen me. May the Lord have mercy on
his soul and may I remember to deal more kindly with the tender
feelings of those who exhibit them. I always thought a great deal
of him, weak and irresolute as he was, for he was the first to help
dispel the dark clouds that had settled on my young life, and treated
me with the courtesy and delicacy of a true gentleman altho' he
knew the whole base slanderous lie that had blackened my life, and
offered me his love even while his companions were rehearsing it
the lie in his ears. Gentle, kind and tender as a woman, if he was
not of a decided character, he preserves my faith in human nature.
I earnestly hope he has gone to rest. Peace to his ashes!

The letter gives me a great deal of news. Mr. Harris is dead &
Lee West is not expected to live; the School Board as yet have failed
to elect teachers. I wonder what they mean by it? Received a letter
also from Mr. Countee in which he informs me that they are unable
to employ me regularly as correspondent, which I knew before &
can't conceive his object for writing, if that was all he had to com-
municate. He could hardly have received my postal when he wrote
and I can't fathom his object unless to inform me he doesn't want
me to write any more for them. Received and answered a letter
from Mr. C[oles]. He is jubilant & confidant of my securing a po-

sition there. Informed him of Mr. Y[ates]'s promise to assist me. Also received a letter from Mr. Walker of Bakersfield who informs me of his house & stock worth $1200 getting burned up. Sent a letter to Mr. Y[ates] to meet him when he gets home. I regret more and more every day that I sold my ticket. If I had it, it would not be a hard matter to borrow money to take Annie away. Sent a letter to the Gate City Press. Also received a Living Way with my first letter in it.

Sunday, August 22

Received a letter from "Charlie boy" on the very day I mailed him the plot (?) of our novel and it has the usual platitudes & I answered immediately & told him of my hesitating between marrying and staying here to raise the children. I know he will be surprised at the tone of that letter. Did very little work last week but must do better next. Wrote to Fan[nie] T[hompson] & B. F. P[oole] today, and told Fan[nie] to send me money to come.

THE entry below reveals the diarist's increased ability to analyze and critique her journalistic writing: choice of subject, clarity of expression, and organization of ideas. Wells also describes the difficulty of writing in Visalia, where she is cut off from the social and intellectual currents that had inspired and supported her writing in Memphis.

Robert R. Church, Sr. (1839–1912), was born a slave in Holly Springs, Mississippi. After the Civil War, he acquired property in Memphis, where he operated a restaurant and saloon at 372–74 Second Street. An affluent businessman and dedicated citizen, he bought the first bond to restore the city charter after Memphis was reduced to a taxing district following the yellow fever epidemics of the 1870s. Wells was counting on his magnanimity when she requested a loan:

> I told him the circumstances of my condition—that although he did not know me he could find out by reference to the board of education that I was a teacher in the public schools and would thus be able to repay the money. I told him that I wrote to him because he was the only man of my race that I knew who could lend me that much money and wait for me to repay it. I also told him not to send the money unless I had been reelected, as otherwise there would be no need for me to come back to Memphis. (Duster 1970, 25)

Thursday, August 26

Finished & at last mailed to the A.M.E. Church Review on the 24th, my article on "Our Young Men" not because I was satisfied with it or thought it worthy publication by reason of the lucid exposition and connected arrangement, but as a trial to get the opinion of others. I never wrote under a greater strain, but kept at it until it was finished, anyhow. I think sometimes I can write a readable article and then again I wonder how I could have been so mistaken in myself. A glance at all my "brilliant?" productions pall on my understanding; they all savor of dreary sameness, however varied the subject, and the style is monotonous. I find a paucity of ideas that makes it a labor to write freely and yet—what is it that keeps urging me to write notwithstanding all? Messrs Brown & Graham have about received the letters I wrote them last week. Wrote a letter to Mr. C[hurch] asking the loan of one hundred dollars. Received letters from Mrs. Rice, Mr. F[roman] and a card from "Charlie" this week. "Pap" tells me not to think of staying here, till my railroad suit is over then I can come back; that only intensified my desire to go back & I answered immediately telling him what I had done also a card to Mr. Rutherford asking him to find out the price of return tickets. Will take Annie back if no more— that is, if I get the money. Am making a dress for Aunt F[annie] this week.

THERE *is no evidence that Wells published the short story mentioned below or the novel that she and Charles S. Morris started.*

Wednesday, September 1

Have received an answer from Dr. R[utherford] who informs me the price of tickets at the scalpers is only a little less than usual fare from this place. No letter from L[ouis] M. B[rown] yet or Mr. H[ackley] either. I can't imagine the latter so rude as to fail to answer my letter purposely. I would write again but it would have the appearance of eagerness. Sunday passed in the same dull way. Monday I sent a letter to Mr. Y[ates] & $3.00 subscription to the Gate City Press for two persons at this place. Found a letter from him &

Mr. C[oles] also at the office; both of them assuring me of their assistance in procuring a place in the schools. Mrs. Turner wrote also to say she had received my letter & had sold the things for $4. A letter from Mrs. J. T. S[ettle] yesterday morning acted like a tonic, it was so newsy & chatty. I wrote Saturday to Mr. F[roman] telling him to use authoritative measures in regard to my return & see Mr. C[hurch] immediately & have him to forward me the money. I know not if he will do so but I am very eager to get back home. I have not seen Mrs. R[ice] yet nor answered her letter. Have made two dresses for my aunt this week & want to do more sewing.

Today witnessed my first essay in story-writing; I have made a beginning. I know not where or when the ending will be. I can see and portray in my mind all the elements of a good story but when I attempt to put it on paper my thoughts dissolve into nothingness.

Saturday, September 4

Have finished the dress I was making and answered Mr. C[oles]'s Mrs. Rice's and Fan[nie] T[hompson]'s letters. Thursday evening brought a letter from L[ouis] M. B[rown], very quiet and very manly in tone, not a hopeless one so far as love is concerned and signing himself as "mine to command to service." He is developing symptoms more to my ideas of what becomes an earnest man and I told him so, as well as that if he succeeded in his new venture & in winning my love in the meantime, I would help him prove to the world what love in its purity can accomplish.

Exactly 13 days since I mailed my letter to C[harlie] and as I predicted the answer came immediately. I received from him last night the most lengthy letter I've ever gotten from him, containing an outline of our projected novel with which I am not much attracted—it is too much on the style of other novels—rather sensational. There was also some good advice as to marriage, only marred by a preface that reflected somewhat on my common sense especially after I had requested the advice and I naturally resent that. Have not answered it yet. Dreamed about Mr. P[oole] last night. Received a Denver paper from Mr. H[ackley] containing an account of his nomination as a representative to the State Legislature by the Republican party. Hurrah for Edwin! but as he has not answered my letter yet I don't know that I shall write to congratulate him. Wrote a dynamitic article to the G[ate] C[ity] P[ress] almost advising murder! My only plea is the pitch of indignation to which I was carried by reading an article in the home papers concerning a great outrage that recently happened in Jackson Tenn. A colored woman accused of poisoning a white one was taken from the county jail and stripped naked and hung up in the courthouse yard and her body riddled with bullets and left exposed to view! O my God! can such things be and no justice for it? The only evidence being that the stomach of the dead woman contained arsenic & a box of "Rough on Rats" was found in this woman's house, who was a cook for the white woman. It may be unwise to express myself so strongly but I cannot help it & I know not if capital may not be made of it against me but I trust in God.

WELLS wrote in her entry of August 18 that she had received a letter from Will Walker of Bakersfield, informing her that his house and stock worth $1,200 were burned up. He must be a native of Holly Springs because he knows Wells, visits her in Visalia, and invites "everybody" to move to Bakersfield, where he is prospering. Bakersfield, near the southern end of the San Joaquin Valley, is located about fifty miles south of Visalia.

Tuesday, September 7

Earthquakes have been shaking the southeastern part of the U.S. ever since Tuesday Aug. 31st, and Charleston, S.C. has been a great sufferer by them; many people have lost their lives & others their houses. Wrote a letter to Mr. Tipton apprising him of my intention to go back & asking what he thought of it. A[nnie] has said point blank that she will not go back & L[ily] is not far behind. Will W[alker] was up yesterday from Bakersfield where he is flourishing & wants everybody to come & do likewise. Received letters from Fan[nie] T[hompson] & B. F. P[oole] last night & answered both today; to the latter I related my dream concerning him & myself. Fan[nie] tells me George is thinking of marrying & was very impudent to her. I earnestly hope he will get over this season of infatuation safely & do nothing to his own or any one else's discredit.

THE next entry indicates that the school superintendent of Visalia, which had a dual public school system, was anxious to hire an experienced Black teacher for the colored school. In the late 1850s, the California State Legislature allowed cities and counties to raise funds to open segregated schools.

Thursday, September 9

How much can be compassed by twelve hours! The past 24 have been very stormy ones with me. At breakfast yesterday morning L[ily] brought me a card from Fan[nie] B[radshaw] & a paper from Fan[nie] T[hompson] both apprising me of the result of the election. After knowing for certain I was elected I went up town & telegraphed to Mr. Y[ates] to lend me $50. & send immediately. I also saw Mr. G. (one of the School Board at this place) and asked for the certificate I had sent in with my application. He promised to hunt it up and send me & I came home jubilant with the idea of soon again meeting friends. Wrote a card to Fan[nie] B[radshaw] telling her I'd leave here on 15th, & for her to wait for me. After sending it—a card was brought to me from Mr. Murphy, school superintendent, & the result of his visit was an offer of the school here to begin Monday & teach until the examination for nothing & if I passed examination to get $80 per month to compensate me for the months I received nothing. He offered all the advantages possible & his eagerness to secure me backed with my aunt's importunities made me yield, tho' very reluctantly. He had the contract drawn up and signed & delivered to me by three o'clock. It was all done so swiftly there was not time to think & when I realized it all I shed bitter tears of disappointment; but my calmer sober judgment coming to the rescue I see it will be a better money plan than if I go home. I'll have no board to pay for the children nor myself till after Christmas, & I'll have over $300. clear to take home; for I am determined to go to that railroad suit, if I come back. I see all that but don't like to acknowledge it & have been very slow in doing so. Wrote to Mr. F[roman] today telling him all about it, & sending a petition for leave of absence, by him, to the Board. Received an answering telegram from Mr. Y[ates] today responding promptly to my request. Bless him! Must write him a letter tonight. I don't feel like writing to anyone.

Have had another fit of indecision about staying but I believe I have entirely recovered now and will send the letters announcing my determination to Mrs. S[ettle] & Mr. Hawkins that I wrote to mail yesterday but did not. I send Mr. H[awkins] my picture also. Wrote F[annie] J. B[radshaw] a card rescinding my decree about leaving here 15th, & one to C[harlie] S. M[orris] apprising him of later developments. I know Mr. F[roman] will be disappointed but I can't help that. I feel more & more that my first duty is to my sisters & my aunt who has helped me when I had no other helpers. And I will stay this year if it were ten times more unpromising than it is and at whatever personal cost to myself. Once I've made up my mind, I will have little difficulty in adhering to my fiat. I will begin school tomorrow and not be so ungrateful for the blessings that come to me on every hand. Received a letter from Mr. H[ackley] written the day after mine of congratulations to him. He is profuse in apologies and frankly acknowledges his fault with the one excuse of politics to offer. I excuse him as requested but his apparent sluggishness has cooled my ardor and taught me a lesson: to make haste slowly. Shall wait for a return of the answer to mine of the 4th, which he will send to M[emphis] and I will receive in about two weeks from now ere I answer this & then very cooly. It is a good letter tho'. "The Watchman" informed me of L[ouis] M. B[rown]'s leave for K[ansas] C[ity] to settle & practice; it also contained a clipping from Washington D.C. Advocate reverting [*sic*] to my being in the west & drawing conclusions thereby because L[ouis] had made known his intention of coming west & closing with a wish for us to live long & prosper. L[ouis]'s reply was just below & was intended as a rebuke. He also sent me the "Advocate" itself that I might see the original & wrote Mr. J[ones]'s address at the top. He need not have bothered himself to do that as I shall take not the slightest notice of the cur. He would be only too happy to have me do so.

I regret so much writing that last letter to B. F. P[oole]. What must he think of me? I gave way to a transitory morbid state of feeling and let my pen run riot. I shall occupy my mind with other things and let that matter that has occupied so much of my time rest in the hands of Providence.

Wrote to George today as this is the occasion of his birthday &

gave him a good plain talk on the subject of marriage. I hope it may do him some good. Wrote also to Mr. Taylor & then answered Mr. Walker's letter.

Must get to bed as school begins tomorrow. God grant I may prosper and be led by His Hand.

WELLS *does not describe her first day of teaching in Visalia—Monday, September 13, 1886—but she writes the following in her autobiography: "I went to school in Visalia on Monday and registered eighteen pupils, all the colored contingent of the town. The school was a make-shift one-room building . . . [and the students] had been given the second-rate facilities that are usual in such cases. . . . Another dreary day went by and I tried my best, with no facilities to get the school material straightened out" (Duster 1970, 25–26).*

Although short and sketchy, the character study of Lutie Rice is one of Wells's most fascinating treatments of women, for she describes Lutie's age, class, tone of voice, and style of living. Surprisingly, Wells, an independent, assertive, and isolate woman herself, seems to criticize those very qualities in another woman. She attributes the older woman's ability to live "within herself and on her own resources" to pride and an air of superiority. Mrs. Rice was, like Fannie Butler, a native of Holly Springs. It was unusual for Wells to address an older, married woman by her first name; in this case, it suggests familiarity or a lack of respect.

In her autobiography, Wells describes her decision to accept the offer in Kansas City: "I finished my day's work at the school [in Visalia] and after cashing my draft [of $100 from Mr. Church], went to the telegraph office and sent this telegram to Mr. Yates in Kansas City, "Leaving tonight. If too late to secure position there, will go on to Memphis. Ida B. Wells" (Duster, 1970, 26).

Tuesday, September 14

Letters from "Pap" F[roman] & Mr. and Mrs. Bowser yesterday upset all my resolutions and on the former's assurance that Mr. C[hurch] had lent the money, I made up my mind again to throw up the school & came home bent on seeing Mr. M[urphy] & resigning. Found Mrs. R[ice] here and we pleasantly whiled away the evening in earnest converse. "Lutie" is lower than I imagined and looks older and more settled. Her face, except when lighted up in converse, is hard. She has a (to my eye or ear, rather) slightly affected drawl to her voice, and her continuous isolation has given her a more precise manner than she would otherwise have; also an unconscious tone of superiority and pride in a fact she often repeats; of living within herself and on her own resources. Her remark that it was too often the case that people could not do so, following my remarks of dissatisfaction and isolation seemed somewhat of a rebuke to me. Her advice: "to do the duty that lies nearest," and a seed let fall now & then about my aunt's working so hard had the desired effect of reconciling me to my lot & I came home almost determined to stay & take the chances. Aunt F[annie] talked very determinedly telling me to go & what she would never do again and then turned about and cried half the night & all the morning. I know I owe her a debt of gratitude but she makes it so burdensome for me as to make it very distasteful. Forced acts of gratitude are not very sincere I should say. I thought I had exorcised the demon of unrest and dissatisfaction but two telegrams from Messrs C[oles] & Y[ates] were brought me informing me of my election there in K[ansas] C[ity] that roused me with full forces again. After a final conflict with myself I sent another telegram thanking them a thousand times but resigning & telling him it was impossible for me to come. I write a letter tonight explaining, but will my explanation be acceptable? I know not if I will ever have another chance yet I try not to be rebellious but extract consolation out of the thought that My Heavenly Father will reward and bless me for doing what is right and just and if I did nothing, sacrificed nothing in return for all that has been done for me, I could not expect his blessing and sanction. Help me & bring success to my efforts I pray.

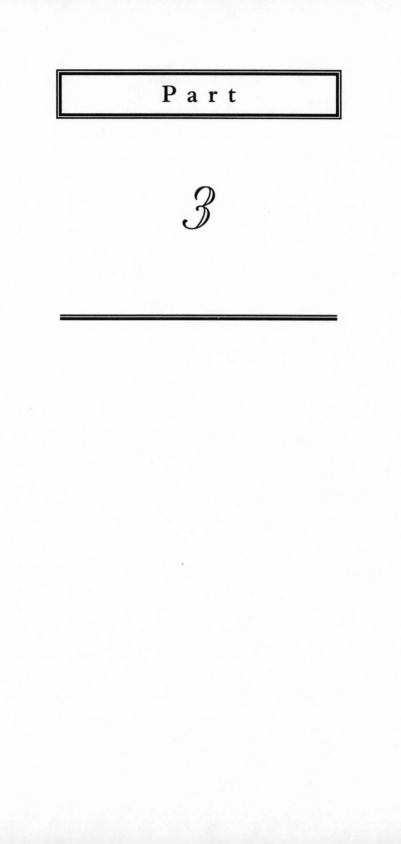

Part

3

Standing Face to Face with Twenty-Five Years of Life

October 2, 1886–September 18, 1887

*A*LTHOUGH she begins this part of her diary in the fall of 1886, after her return to Memphis, with an account of her experiences at the Lincoln School in Kansas City, Missouri, Wells seldom describes her work as a teacher. Instead, she writes frequently and enthusiastically about her journalism, noting letters to and from newspapermen, articles published in Black newspapers throughout the country, and attendance at a press association convention. During this period, she wrote biweekly "letters" on such subjects as "Our Young Men" for the *American Baptist*, edited by Dr. W. J. Simmons; an article for the *Scimitar* on Memphis theater, which was reprinted in the *New York Freeman*, the *Kansas City Dispatch*, and the *Living Way*; another essay, "Our Women," published in the *New York Freeman*; a letter to the *Memphis Watchman* on the Knights of Labor, which was extracted by the *Detroit Plaindealer*; and an article for the *Headlight and Sun* of Arkansas.

Her services as a journalist are much in demand, and she is even beginning to receive compensation for her writing. Mr. Coles of the *Kansas City Dispatch* asks her to serve on the newspaper staff, and the editor of the *Chicago Conservator* also wants her to write for that publication. When the editor of the *Indianapolis World* asks her to serve as a paid contributor and then "pays" her with a two-year subscription, she writes, "Cheeky, that," and refuses to write for him again. Dr. Simmons offers to pay her $1.00 for weekly articles and then promises to cover her expenses to the national convention if she will write two short articles a month. He actually places her under contract and then complains when she also writes for another newspaper. She notes that she has also been elected "editress" of the *Evening Star*, a newsletter produced by the Lyceum, a Memphis literary society.

Now a young woman in her mid-twenties, Ida B. Wells clearly demonstrates the leadership skills that will bring her fame, if not fortune, in the 1890s as a journalist, clubwoman, civil rights advocate, and antilynching crusader. In 1887, she organized and led a Sunday school class for young men at the Avery Chapel A.M.E. Church. She planned a storm party for teachers at her school and asked P. B. S. Pinchback, a noted Black politician, to lecture to the Lyceum. She gave spirited readings, sometimes in costume, at socials and concerts. She served as chair of a committee to form a dramatic group and even performed in a play at LeMoyne Normal Institute. Elected by her contemporaries to edit the *Evening Star*, she was also asked to serve as a delegate to the National Press Association Convention, where she read a paper, gave a response to "Woman in Journalism," and had her picture published in the *Louisville Courier Journal*.

Wells seems to sense that she is destined to become something more than a Memphis schoolteacher. She feels, intuitively, that hers will not be a conventional life as wife and mother, although the pressure for domestic conformity is mounting. During the fall and winter, she attends or participates in several weddings and becomes increasingly conscious of her single status, pointing out that she is the only unmarried female teacher at her school. Her colleague and suitor, I. J. Graham, also marries soon after it is reported that he and Wells were dismissed for immoral conduct. Rumors about Wells, a nonconventional single woman, become increasingly vicious as she gains more visibility and prominence. Apparently, the rumors that she has been dismissed and that her eleven-year-old sister, Lily, is her illegitimate daughter undermine her integrity as an unmarried woman by attacking the most vulnerable area of her private life— her sexuality.

Such attacks, however, do not detract Ida B. Wells from her lofty goals, so she begins 1887 with a prayer and a resolve to organize a Bible class. She complains, occasionally, about depression, but seldom experiences the acute loneliness, self-doubt, and social isolation that plagued her the previous year. She has personal problems—with Lily, her brother Jim, and her landlords—but she is more concerned about the social, economic, and political difficulties that faced African Americans in the 1880s. On April 11, 1887, she discovers that the Tennessee Supreme Court has ruled against her in the railroad suit, and, a week later, she attends a meeting of the Negro's Mutual Protective Association, a group organized to defend the civil rights of Black Memphians.

Articulate, intellectually gifted, and committed to racial uplift, Ida B. Wells becomes increasingly involved in the struggle for racial equality. She attends lectures on the plight of indigenous Africans, and she presents a paper, "What Lack We Yet?" to the Lyceum at LeMoyne Normal Institute. In 1887, she wrote newspaper articles on topics like "Race Pride," "Iola on Discrimination," and "Our Women," which illustrate the intellectual vigor and analytic depth of her writing. Although she may not realize it at the time, she is honing the writing and speaking skills that will force her into a wider, more activist role in the 1890s. On July 16, 1887, the diarist, now a mature, confident, and independent woman, takes stock of her life and accepts responsibility for her failures: the missed opportunities, educational deficiencies, and un-Christian acts of omission. At twenty-five, she understands the significance of her losses and is philosophical about her future.

IN chapter 4 of Crusade for Justice, Ida B. Wells gives more details about her experiences in Kansas City, Missouri. J. D. Bowser, editor of the Gate City Press, campaigned vigorously for her appointment to the Kansas City public schools, in part, because he wanted her to work as associate editor of his paper. When she arrived in Kansas City on Tuesday, September 21, a day after school had opened, she discovered that a local woman, Callie Jordan, had been appointed to teach after Wells had declined the offer. School officials wanted a more experienced teacher, but Jordan's friends resented the preferential treatment accorded an "imported" teacher. In Crusade, Wells describes her experiences at the Lincoln School:

I went right to school that day and was given the fourth grade room. The principal and most of the teachers were friends of Miss Jordan's, and they showed themselves to be hostile and resentful. Being very sensitive, I was much hurt over their attitude. When I thought of how united all these friends had been in entertaining the Memphis teachers when we had passed through on the way to the National Educational Association two months before, I could not bear to be a disturbing influence.

I taught through the day, however, and held my room until quiet and order had been established; then I dismissed it as if I were coming back next day. I went straight to the principal's office, wrote out my resignation and gave it to him, then went home to face Mr. Bowser, Mr. Yates, Mr. Coles, and others. They felt I had deserted them, but I stood firm and insisted on leaving for Memphis. I did not tell them of the attitude of the teachers. There was no use in making them enemies of each other. These men were all principals of schools in Kansas City, and I believe they were honestly trying to get experienced teachers in the school. (Duster 1970, 30)

When she reached Memphis, Wells was assigned to the Clay Street School (renamed the Kortrecht Grammar School), where she heard rumors that she and I. J. Graham had been dismissed for "immoral conduct." Later, she met the Reverend William J. Simmons, who had a profound impact on her journalistic development.

I 8 8 6

Memphis, Tennessee
October 2

Nearly a month since I wrote in my diary and despite all my professions of resignation in the last entry I am back in Memphis again. I taught four days in Visalia & received the remittances from both Messrs Church & Yates.

On Thursday, Sept. 16 I determined to come home & telegraphed Mr. Y[ates] to that effect; I told him if too late for K[ansas] C[ity] would come on to M[emphis]. Left that night & thro mistake was brought around by Los Angeles, Tuscon Ar[izona], El Paso, Tex. across to Fort Worth, up thro' Indian T[erritory] & Kansas to the city of Kansas where I arrived without more than an hour's stop Tuesday morning, 21st ult. I saw there was a spirit of constraint visible & of course was constrained myself. I learned also that Jones &

Co. foiled in all their efforts, & angered that others succeeded in doing what they offered to do—had published a card in the papers calling a mass meeting of the citizens to protest against the employment of "imported teachers" to the exclusion of home talent. I immediately declared off & proclaimed my intention of coming on, but Messrs B[owser] & Y[ates] would not hear of it, and urged me to pay no attention to it, but go on & teach next day as my room was waiting for me. I yielded & went but my extreme sensitiveness caused me to determine to come home & I told Mr. B[owser] so that night. He was very angry & that grieved me because I did not want him to be or to think I was ungrateful but I saw him no more that night. L[ouis] M. B[rown] came in shortly and he undertook to persuade me, but I was firm & he was in high dudgeon about it. He took one of my pictures. I had told Mr. Bailey, the principal that I would not return the next day so I occupied myself packing my trunks. L[ouis] M. B[rown] came home about 10 o'clock and remained all the morning pleading but nothing he said moved me. Mr. B[owser] came home at noon & we talked and parted in a better frame of mind.

Mr. C[oles] stood by me till the last and was the last person I saw as I left, but I breathed freer after it was all over & I turned my face to the only home I know.

I arrived here next day at 4 o'clock & found the people all unsettled on account of Mr. Matthews' death.

Was at the teachers meeting next day & assigned to Clay st. building. Mr. G[raham] informed me that a letter was sent to him to get information concerning our moral status as it was there rumored that we had been dismissed for immoral conduct, here. Paul J[ones] wrote it also one to Mr. Sampson in the same strain. I had not expected anything like that & it angered me somewhat. I have sent a letter to Mr. B[owser] telling him I would like to know if there was such a rumor afloat, that I might know if the K[ansas] C[ity] people would attempt to blacken the reputation of those who desired to sojourn among them. Have written also Messrs Yates & Coles only in K[ansas] C[ity]. Found letters from Messrs Hackley, Morris, B. F. P[oole], Miss Barnes & have answered all but the next to the last. Met Rev. Simmons, pres. of East Press Convention and he came home with me; he wheedled a picture out of me & a promise to write for him. He is very lively & jolly. Have been at work all the week with 70 pupils. Had three callers this week, Messrs Jackson, Graham, and a Prof. Wilson of Ohio. G[raham] was here Tuesday night & was disappointed in me; he thinks I've lost my heart to some one else and writes today to tell me he is afraid such is the case. Saw Harry L's mother today & she says the first thing H[arry] said was to ask where I was.

O, I wish I could have seen him!

Fannie H[amilton] came to see me yesterday & she will be married in two weeks & invited me to the wedding. Received an invitation to Mr. Moseley's marriage which takes place week after next also.

Have nothing to send. Have spent several dollars this week & owe Menken $4.00 & Williams $1.05.

WILLIAM J. SIMMONS edited the American Baptist, *a religious newspaper with a national circulation.*

Wells paid a high price—isolation, criticism, and calumny—for her professional ambition, the freedom with which she conducted her personal life, and her failure to comply with social expectations for women of her class. By age twenty-four, she should have been married, like other female teachers—Mrs. Hooks, Mrs. Lott, Mrs. Bradshaw, and Mrs. Cassels—and had a child on the way. Since she was not, she became the object of vicious rumors: that she was involved with a White Holly Springs man "for money," that she and a male teacher were "immoral," and that she had an illegitimate child. The rumors were fabricated by men. When several males accused her of being a "heartless flirt," she wrote, "I have been so long misrepresented that I begin to rebel." She realized that she was subject to misrepresentation because she was a single woman, unprotected by male kin. She wrote in her autobiography, "[M]y good name was all that I had in the world, [for] I had no brother or father to protect it for me" (Duster 1970, 44).

Tuesday, October 12

Mr. Mosely marries tonight. Have received several press comments and a very flattering notice in Mr. Simmons paper. I sent him the article Mr. L[ott] returned to me & he promises to print it in full.

The Editor of The Indianapolis World wants to engage me as a pay contributor to his paper, also to engage in correspondence. My experience with P[aul] J[ones] & Co. has been of such a nature, I hesitate about it. They have written letters to others besides Capt. C[hurch] and even sent a forgery to get evidence to convict us of immorality. Mr. B[owser] advises me to keep cool but when he tells me that McG[ee] has circulated the report that Lily is my child, instead of my sister, I could not help getting furiously angry, but have controlled my anger. Received 3 letters from the same place, of the same date and at the same time. L[ouis] M. B[rown] wants to know why I have not written. Answered today. Fannie H[amilton] marries tomorrow night, but I've nothing to give her. I am not able. Dr. told me I had catarrh & I must attend to that. Stella will marry next month & wants me to wait on her but I fear I'll not be able. Sent G[raham] a short, unsatisfactory note in which I told him my feelings & I've not seen nor heard from him since. F[annie] J. T[hompson] told me he wanted to send a message by her, but she thought she would not see me. It was to the effect that he could not go to the wedding tomorrow night. He ought to have sent me word sooner.

The superintendent of schools, C. H. Collier, transferred Wells from the Kortrecht Grammar School (the Clay Street School) to the South Memphis School.

Many of those close to Wells are getting married: A. A. Moseley, her cousin Stella, her friend Fannie, and her brother George. The most interesting turn of events, however, is the sudden marriage of her beau, I. J. Graham, with whom she has had a stormy relationship for the past year. She dismisses him with a cool, "Mr. G. was married very unexpectedly last week," and then fails to mention him ever again. Perhaps Graham, an ambitious, money-conscious young man, felt compelled to marry because of the rumors about his "immoral" relationship with Wells. Several years later, G. P. Hamilton wrote the following about Mrs. Graham: "His devoted wife is an alumnus of Kortrecht High School and one of the most intellectual women ever honored with a diploma from that institution" (1908, 264).

Wednesday, October 20

It rained so I could not go to Fannie's marriage but I sent her a pair of vases costing $1.50. Wrote to aunt F[annie] (who has heard something I should say about the children & has not written). Mrs. K., my old friend J. G. Johnson, Ida Overall, J.D.B., and a note to I. J. G[raham] asking to be excused from going to the wedding, the day after the wedding was over. Mr. C[ollier] changed me to No. 3, yesterday and I've had a tough time with tough pupils ever since. Wrote a letter on the Knights of Labor demonstration at Richmond Va. but have misplaced it. Wrote one to the Scimitar concerning the theatre here & it is published in this afternoon's paper. Mr. G[raham] was married very unexpectedly last week. I wish him joy. Have done no sewing yet this week. A letter from L[ouis] M. B[rown] was answered this morning, also one to Mr. C[oles] & a card to Mr. Simmons. Have received neither of my papers this week. J. Mason came home with me from F[annie] H[amilton]'s Sunday evening and stayed & talked a long while. George was in to see me Sunday & seemed somewhat constrained in his manner. I earnestly hope he is not thinking seriously of marrying.

WELLS does not elaborate on her election to the editorship of the Eve-ning Star, a Black Memphis newspaper that contained items of news, gossip, and literature, but work on the paper launched her on a career in journalism. In her autobiography, she writes that the editor took a job in Washington, "leaving the Evening Star without an editor. To my great surprise, I was elected to fill the vacancy. I tried to make my offering as acceptable as he had been, and before long I found that I liked the work" (Duster 1970, 23).

Sunday, October 31

Letters from C[harles] S. M[orris]—J.G.G., J. A. A[rneau]—E. H. H[ackley]—Aunt F[annie]—L[ouis] M. B[rown]—& Professor J. H. B[urrus] and have answered none. Mr. Johnson called last week & we spent a very enjoyable evening. Was elected editress of the Evening Star. Wrote a letter to the Scimitar concerning the the-atre which they published & the Free Lance published. Haven't

joined the Chatauqua yet. . . . bro. Ayers this morning, & went to
Avery Chapel S[unday] S[chool] this afternoon, from there to Mrs.
Love's.

Sunday, November 7

Few letters last week. Answered Mr. A[rneaux]'s, E. H. H[ackley]'s
during the week & wrote to Aunt F[annie], L[ouis] M. B[rown],
R. T. C[oles] and Wm. J. S[immons] tonight. The last published
my article "Our Young Men" last week—wrote for several copies.
Sent $1.50 for "The Chatauquan" & 50 cts. to the C.S.L.C. for
membership yesterday. Broke my $10. to pay for my hat & get
some other things yesterday. Bought $6.00 worth of lace to go on
my dress last week & will have to pay about $4 to get it made over
besides slippers, gloves etc—such a nuisance but it must be done, I
suppose. Bought L[ily] $1.35 worth of books last week also. Met
Mr. Collier yesterday & he advised me to study up & get a principal's certificate & he would give me a school. I believe its worth
the trial. Am going to studying in real earnest after this is all over.

I kept expecting Rev. Johnson back but conference has sent him
to Clarksville. I wonder when I'll get my scrapbooks? I had begun
to hope to hear from or see him often; he is delightful company.
Heard George was going to marry B.P.'s daughter, so wrote him
an urgent letter to come in today & he did so I talked to him long
& earnestly.

Sunday, November 15

No letter from H[ackley] yet—I think he is defeated tho'—by what
I can get from the papers. Have not written to C[harlie] yet. Will
some time next week. Received letters from Mr. Johnson, L[ouis]
M. B[rown]—Wm. J. S[immons] Mr. Lawson & others. The Lyceum was interesting last Friday evening if there were only a few
of us. Ripped up my blue silk dress & took it to the dressmaker to
make over this week. Bought Lily a pair of shoes $2.50. Received
a card from Miss Kimball notifying me my 50 cts. had been received, but no communication yet from the paper. Books will cost
seven dollars. Wm. S[immons] sent me 4 copies of the paper, Arneaux sent two of his own & two of another that had a sketch of

his life. So far work is progressing pleasantly. To Cong[regational] church this morning & Mrs Hill's to dinner, home late this afternoon & letter writing tonight.

WELLS read a wide variety of books, including Rienzi: The Last of the Roman Tribunes *by Edward Bulwer Lytton (1803–73). When she calls the characters "superstitious," she implies that they were pagan or non-Christian.*

She gives no details of the "misunderstanding that occurred at the Lyceum," but it was serious enough to have made her "indignant."

Although she uses a few (ungrammatical) French phrases in her letters to Charlie, it is unlikely that she studied French at Rust, where only students in the classical program studied foreign languages.

On Thanksgiving, she visited a friend and attended service at the Stranger's Church, a White church on Union Avenue, which admitted but did not welcome Blacks. The evening before, on November 23, 1886, she served as maid of honor (the "first" of three bridesmaids) at the church wedding of Isham F. Norris and Stella Butler. Wells's failure to elaborate on Stella is one of the most provocative silences of the text because Stella Butler is her relative, her contemporary, and her colleague (listed in the 1886 city directory as "Stella Butler, c teacher"). Even more astounding, Stella moved to Memphis the same year that Ida did, and the two young women boarded at Mrs. Hill's house on Tate Street. The relationship between the two women became clear in a rereading of Wells's autobiography: "Hon. I. F. Norris, a former member of the state legislature, whose wife was a relative of mine, suggested that I go out to Oklahoma. . . . I accepted the suggestion and left Memphis with them" (Duster 1970, 57). Mrs. Norris's family name, Butler, was also the married name of Fannie Butler, the widow of Ida's uncle, so Ida Wells and Stella Butler must have been first cousins, "whole" or "half."

Often slave women had two sets of children: the first carried the name of the White slaveowner-father, and the second took the name of the Black husband that the woman later married. Ida's grandmother married after giving birth to Jim Wells because Ida writes, "She and her husband owned and tilled many acres of land." She also had other children, for Wells adds, "My grandmother, aunt, and uncle . . ." (Duster 1970, 9, 10). Since Stella Butler and Fannie Butler do not interact as kinswomen, Stella must have been the daughter of an older uncle, and Fannie must have married a younger uncle of Ida's. Stella first appears in the city directory of 1885 as a seamstress living at 22 Tate Street, the address of the Hills. On February 14, 1886, Wells wrote, "Little Louise Cage is very ill with scarlet fever and we are just across the street from them." (The Cages lived at 19 Tate Street.) The "we" to which she refers must have included her cousin Stella as well as two of Mrs. Hill's other boarders—Ella and Boots—mentioned in previous entries.

Why, then, does Wells seldom write about her cousin? Actually, she rarely wrote about any of her family—Jim, George, Lily, or Annie—unless they were problematic to her. She continued this practice in her 1930 diary, where she discussed at length her son Herman, who disgraced the family with his gambling, but she hardly mentioned her husband, Ferdinand.

Sunday, November 28

Two weeks since I've written & yet I was home all day last Sabbath, for it rained the whole day. I was occupied reading "Rienzie" by Bulwer Lytton. It is a fine book. Finished it sometime during the week. All of the author's heroes are learned, superstitious men—at least—all I've read. I had no callers at all last Sabbath. Nothing of interest to write of the week before, except a misunderstanding that occurred at the Lyceum, at which I was very indignant. The School Board paid us for Sept. & Oct. Saturday Nov. 20. $70 was my share. After paying Menken $12.—Lowenstein 8—Williams 2—Mrs. Settle $17.50. Mrs. Hawkins $4—& Dr. Burchett $1, I had very little left to put in the bank or send for books. Have not sent for them yet but must next week. Received a paper published in Aug. from Chatauquan headquarters but no others yet. Letter from Mr. J[ohnson] who was then at Clarksville instead of Ohio, which was answered immediately also one from L[ouis] M. B[rown] who wrote pages because I had called him, in my letter, "Mr. Brown" instead of "mon ami" or "Ma chere frere" as I was wont. He rants about friendship when he didn't need it & friendship when he does need it and hastens to decline to do several things before they were asked of him. At first I was angry that so slight a thing would call forth such zeal & was for sending him a cutting letter in return, but on reflection I did not—at least I should not call it one. But I manifested my displeasure by sending him a half sheet in return & told him I did not need to defend myself against the silly accusation of turning my back on a friend simply because he was "down in the world," had changed his occupation, & therefore would not at this time make an assurance one way or the other, & closed by telling him to "be a man, a strong, liberal minded man, or be none at all." Have no answer to it as yet. I suppose he is angry. Wrote a short letter to C[harles] S. M[orris], asking for my pictures. Received letters this week from Ida, L[ouis] M. B[rown], who thinks of coming here Christmas, Mr. J[ohnson], who will be in the city today & expects me to furnish him a paying audience to lecture to next Friday evening, according to a rash promise of mine—The editor of "The Indianapolis World" has at last decided on the remuneration I shall receive for the article I sent him & gives me 2 years subscription to his paper, sending me the receipt for one—after placing my name on his roll book as an honorary subscriber! Cheeky, that. & last but, anything thing [*sic*] else but least Mr. Hackley's letter came to hand Thanksgiving Day. He enlarges on the causes of his defeat & draws valuable lessons therefrom. Visited Miss Rosa Sheppard Thanksgiving also went to the Strangers Church & heard a good sermon & witnessed practical evidence of "white folks' christianity," in the haste with which they passed us by when choosing a seat. Wednesday evening was the day of days, the night of Norris & Stella's marriage. The church was crowded & the house was packed, and the presents were many & beautiful. There were three bridesmaids each, of which I was the first. Everybody said we looked "sweet" & I guess we did. The bride was simply lovely. Friday evening found me at home early to work on the "Star" & I found a letter from H. T. J[ohnson] awaiting me, informing me of his coming & urging on me to secure the audience for him for the following Friday evening. I did so, but the notice was too short to charge any admission. Saturday I did not go out of the house all day but stayed home & finished my dress. Sunday (today) I wrote to Mr. H[ackley] & then went again to see Miss Sheppard where I met Mr McAlwee. From there I went to Stella's & remained all the afternoon. Had a pleasant time. Came home early & found the elder awaiting me. On the impulse of the moment I simply bowed & passed thro', but recollecting myself I went back and shook hands with the gentleman.

We went to Fan[nie]'s & from there went to church at Providence where he preached a very good impromptu sermon. He will come tomorrow night to take me to the lecture at Beale s.

In early December, Wells attended a lecture on Africa and, a year later, wrote an article bemoaning the "degraded and ignorant" condition of Africa. By 1892, however, her views on the continent and its people had changed, and she supported the return of Blacks to the motherland. In "Afro-Americans and Africa," which appeared in the A.M.E. Church Review, she wrote, "Why should not they turn to Africa, the land of their forefathers, the most fertile of its kind, . . . where they would be welcomed by their race, and given opportunities to assist in the development of Africa, such as are not possessed by any other nation waiting for a foothold?" (July 1892).

Like other nineteenth-century, middle-class women of color, such as Maria W. Stewart, Charlotte Forten, and Frances Watkins Harper, Wells practiced Victorian social customs and conformed to a strict code of ethics. This code mandated that, like their White counterparts, Black women be noble and refined; they had to "uplift" the race (notably men) by eradicating vice: drinking, gambling, and fornication. Wells was determined, in this regard, to reform her "wayward" brothers, Jim and George.

A major threat to racial uplift was the figure of the Black Harlot, the invention of White Southern novelists. In December, Attorney Settle, her landlord, reported that G. P. M. Turner, editor of a White Memphis newspaper, had declared that "it was not now as it had been that colored women were harlots." Wells then wrote a letter to the Scimitar, *on behalf of "virtuous colored women" of Memphis, commending Turner for his defense of Negro womanhood. The* New York Freeman *reprinted the letter with the title "Our Women." (See "Selected Articles.") In 1887, Turner, a former general in the Union army who was attorney general of the Criminal Court of Shelby County, appointed Josiah T. Settle assistant attorney general.*

Saturday, December 4

Found a letter from "Charlie boy" when I came home Monday evening. He fails not to express himself at my waiting a month before answering him & supposes that I have a more interesting correspondent & have grown indifferent to writing to him—or I have allowed my "love of repose" to get the better of me too much for my own good or the happiness of my friends. I answered two days later & told him my delay was intentional & why it was so, but sent him a good long letter. I don't imagine he pines very much as he hardly has time. I concluded when he sent me that half sheet, that if he had time to visit etc, he certainly had time to write me a decent letter. Went to the lecture Monday evening & was highly entertained & enthused. I never was so touched for Africa before, as when he pictured the thousands bleeding & dying in ignorance & sin, & their eagerness for the gospel, and incapability to learning. Mr. J[ohnson] proposed that I join with him in the edition of a book & outlined his plan.

I gave him no satisfactory answer & he grew warm enough to express himself as to what he would do in case I did not. I was surprised to think he would suppose such a course would have any effect with me & I answered him coldly in consequence of his temerity in thus addressing me. I worked all Monday afternoon for his lecture & was told by Prof. Sampson Wednesday morning that the gentleman would leave that night. I immediately replied that if he did, I would never speak to, or recognize him again. He came that evening and brought the African lecturer, T. L. Johnson, but I noticed that he was singularly reticent & brief in his replies & surmised that Mr. S[ampson] had told him what I had said. Which was true as I found out. He concluded to remain & left to attend a lecture of his own. Next day in Mr. S[ampson]'s office he showed me a portion of a letter that greatly excited my curiosity, but he would not satisfy it. He then stated that I call a concourse of the members together & get them to agree on what they would give.

I told him that he had been so undecided all the week we had not formulated any arrangements, & consequently must be content with whatever was given. It was all a failure, tho, for it began to snow in the afternoon & continued so that when we started out, it was fully 6 inches deep. Of course nobody was there & after waiting a while returned home. He was disgusted & silent, I was cold & my nether extremities decidedly uncomfortable from contact with the snow. His visit has been something of a disappointment to me, for every thing seems to have gone awry this week. I have not been happy in my expressions & several awkward things have transpired & I know he goes away with a greatly modified opinion of my womanly equipoise & dignity; even my last speech was an ambiguous one. Received a card from editor of C.P.L.C. informing me, my $1.00 had not been received but sending me the two numbers previous. The money is lost I know and all for my stupidity. I might have known it. My brother Jim came to see me Wednesday & talked fully and freely with me; he has been roaming around & has been following a passion for gaming. I talked long and earnestly with him & begged him to promise to quit. He said he would consider it. I told him of the depths to which he would sink & when he said the passion would never get such a mastery of him, I asked him to promise to quit & let the adherence or the struggle be the test of the power it had already acquired over him; & he might judge of the future from that. O God, hear my prayer & help my wandering boy to come back to the innocence of his childhood! Let me be a feeble instrument in Thy Hands to reclaim him! I have thought of prevailing on him to stay here & help me with my project—i.e. to start a chicken farm, & for us to go housekeeping. He went out to see George & find out about him & his marrying, & promised to return yesterday, but it turned so bitterly cold, I guess he concluded to stay. Snow everywhere—an unusual sight for us before Christmas. I do hope he will return. Letters from Annie & aunt Fannie. Have written to Dr. S[immons]—Mr. T.—Charley—Cranston & Stowe, publishers (for my books).

Mr. Settle remained up town until 12 o'clock last night & tells me this morning that Gen. Turner, editor of the Scimitar, made one of the most eloquent pleas in behalf & defense of respectable colored people he ever listened to; that he declared it was not now as it had been that colored women were harlots, etc, whose virtue could be bought or was a thing of jest—a byword & reproach that there were as decent among them as among their own race; that there were some who were disgraces to their race, but that the white race had no room to talk. The same was true of them.

A. SIDNEY J. BURCHETT (1862–1916), who graduated from Meharry Medical College in 1884, was a handsome man and lifelong bachelor, who was known for his stylish dress and elegant horse-drawn carriages.

William J. Simmons engaged Wells to write for the American Baptist. *She explains the terms of their agreement:*

> He wanted me as correspendent [sic] of his paper and offered me the lavish sum of one dollar a letter weekly! It was the first time anyone had offered to pay me for the work I had enjoyed doing. I had never dreamed of receiving any pay, for I had been too happy over the thought that the papers were giving me space. Dr. Simmons also wanted me to come to Louisville next year to represent his paper at the press convention. (Duster 1970, 31–32)

Simmons was a powerful man: he was president of State University; he founded and served as president of the National Baptist Convention; he was president of the Colored Press Association; he published Men of Mark *([1887] 1968); and he traveled throughout the South as an agent for the American Baptist Home Mission Society, a White philanthropic group. Wells acknowledged his support: "[W]hatever fame I achieved in that line I owe in large measure to his influence and encouragement" (Duster 1970, 32). Unfortunately for his protégé, he died suddenly in 1890.*

Tuesday, December 21

Over two weeks since I wrote! I do not like to be so long as I am sure to forget something, but it seems I cannot help it. Went to Elsie C.'s marriage Dec. 8th & received a severe shock of fright by the floor of the room I was in falling. Mr. F[roman] came for me in a hack but I was gone; he brought me home tho'. Jim returned with George & they both went to Millington; he says there is nothing of George's marrying. They have concluded to make a crop up there this year & by that time I hope to be able to start my project. Received a letter last week from Mr. J[ohnson]. He was then in Baltimore, had waited two weeks before he wrote in accordance with my request. Was in Chattanooga 4 days & showed my picture to Prof. W. Hoped I was getting on with my work, etc, etc. I answered immediately so he might not depend on me, to let him know I could not do as he asked me & telling him I was seriously offended at his showing the picture (which, by the way, he has without my consent as Mrs. Settle was so yielding to let him have it). There has been time to answer but he has failed to do so. I know not what inference he left with Prof. W. and where he told me they "discussed me," my blood was afire. That reminds me of another picture episode. I took the picture I loaned Dr. B[urchette] from his album the night of the wedding & he says I did so because I was jealous of he and S. I gave him a piece of my mind concerning so untruthful & ungentlemanly a trick & he denied it every bit. The soft cake! Received the first of the series of books from Cranston & Stowe also the Dec. No. of Chautauquan. Am not keeping up as I could wish but will resume after Christmas. Have concluded negotiations with Simmons touching the ticket to Press Convention. I am to write short-twice-a-month articles for him exclusively until August & the price of my ticket will be forthcoming. "The World" sends me 2 years' subscription to The World as pay for my article. I sent them to Jim, & will write no more for them. They write to ask a communication for Christmas but they will not get it. I may write them something for New Years. Jim says it takes time to break up a habit that has been forming for years, & signs himself "your wild & reckless brother." It is a good hopeful letter. Received my pictures & a long letter from Charlie Friday, & answered Saturday. My letter had a motherly tone that I suspect he will not like. Received a short note from Mr. Hackley also, who only wrote in answer to my inquiries concerning Mr. Humbert (who is dead, poor man) & yesterday brought me a fuller missive. Will answer soon. All of last week was occupied in soliciting money from the Lyceum to get something for Mrs. B[radshaw]. The pin I got her cost $5. all of which I collected but 75 cts., which I paid myself. The presentation was made in good style, I think. Her sister was present & addressed us. Went out with Fan[nie] & Mr. F[roman] to look at some property Sunday afternoon, & to church with the same young lady & her escort, the younger F. that night. Am told we will get no money this Christmas. L[ouis] M. B[rown] has a letter in this weeks "World." He doesn't write to me any more.

   Mr. Carr came out to call tonight & we spent an enjoyable evening together. He promises me a Christmas Gift.

OVER the Christmas holidays Wells heard a rumor that "causes the iron to enter [her] soul," but, again, she does not elaborate. Alfreda Duster recalled in an interview that one of the rumors that galled her mother was

that she was the mistress of the Reverend Taylor Nightingale, with
whom she was later professionally associated.

Lide Meriweather and her sister-in-law Elizabeth were outstanding
suffragists of the period. Wells published her account of the meeting at
which Lide Meriweather spoke in the January 15, 1887, issue of the
Memphis Watchman: *"Every one who came was welcomed and every*
woman from black to white was seated with the courtesy usually ex-
tended to white ladies alone in this town. It is the first assembly of the
sort in this town where color was not the criterion to recognition as ladies
and gentlemen."

Tuesday, December 28

Christmas has come & gone & brought with it the good cheer incident thereto. I have had a good time but the pleasure has not been
wholly unalloyed. I have heard things that causes the iron to enter
my soul but I must learn to bear them & meet them in a more unmoved manner; to be more calm & philosophical. I rejoice in good
health & fair prospects. Received a whisk broom, a photography
album from my brother G[eorge], a box of paper from Mr. C[arr].
Today's mail brought me a beautiful autograph album from Mr.
J[ohnson] & I am expecting a book from L[ouis] M. B[rown] & my
expectations of Christmas will have been fulfilled. I gave Mrs.
T[hompson] 1.00 Mrs. Page the same, Mrs. M. a handkerchief &
Susie a pair of stockings, George a pair of gloves. Received a letter
from California Friday Dec. 24th, with a christmas Gift of $3.00 for
Lily. Received a month's pay the same day. I paid Mrs. S[ettle] $20.,
Mrs. H. $2. and put $50 in the Union & Planters Bank. Will send
Aunt F[annie] $5 for her things. Had Miss B[arnes] here to supper
that evening & we went to the Christmas tree. Went to Episcopal
Church service Christmas morning & was on the go all day. Mr.
Mosby called in the evening; afterward Mr. R. & I went to Collins
C[hapel] to a christmas service, & had a splendid time. Sunday went
to church, remained to S[unday] S[chool], went from there to Miss
B[arnes]'s to dinner, came home, then went to the Knights of Labor
to hear Mrs. Lide Meriweather speak. It was a noble effort. Mr.
Alexander accompanied me. I like him very much. Remained home
all day Monday scribbling. Monday evening Mr. R. & myself went
to call on Miss Baber & spent a very pleasant time. From what he

tells me, I believe him to be a sincere friend of mine. I must try &
curb myself more, and not be so indifferent to the young men; they
feel & resent it. I will find less business up town & be more careful
than I have—so I may give no cause whatever for uncharitable remarks. Wrote to Mr. H[ackley] & mailed the letter today. He is
traveling thro' the north. Wrote a letter for the American Baptist.

*WELLS, often outspoken and critical of others, no doubt alienated both
her male and her female friends. For example, after he had engaged her
as a paid correspondent, she told the Reverend Doctor Simmons that his
manner of writing his name was "superfluous."*

*In this entry, the first one of the new year, Wells reviews her past fail-
ures and resolves to be a better Christian and do more good works for her
Master. She was a deeply religious woman, whose pious apostrophes to
God establish, in a call-and-response pattern, a textual dialectic of
transgression and supplication. Whenever she breaks conventional codes
of behavior, of linguistic propriety, or of social decorum, she appeals to
God for assistance and guidance. Her many prayers, which recall the
formulaic and ritualistic incantations of the Black church, serve as fram-
ing devices in some entries and as acts of closure in others.*

I 8 8 7

Monday, January 3

The new year is three days old ere I find time to make entries concerning its arrival. Mrs S[ettle] & I had intended doing many things
& paying numberless calls last week but the pavements kept so
glassy the greater part of it, that we were afraid to venture. So
the week passed & we went nowhere but to Florence's marriage
Wednesday night. Messrs Carr & Mann & Mrs Phillips were the
only callers I had. Received letters from L[ouis] M. B[rown] & Dr.
S[immons]. The former in response to my card, the latter sending
money, contract, etc & our contract is sealed; for I returned the contract signed & began to carry out his instructions immediately for
I called his attention to his manner of signing his name "Rev. Wm.
J. Simmons D.D." as being superfluous. Don't know how he will
take it.

Answered L[ouis] M. B[rown] very stiffly requesting my pictures. Was at Cong[regational] Church yesterday & took sacrament. While there I reviewed my past year of existence & I am so overwhelmed with the little I have done for one who has done so much for me, & I resolved to connect myself with the S[unday] S[chool] forthwith & work for the master. I think I shall ask for a class of Youths & see if I can not influence them in a small degree to think on better things. The bible & its truths are dealt with too flippantly to suit me. God help me to try. I shall begin this year with that determination, so that another year may find me with more to offer the master in the way of good works. God help me to be a Christian! To so conduct myself in my intercourse with the unconverted. Let it be an ever present theme with me, & O help me to better control my temper! Bless me for the ensuing year; let me feel that Thou art with me in all my struggles. May I be a better Christian with more of the strength to overcome, the wisdom to avoid & have the meekness & humility that becometh a follower of Thee. Wrote to my brother also to Mr. Johnson thanking him for the beautiful autograph he sent me, for Christmas.

In her personal and professional life, Wells's most significant relationships were with men: mentors like Alfred Froman and William J. Simmons; beaux such as Charles S. Morris and I. J. Graham; and newspapermen (Countee, Arneaux, Fortune, Bowser, and Fulton) who encouraged her writing and supported her journalistic initiatives. It is not surprising, then, that she organized a Sunday school class exclusively for young men, which she describes often and proudly.

Tuesday, January 18

Received an answer from Wm. J. S[immons], D.D. proving him to be in the right & I in the wrong. Have written two letters for him already & two for the Watchman here to which he has objected as being a violation of our contract. The Freeman & K[ansas] C[ity] Dispatch & Living Way copied my letter to the Scimitar; the first named & The Detroit Plaindealer have an extract from the Watchman letter relating to the K[nights] of L[abor]. Wrote nothing last week as I was sick all day Saturday. Spent the second Saturday &

part of Sunday at Woodstock with friends. Mr. Harrison came to the school to hunt me up the week previous & I promised to go then & I did for the first time in nearly 3 years. Went to see Mrs. P[ayne] & got her husband to promise to send their daughter in to school. He was here last week & says he will bring her Monday. I am glad of it. Promised Mr. A[lexander] to go to the theatre with him & went but I felt like a guilty thing for breaking my word. The play was "Monte Cristo." Already I've had it thrown at me for so doing, & I regret having yielded.

Found a letter from Mr. H[ackley] awaiting me Sunday a week ago. & very interesting it was. I answered immediately. He has been having a gay time in Cin[cinnati]. No letter from Charlie yet. A short letter from H. T. J[ohnson] requesting his MS. Sent to him Saturday. Mr. T. writes to know when I can come to N[ashville]. Read a paper at the Institute Friday entitled "What Lack We Yet?" Friday night we went to hear Bishop T. preach & Mr. Woodford came home with me. Mrs. Rickman has given me a tempting invitation to accompany her home this summer, but alas! I cannot on Lily's account. I like not the idea of sending her away from me & to strangers at that. No, that will have to go as many other such offers have done. I cannot accept it. I will teach this summer. She is a good woman tho', & I feel as near to her as to a mother. Saturday I received a letter that had I got it 6 months ago I would have been better off in pocket than I am, if not experience. The letter Aunt F[annie] wrote just before I left for California advising me not to come. Where it has been all of these months is hard to say. Sunday tho' still weak, I went to Avery Chapel S[unday] S[chool] & organized a class of young men or rather youths, just merging into manhood. I talked to them & got them to say they would come every Sunday. I am so thankful & more than delighted with my success, so far & pray for it to continue. But I seem to be a failure so far as my own brother is concerned, for I speak harshly or indifferently & repulsively to him before I think of the consequences. I can get along well enough with other boys but am too hasty & impatient with my own. God help me be more careful & watchful over my manners & bearing toward him. Let not my own brother perish while I am laboring to save others! Have heard nothing from Jim since I wrote him last. A number of papers & a letter from H. T. J[ohnson] yesterday. A letter & my little picture last week from

L[ouis] M. B[rown]. He gratuitously declines to do many things that were not asked of him as well as refuses to send my other picture. As there is a repetition of the same old gasconade concerning qualifications of friendship, I'll treat it with the silent contempt it deserves.

Tuesday, January 25

The week passed swiftly & pleasantly if not profitably. Wednesday evening Mr. M[arcus] came over & we went to hunt up Fan[nie] whom we found at Mrs. T[hompson]'s, to go with us to Miss B[aber]'s. We went but she was gone to the theatre. Returned to Mrs. T[hompson]'s & made a night of it. Thursday evening Miss T. & Mr. Carr called & spent the evening agreeably. Friday remained at the Institute till late but went nowhere that night. Received & answered a letter to Mr. Yates giving him a good scolding for waiting so long. One to Prof. Johnson also one to Eli. Received letters from Mr. T[aylor] & Aunt F[annie] Sunday. Went to Avery S[unday] S[chool] & had a class of eleven; our name is Excelsior.

VICKIE O. *is Victoria Owens, a public school teacher, who lived at 445 Vance Avenue.*

Tuesday, February 1

Expected to attend a party given last week but my escort did not come. He not only did not come but has told others that I wrote his name on the invitation & intended subjecting it to an expert to decide if it was my handwriting. I spoke to him about it this morning and he acknowledged that he said "some" of it. I thanked him that he had so early shown me my mistake in supposing him a high-minded gentleman who could discriminate between the false and the true & would scorn to lend himself to wrong and injustice. I feel so disappointed in them all! He made no excuse last week & I asked for none. Thursday we, Fan[nie] & Jim came by & played parcheesi till late. Friday was occupied in finishing the examinations. A letter from Mr. C[oles] that evening wishing to engage me on the Dispatch staff. Vickie O. was married Thursday of last week. I am the

only lady teacher left in the building who is unmarried. Letter from
H. T. J[ohnson] Saturday. Went out to Mrs Hill's & stayed all night
Saturday & came to church next day. Went to Avery Chapel
S[unday] S[chool] after church & had three members in a class! I
hope for the best tho. An account in last week's Scimitar of a
woman who mashed a white man's face to a jelly that was trying to
enter her house & shot her husband in the attempt. He was so badly
hurt, he died in a few moments. Wrote to Messrs C, P[oole], H. T.
J[ohnson] and Eli. Wrote to Mr. P[oole] in answer to a letter I received from him yesterday wishing to know if I was to be married
declaring how he was affected by it & conjuring me to tell him, "by
memory of what had been" if it were true.

I sent a few lines merely stating that if he desired my happiness
to come home & help make me happy. I know not what he will
think of it, but I feel singularly lonely & despondent and wrote on
the spur of the moment. Stayed at Mrs Hill's L[ily] & I, last Saturday night & came to church Sunday morning. Had one caller in
the afternoon in the person of Mr. Dunlap, who took me to church
that night at the Cong[regational].

*WELLS describes a scandal involving prominent White Memphians; she
suggests that the punishment fits the crime because the lady has been de-
famed by her lover. According to the February 1 Memphis Appeal,
J. T. Dalton "had been having improper relations with [Mrs. Annie
Polk, the daughter of John R. Godwin, a prominent cotton merchant],
taking her to assignation houses and following her to a watering place."
Her brother, Russell Godwin, avenged his sister by killing her lover in
the lobby of the elegant Peabody Hotel.*

The noted actor Edwin Booth was scheduled to appear in Richelieu
on February 10, Hamlet *the next night, and* Hamlet *and* Othello *the
night after that. Performances were held at the Memphis Theater, where
tickets sold for $1.00 and $2.00.*

Tuesday, February 8

Another week has slipped away & I've done nothing. Interest has
been & is still centered in the Godwin case that has brought forth
some shocking developments concerning the morals of high life. A

silly woman forgot her marriage vows for an equally scatterbrained boy; who boasted of his conquest in Nashville, St. Louis, Marianna, as well as here, as a result he lost his life. The brother of the woman taking this revenge on him. It seems awful to take human life but hardly more so than to take a woman's reputation & make it the jest & byword of the street; in view of these things, if he really did them, one is strongly tempted to say his killing was justifiable.

Letters from Messrs Simmons & Hackley who was in K[ansas] C[ity] at the time. Answered yesterday. Went to church at the eleventh hour Sun.; from there to Avery S[unday] S[chool] and 8 of my class came back again. My Sabbath evening callers were Mr. & Mrs. Henderson, Messrs Lee & Phillips, Fan[nie] & Jim who wanted me to go to church.

Mr. C[arr] was out Friday & made arrangements that we go & see Booth play Richelieu. But I am afraid he will wait too long to get the tickets & thus we be crowded out. Mr. Mann promised to see what he could do & let me know last evening but he came not. Mr. Settle is sick with pneumonia & Lily has stayed with him while we were at school. Am going to speak to Mrs. S[ettle] about her next pay time. Letters from Eli & Nathan. Mr. C. has said nothing about going to see B[ooth] & I will say nothing to him.

Monday, February 14

Wednesday evening went up to Fan[nie]'s & spent a pleasant evening in company with Mr. C. A. Thompson playing parcheesi. Thursday night Mr. C[arr] sent a note to say he could not get the tickets but would go to the Odd fellows entertainment. Was much disappointed but I went to the latter place with him; spent a miserable evening there. Wrote to Mrs. Bowser & Mr. Arneaux congratulating him on his success. Next night, Friday I went in company with Miss Baber & her cousin to see Booth play "Hamlet." It was a superb rendition & as the first time I saw either the man or the play I could form no comparison between other actors & "the greatest living actor." I saw him also the next night, in company with Miss F[annie] J. T[hompson] & Mr. Froman, play "Iago." I do not like that near as well as the former. There was an incongruity as well as an ordinariness about it, that showed little if any of his genius. Came home thoroughly done up as I was out all the night before. Miss Baber, Mrs. Woodford, Turner, Jackson & Mance & myself went out to Fan[nie]'s after the theatre Friday night as Miss B[aber] expected to leave the next night, and spent the rest of the night in fun & games. Enjoyed myself nicely but have felt very badly ever since from its effects. A caller Friday at school, Mr. Balay, by name, with an introductory letter from Dr. Wm. J. S[immons]. He was at S[unday] S[chool] Sunday and accompanied me home. We spent the afternoon in pleasing converse & I was loath to see him leave. Had my class as usual and tried in my feeble way to talk to them. I earnestly pray for faith, wisdom and patience to accomplish what I have undertaken. Let my work prosper in Thy Hands my Father & let me not trust in myself, nor forget the lessons of humility Thou hast taught. Bless me in *all* undertakings my Father & O guard my tongue from evil. Answer to my mad letter to B. F. P[oole] today & he asks if his coming will really contribute to my happiness. I know not what to write; he seems so surprised at my writing so & that I have not forgotten him. Shall write & ask him to forget & send me back those letters. Letter also from Aunt F[annie]. Wrote to H. T. J[ohnson] this day.

THIS entry indicates that, in the 1880s, Black men created a model of bourgeois social respectability; they established and enforced codes of "proper" womanly behavior. When a group of men decided that attendance at the theater was inappropriate for a teacher, Wells accepted the criticism and vowed to be a better example to her students.

Sunday, February 20

Letter from J. A. A[rneaux] of New York City in answer to mine of congratulations; he presumes to familiarity. Did not answer. Wednesday evening went to Bettie B's funeral & that night to the wedding of Miss L. Wright. Thursday morning Mr. Carr came to see me at school & brought me a ticket. Friday the suggestion entered my head to get up a storm party among the teachers & I believe it will be a success.

School Board paid for two months yesterday. I also drew out $20 from the bank in order that I might pay Mr. Church & have enough to foot my other bills also. Bought L[ily] a pair of shoes $3.00.

Paid Menken $5.00, Mrs S[ettle] $20. & the rest belongs to Mr. C[hurch]. I regret it but it is not to be helped now. If I could only take that money as my own! Was to have gone to LeMoyne last night to practice a drama in which I have taken part, but I had no one to go with, so went up to Fan[nie]'s & stayed all night. Mr. Hunter came after I had gone, but they did not tell him where I was. Miss B[aber] sends word there will be a rehearsal tomorrow night, & I guess I'll have to go. Went over to Mrs H[ill]'s this morning & met Fanny there. She looks very badly; I fear she will go into consumption. Came from there to S[unday] S[chool]; had 10 in the class & our collection was 65 cts. Mr. Dardis Jr . walked home with me & read me a severe lecture on going to the theatre; he showed me how his father Prof. Thompson, Mr. Greenlee, Mr. Selectman, Dr. Burchett etc regarded it, & that he now considered that I was one who failed to practice as I preached. I regretted it more than I can say all along, but not so keenly did I see the wrong, or think of the influence my example would exert until then. I had not placed so high an estimate on myself. He certainly gave me food for thought and here after when I grow weary or despondent & think my life useless & unprofitable, may I remember this episode, and may it strengthen me to the performance of my duty, for I would not willingly be the cause of one soul's being led astray. O thou Help of the weak & helpless! help me be firm and strong for the right & watchful for my own conduct. Guard me aright, and grant me success.

In the following entry, Wells hints at the reasons for her decision to move, suggesting that the Settles are "parsimonious," particularly in their treatment of Lily. She and Theresa Settle, however, continue to socialize together.

Ellen Dickinson taught with Ida B. Wells at the Kortrecht School, and John Carr was a barber, located at 59½ Beale Street. M. W. Dogan, her hairdresser, was originally from Holly Springs and made frequent trips there.

Tuesday, March 1

Paid at last. I went up to Mr. C[hurch]'s this morning before breakfast and paid him one hundred dollars, leaving 45 cts, still unpaid.

Did not call for a receipt or think one necessary. Now when I pay Mr. Yates I will be all right. Had I only been ready could have gone to housekeeping this week, at a location just suited to me, but I had no furniture & there was no time to consult Mrs. Matthews. I am dissatisfied here, and much as I dislike the way things are arranged, I have decided to make no other break until I start out for myself. I believe in everybody's saving what they can, but I don't believe in one's being too parsimonious & when it comes to a point of offering to sell a pair of shoes to a child—that might easily have been given away & taking dimes promised them & paying their way on the street cars when going on errands for them. I'll not rest till I am out of the house, as I've lost my interest in it. Not many letters last week—in fact only one of special interest & that was from Mr. H[ackley]. He writes with his usual happy style & proposes to introduce me to a lady friend. Have not replied as yet—will wait & curb my impatience. While I received none, I wrote more than for many a day. To Mr. P[oole], Mrs. Bowser, Mrs. Wells, Messrs Ousley, Harrison, Lewis (& a bundle of papers) Morris and Mrs. M. Later I wrote to Mr. B. & Rev. Wm. J. Simmons. Still owe Messrs Taylor & Coles letters. We had a holiday last week & Mrs. S[ettle] and I went calling—a thing I've not done before since I've been in Memphis. We paid 22 calls in all & came home in the evening tired out, & then did not get around. Monday night 5 of us— all that came of the large number expected—went down to Ellen D[ickinson]'s & spent a very pleasant time. Tuesday night, the Messrs Bryant came & spent the evening playing parcheesi—they left next night. They are very pleasant. Mr. Carr came that evening also & brought a Mr. Stewart with him. He seemed somewhat constrained, in the presence of the others, but said he would be here the first Sunday in the month. Practiced Wednesday night again, & the rest of the week tried to make up for any loss of sleep. Spent Saturday in writing for the American B[aptist]. Sunday went to church after a call from M. W. Dogan who took a picture I sent by him to Mrs. Rather. Had 10 in the class Sunday & my contribution was 75 cts. I am so proud of my success. Father help me, I pray be more thoughtful & considerate in speech, and in action be consistent. May my labors be attended with success & guide my pen in ways of wisdom & peace: and may my prayers be answered & may I be submissive to thy will.

WELLS promises Mr. Ousley to spend a month at his home in Wood-
stock, a town in Shelby County.

Sunday, March 6

No S[unday] S[chool], no church, no nothing today but a steady
downpour of rain; so no one has been out but L[ily]. Letters from
Mr. H[ackley] (nearly two weeks ago), Mr. J[ohnson] Friday and
"Charlie" yesterday. He started to write in answer to my peremp-
tory card but was taken sick & the letter was concluded in a different
handwriting & stated that he was sick. All anger & resentment dies
away & I write him immediately solicitously, inquiring for his
health. Was out every afternoon & night last week practicing my
drama. We are getting along nicely. Bought a pair of shoes for myself yesterday for $4.50 and a writing desk for Lily for 90 cts. Want
to have my dress made soon, but I've no money to spare. Have not
made Lily's dress either & tomorrow is her birthday. She will be 11
years old. Fan[nie] T[hompson] Mr. Mann, and Mr. Carr came to
call this evening. Have not moved yet & hardly think I shall now
until school closes anyway. Will have to put up with it, and if the
Father prospers me, will go to housekeeping on my own hook. No
letter from Mrs. Matthews yet. Mr. Ousley was in to see me yesterday & I agreed to go out when school is out & stay a month.

FLORENCE COOPER taught at the Monroe School, and J. L. Fleming
was a journalist who moved to Memphis from Marion, Arkansas, where
he edited the Marion Headlight.

Monday, March 14

Letters from Mr. B. Mrs. A. W. M[atthews], Eli, Jim, Mr. Yates.
Wrote to Messrs Johnson & H[ackley] last Monday. Every after-
noon last week we practiced and Friday night the long expected
event transpired & was an artistic & financial success. Wrote the
American Baptist Saturday. I find myself running out of subjects.
Will have to check up if I expect to hold out till Aug. Called on Mrs.
E. W. Mosely who with her husband has been in town two weeks,

in company with Mrs. Cooper Misses Thompson & Felton, week before last. Last Tuesday evening I went to the first named lady's to a sociable to meet her. Had a pleasant time. Mr. Marcus was my company. Our preacher is here and I heard him preach first Sunday. So far I like him except he assumes too much for a stranger. Went to Mrs H[ill]'s to dine & was too late to meet my class. Hated it badly, as I had to miss last Sabbath. Mr. S[ettle] went to the office yesterday & brought me a letter & card from B. F. [Poole] & Dr. S[immons] respectively. The former sent my letter & talks as tenderly as usual. I wonder if there is nothing to him but words. Heaven knows I would gladly help him, but he seems content to remain as he is, despite his tone and I cannot show more anxiety than he. Wrote to Mr. Taylor, Jim, Mr. P[oole] and Mrs. M[atthews] last night. Took my dress & trimmings today and spent 3.22 in the store besides the money I'll have to pay for my dress. Dr. Braden of Nashville visited the school today—also had a call from Mr. Fleming.

Tomorrow is the day of the drawing—I wonder if 71796 will get anything, or if my approaching case in the Supreme Court will bring me any thing? A little help now would do wonderful things. I trust I may be prospered.

WELLS's grandmother Peggy had at least one child, Jim Wells, by her slave master. She married (probably a man with the surname Butler) and had several children, including Margaret, her only daughter. Following the deaths of Jim and Lizzie Wells, Peggy, who did day work, took care of Ida's brothers and sisters until she had a stroke and moved in with her daughter (see Duster 1970, 8–11). It is surprising that Wells had lost touch with her relatives and did not realize that her grandmother was still living.

Apparently, Fannie Butler owns property in Memphis, which, as she writes in a later entry, Wells wants to buy. Perhaps it is property that Fannie inherited after the death of her husband because the place has to be "probated."

Wells was elected editor of the Evening Star, *a newsletter issued by the Lyceum, a literary society that met at LeMoyne Normal Institute on Fridays.*

Sunday, March 20

I am not happy & nothing seems to make me so. I wonder what kind of a creature I will eventually become?

A letter from Aunt Margaret last week that informs me grandma just died March 1st. I was very much shocked to know she had been alive all this time & I never knew it or where she lived. I wrote immediately asking for particulars. A letter from Aunt F[annie] who still wishes to know what it will cost to have the place "probated" to her. Must find out what she means before I write. One also from Mrs Rice who has a little girl. The new preacher called & we went to prayer meeting last Wednesday evening after supper. I like him rather well save a few mannerisms. Tuesday night Mr. Greenlee called. Friday night went to the Lyceum & was reelected as editor. Learned that George is at Mr. Payne's. I fear I've driven him away with my tongue again. Will write him. Mr. Carr was out calling Friday eve & went to the L[yceum] with us. Mr. H. came home with me from the Institute. He's a nice little fellow. Added another dollar to my already long account at Menken's this afternoon. Am determined it shall be my last. Can buy things cheaper at other places & I'm going to do a cash business after this so help me.

Tuesday, March 28

Letters last week from Aunt Fannie, Mr. H. T. J[ohnson], Mr. E. H. H[ackley] "Charlie" & Mr. Lawson. Wrote to George, Jim, Aunt F[annie] Mr. Taylor, Bowser & Simmons. Bought a hat costing $3.50 that I am sorry for now. Fan[nie] & J[im] were over one night & played parcheesi. Friday night went to Lyceum & Saturday made a dress for Lily. Must make her some skirts. Mrs. Matthews was up yesterday and I went with her to her church & missed my own service, but we had a very affecting meeting. Mr. I[mes] preaches with such fervor. I wish to attend the series of meetings there this week, but I have no one to escort me. Went to meet my class in S[unday] S[chool] at Avery at one o'clock. Father help me to have some influence over them and use that influence for good! I want to be of use to them, show me the way, I beseech Thee. Mr. Imes preached about our religion costing us something & I thought of the beautiful Easter time coming, that my thoughts had strayed away from the true significance of the time to less important matters of dress; that I have made no preparation for an Easter offering, but must do so and instead of spending my holiday in fun & pleasure for myself will fast for my many sins of dereliction & remain home to work, watch and pray, and praise for the wonderful goodness of my Father to an unworthy servant. Went to see old man Bostic who has been sick so long, last week & was greatly refreshed by my visit. Mr. Carr brought a good motherly lady Mrs White from K[ansas] C[ity] to see me today at school. Paid Judge Greer $10. today to continue the case; with what he has, makes $15.

J. PENNOYER JONES was a Black politician from Desha County, Arkansas, who urged representatives to the Colored Republican State Convention in 1883 to break with the "party of Lincoln" and support the Democrats.

Monday, April 4

Last Tuesday evening Mr. Marcus took me to call on Mrs. Means & we spent a very pleasant evening. Wednesday night Messrs Carr & Woods called to take us to call on Mrs. White. We had a fine time going thro the rain and spent a very enjoyable evening. Mr. Wilkins was out to see me Tuesday evening & borrowed an American B[aptist]. Thursday evening went up to Mrs Hooks to meet the "Hon J. Pennoyer." He's a gas bag if not worse. Friday night to the Lyceum with my work unprepared. Was excused till next time. Saturday sewed most of the day, went to Fan[nie]'s in the afternoon and stayed quite a while in company with J[im]. Mr. C[arr] called that evening & we went to Mrs. Turner's for a moonlight walk. Fan[nie], Abbie, J[im] & Ike D. came by and serenaded me as a last goodby from J[im] for he left yesterday morning before I opened my eyes. To take a morning walk we went out to Mrs. Love, Fan[nie] and I—and I spoke about moving as Mr. S[ettle] & Lily don't seem to get along well together. Made hurried calls on Mesdames Page & Turner & returned in time to get Lily ready for S[unday] S[chool]. To church in the morning, from thence to S[unday] S[chool] then home where I found Lula Stanford awaiting me. Before she left Mr. W[ilkins] came & I spent a very pleasant afternoon in his company. Mr. Orr came home with me & made an engagement to call next week. Fan[nie] & I went to church at night alone.

WELLS records rather matter of factly the death of Louis Payne, her mentor in Woodstock, before reporting the loss of her suit against the railroad.

Henry Rider Haggard's She: A History of Adventure *was a popular novel published in 1886 by Harper's Brothers.*

Monday, April 11

Nothing of especial interest to record for the past week. Wednesday evening went to Mrs. Love's & from there went to prayer-meeting. I asked the prayers of the church for my aunt. Went again Thursday night in company with Mr. & Mrs. Tate & Mr. A[lexander]. Mr. Orr came but he did not come on to the church as I requested him in a note I left for him. Received a note since, in which he says he went to the Christian Church instead. Letter from "Challie Boy" Thursday. Answered immediately. Letter from Mr. T of Nashville. He intends coming this way soon. Friday night Mr. Hart was in and informed me of Louis Payne's death & Fan[nie] & I went out there next morning, but were too late for the funeral. Sunday was Easter—the day celebrated for that on which our blessed Lord was risen. Went to morning service S[unday] S[chool] and back home— the usual routine except that I went to Mrs. Herman's for dinner. No callers in the afternoon but read or began to read the novel "She" that is creating such a stir. Letter from my dear Aunt who was packing to move when she wrote. Will write her before I send the money; I think I can see my way clear to paying back the money if I borrow it. The G[ate] C[ity] P[ress] brought the sad intelligence that Louis B[rown] is paralyzed. I was very much shocked on reading it, and will write him a letter tonight. The Supreme Court reversed the decision of the lower court in my behalf, last week. Went to see Judge G[reer] this afternoon & he tells me four of them cast their personal prejudices in the scale of justice & decided in face of all the evidence to the contrary that the smoking car was a first class coach for colored people as provided for by that statute that calls for separate coaches but first class, for the races. I felt so disappointed, because I had hoped such great things from my suit for my people generally. I have firmly believed all along that the law was on our side and would, when we appealed to it, give us justice. I feel shorn of that belief and utterly discouraged, and just now if it were possible would gather my race in my arms and fly far away with them. O God is there no redress, no peace, no justice in this land for us? Thou hast always fought the battles of the weak & oppressed. Come to my aid at this moment & teach me what to do, for I am sorely, bitterly disappointed. Show us the way, even as Thou led the children of Israel out of bondage into the promised land. To Mr. Yates, Taylor, Johnson, Bonner, and Aunt F[annie] I must write when I'm able to buy stamps.

A WEEK *after the loss of her suit against the railroad, Wells attended a meeting of a local civil rights group organized to fight White violence and the politics of accommodation, which intensified in the decade following the Compromise of 1877. This passage underscores the role of independent Black churches, such as the Avery Chapel African Methodist Episcopal Church, in championing civil rights and the importance of Black ministers and businessmen in providing progressive leadership.*

The Reverend Benjamin Albert Imes was born in 1848 to free Black parents in Pennsylvania. After graduating from Oberlin in 1880, he became the first Black pastor of the Second Congregational Church, which he served until 1892. Edward Shaw (1820?–91) was a free Black who moved, in the 1850s, to Memphis, where he operated a saloon and gambling hall on Linden. A fiery orator and militant Republican, he ran for the Shelby County Commission in 1869 and for the U.S. Congress in 1870. Elected wharfmaster in 1874, he edited the Memphis Weekly Planet, *one of the city's first Black newspapers, and practiced law in the 1880s.*

Monday, April 18

Have just returned from what I consider the best thing out. The Negro's Mutual Protective Association had a public meeting at Avery Chapel tonight and Mr. A[lexander] escorted me down. I was very much enthused as I listened to the speeches and saw the earnestness of the men present. The object tonight was to draw up resolutions concerning John Sherman's action and touching also the competitive drill to be at Washington next month. The Negro is beginning to think for himself and find out that strength for his people and consequently for him is to be found only in unity. The earnest scholarly enthusiasm of Mr. Imes, the dignified patriarchal & stern demeanor and bearing of Mr. Shaw—show that the men of the race who do think are endeavoring to put their thoughts in action for those and to inspire those who do not think. A note from Miss F. informed me Mrs Graham has returned home & I went to find out where she was. Mr. Wilkins & I also called on Mrs. C. and got her consent to sing for us. Went to Menken's & paid him $10. bought a pair of shoes & a dress for Lily. $3.25 & came very near buying a pattern, but refrained. No letters today. Mr. Fleming & Miss P. called on me yesterday afternoon & spent a pleasant afternoon. My Sabbath School class was quite interesting. Must go to S[unday] S[chool] at my own church. Saturday the school-board paid me $120. $50 of which I immediately sent to Mr. Yates & $2.50 to Mr. Johnson for my pictures. Paid Williams 90 cts on acct. & bought 30 cts. of stamps, & Mrs. Settle $40. Owe her 5 more; Mrs. H. $4.00 for last & this month's washing & that about exhausts my pile, but I am thankful it is as well as it is. Ridie M. sent for me Friday afternoon. I went to see her & she told me a horrible tale of cruelty & mistreatment & said she was going home next day. Have not seen her since so can't say if she did. The Lyceum met as usual Friday night, Mr. A[lexander] accompanied me. Wrote Aunt F[annie] Messrs T[aylor], Orr, Bonner Yates. Wrote to Mr. B[rown] last week—after the G[ate] C[ity] P[ress] informed me of his affliction & received the answer Saturday. Glad to know he is better.

IN April, Wells corresponded with the editors of the Chicago Conservator, *the oldest Black paper in that city. In 1893, she moved to Chicago, where she joined the staff of the* Conservator, *edited by F. L. Barnett. She bought the paper in 1895 and the Monday following her June 27 marriage to Barnett assumed editorship of the paper.*

In 1887, Wells's circle of friends increased substantially to include teachers, businessmen, government workers, and their wives. William Davis, C. A. Thompson, and Ellen Dickerson (or Dickinson) were public school teachers. James Willis was a blacksmith with a shop on

Union Avenue, and her friend Mrs. Matthews was the wife of Roland Matthews, also a blacksmith. Samuel Woods and John Selectman were barbers, while Mrs. Alfred Means was married to a hatter. Dallas Lee was a policeman, and Abraham Henderson, whose wife invited Ida to tea, was a letter carrier for the Memphis post office. Madison Wilkins, Thomas Stewart, and Patrick Mann worked for the Memphis and Louisville Railroad. Lewis Speigle worked at Cole Manufacturing Company, Andrew Orr at Floyd and Mooney, George Carr at Bohlen-Huse on Beale Street, and Charles Woodford was employed by J. W. Grant and Company.

In her diary, Wells never names either her minister or the church to which she belongs. "Mr. N." might have been the Reverend Taylor Nightingale, who took over the pulpit of the First Church (later the Beale Street Baptist Church) in the 1880s, probably after the Reverend Countee was forced to resign in 1882. Active in Republican politics, Nightingale was also a journalist who cofounded the Free Speech and Headlight, *in which Wells later assumed an interest. At one time, the office of the* Living Way *was also located in the church. In Holly Springs, the Wells family most likely attended the Asbury Methodist Church. Furthermore, whenever she mentions the Beale Street Church, Wells lists it as one of the churches she visited.*

Sunday, April 24

Have not heard from Mr. Arneaux since I sent him, at his request, my picture and sketch. If he published it, am anxious to see what sort of figure I cut. Wednesday evening Messrs Carr, Jackson & Hunter were out to call. Went to see Mrs. G[raham] Tuesday. She looks very thin & poorly. We formed ourselves into the nucleus of a Dramatic Club & wrote out a list of names of those who we thought would take part—to meet here next Wednesday night. Thursday evening a letter from "Jim" and a call from Mr. Orr. We spent a most agreeable & enjoyable evening. He promises to call again. Friday afternoon brought a letter from Mr. H. T. J[ohnson] who will send my pictures this week. Mr. A[lexander] & I went out to Mrs. Henderson's to tea the same evening & returned to the Lyceum. A letter Saturday from The Conservator managers (Chicago) who wish me to write. Almost finished a dress for Mrs. S[ettle]. Mr. Carr brought me a note from L[ouis] M. B[rown] &

came back this morning early & went with me to the conservatory to get some flowers to send him (L[ouis] M. B[rown]). After sitting up over half the night, was up by six this morning & enjoyed my walk much. The basket of flowers I bought were both lovely & fragrant. I sincerely hope they will help to cheer him in his loneliness. Back for breakfast, dressed, went to Cong[regational] Tabernacle, Beal sts. & personally requested they announce our entertainment. Also sent notices to Avery & the Episcopal Church. Then to my own church to service, from there to Mrs. Herman's, thence to Avery S[unday] S[chool]. Went to Mrs. Henderson's & ate another dinner, from there to Dr. Phillips' with another notice. Home—to church tonight & now to bed. Met Lewis Speigle when on the way & he went back with me. Have spent for the week: Box of berries for Mrs. G[raham] 35 cts. Flowers for L[ouis] M. B[rown] $1.25, calling cards 25 cts, church 25 cts. May all the mistakes of the past week be forgiven & the good deeds repeated.

I want here to speak a word of my delight in our preacher. He is the most energetic man I know. He has made the waste places blossom as a rose and the church is beginning to look up. He is also a hard student and good preacher. The way he handles the beligerents is admirable, for they are becoming as quiet as lambs, and yet they all stick to him and respond when he calls on them. They yet remain his friends. He is certainly a splendid judge of human nature.

Mr. N.

PINCKNEY BENTON STEWART PINCHBACK (b. 1837) was elected lieutenant governor of Louisiana in 1871 and served as governor for forty-three days in 1872.

Monday, May 2

Last Monday nothing unusual occurred; went to the church meeting & everything passed off amicably. Miss P. & Mr. Gaillard called for me. Tuesday eve Mr. A[lexander] called & invited me to attend Mrs. S's concert but I had engagements at home that prevented. Messrs Woods, Carr, & Woodford called & we spent a pleasant evening. Each of the gentlemen bought a ticket for our concert. Wednesday received a letter of acknowledgement & thanks from

L[ouis] M. B[rown]. That evening in response to invitation nearly
a score of young ladies & gentlemen met to form the dramatic organization, & appointed a committee of which I am chairman to
draft plan for permanent organization. Went out to Mrs. H[ill]'s
with Ella & stayed all night. Came home early next morning.
Thursday evening called on & solicited the Hon. P. B. S. Pinchback
to lecture for the Lyceum. He promised to be there & I published it
so. The result was we had a nice crowd out & while they heard
nothing extra as a speech, we got a crowd to make the announcement concerning Judge Douglass. Saturday finished the work of
the previous S[unday]. Had an enthusiastic session of my S[unday]
S[chool] Class yesterday. Mr. & Mrs. S[ettle] went to my church
both morning & evening. Letters from Mr. Yates, Gus. Navers,
Mr. Fleming, Mr. Orr. Spent for the week ending $4.90 at Men-
kens. 25 cts. at church. Received my pictures which do passably
well & exchanged with Miss B[aber]. Wrote Prof. H. T. J[ohnson]
etc. Tonight after a good deal of worry, comes our concert & entertainment. The clouds lower but I sincerely hope it will not rain.
Last Thursday the pictures of the school were drawn; today we had
a sample of them.

Tuesday, May 3

The concert which was a grand success every way is over & done
with. Our program was good (so they so [*sic*]) & they sold out
nearly every thing. I recited "Le Marriage de Conveniance" for the
first time here and every one admired it. Indeed Judge Latham paid
me a very high compliment when he said it was the most artistic
piece of elocution he had ever heard. I felt greatly flattered. Jimmie
W—Mr. Carr—& Mr. Froman were my especial helpers. The last
named gave me a basket of flowers costing $1.10. Taken all together
it was a big success, for I learn we made clear nearly $60. Thank the
Lord for His blessing! Letters from my aunt & Mr. Bowser today.

Thursday, May 5

Part of the Dramatic C[lub] met last evening but we did no work.
Adjourned to next Tuesday night. Bought 65 cts. worth at Men-
kens yesterday; received my bill with the same mistake on it. Lily

& I had a pitched battle this morning for some of her felonious practices. My Father help me guide her aright.

During this period, Wells had to take over some of the household chores because of the illness of her landlady, Mrs. Theresa Settle. Within the next year or so, Mrs. Settle must have died because on March 20, 1890, Attorney J. T. Settle married Fannie A. McCollough, a vocalist and musician, who headed the Music Department at LeMoyne Normal Institute. Miss McCollough, an acquaintance of Wells's, appears in one of the diary entries.

Monday, May 16

A whole week went by without a letter from any one. Finished Mrs. S[ettle]'s dresses & begun on one for L[ily] but had to go to town to be paid one months Sat. so got up early & finished ironing in time to go. Put $40 in the bank, paid Mrs. S[ettle] $5. remaining on board, spent $4.30 up town to finish my dress this evening & I will have to pay $3. for the making. Mrs. S[ettle] has been sick for three days, & I've done the cooking. Mr. Jack—was out one evening last week. Went to the L[yceum] last Friday evening but no meeting. Letter from L[ouis] M. B[rown] Saturday. One from H. T. J[ohnson] today. Wrote to my aunt & instructed her to send a clear deed. Consulted Mr. S[ettle] about it & desired him to work it up. I owe so many letters & am getting too lazy to answer them. Messrs Woodford & Hunter came as callers yesterday.

On Sunday, May 29, Wells joined friends for an excursion to Raleigh, a small health resort with a population of about 1,500. Located on the Wolf River, eleven miles outside Memphis, the town was noted for its natural springs, health spas, historic cemetery, Tapps's Hole cave, and beautiful landscape of fountains, laurel bushes, and rustic bridges. Vacationers lodged at the Raleigh Inn and the Raleigh Springs Hotel as well as at a hotel owned by Blacks.

Monday, May 30

Two weeks since I scratched a line! Since then we have had our concert—was caught in the rain—Charlie sent me home in a hack. Very few letters from any one. Mr. A[lexander] has not called for some time: Mr. Spain was up from Sardis last Sabbath & Mr. W[ilkens] called as well as many others. Mr. Greenlee escorted me to church that evening. Messrs Carr & W[ilkens] were out Thursday evening & the latter perfected arrangements to take me to Raleigh the 29th (yesterday). Friday evening Mr. Froman was out & escorted me to the Lyceum also engaged my company for the concert two weeks hence. Ironed, sewed, went for my dress,—all Saturday made preparations for lunch and all for Sunday and it rained until 12 o'clock. We went to Raleigh tho' our stay was necessarily short.

I enjoyed the quiet of the place very much and the drive was splendid! The Cemetery is a beautiful place. It all had the beauty of novelty to me. Am very grateful for the opportunity to do so. To church last night we went at Avery but I did not enjoy services much. Letter from Fayette Saturday & he is in Colorado Springs, Colo. He is certainly a rolling stone as is also L[ouis] M. B[rown] who, I see by the K[ansas] C[ity] Dispatch is en route for Baltimore. School out tomorrow. I cannot say I am sorry. I don't feel glad. Expenses go on just the same and I don't wish to leave town yet. I wish to get a school this summer if possible.

Friday, June 17

The school board paid its last indebtedness today. With $60, I paid Menken in full ($19). Sent Aunt Fannie ($10). Paid Mrs. S[ettle] $15. and she brings up a months indebtedness of which I was not aware, & shows me to be in debt to her $18. I don't know how it came about, but of course I'll have it to pay. They have been very exact & hard on me in the money way but I'll not say anything about that. But try & do better next year. And I shall also keep strict account of all my expenditures if I live another year. I feel that I have paid, but have nothing to show for it & must pay again. I wish I could have managed better for this month but could not.

I wish I could feel that my money was not so persistently sought after. I wonder if I shall ever reach satisfaction in this world. My Father prepare me in my undertaking I pray Thee. I have secured no school as yet, & fear I shall not.

Wrote 10 letters at a stretch day before yesterday: Messrs Hackley, Morris, Lawson, J. H. Alexander, Simmons, D.D., Wells,

McAlwee, Mann, Aunt Fannie, Mrs. Overall. A card to Mr. Ousley & a letter to Mr. Arneaux last week. Answer to the last today brought a picture in costume, of the writer. Attended the Institute all of last week, & went to the picnic Friday evening where I remained till late. Was at Mrs. Hill's yesterday & calling at about 5 other places today. I'm very much dissatisfied about the way money matters have paid out.

Had to whip Lily severely this morning for her second peculation. I earnestly pray such may never happen again.

WELLS *spent almost a month near Woodstock, a small farm community in Shelby County, where she once taught and still has many friends. Located on the Loosahatchie River about ten miles north of Memphis, in the 1880s the community had four general stores, a combination flour mill and cotton gin, and one physician. The Chesapeake, Ohio and Southwestern Railroad, which Wells sued, linked the town to Memphis, the county seat. Mrs. Nannie Wallace, mother of nine, was the wife of Lyman Wallace, the first Black alderman in Memphis and a former member of the Board of Education. Mrs. Cassels was the wife of Thomas Frank Cassels, who served in the Tennessee General Assembly from 1881 to 1883. He was Wells's first attorney in her suit against the railroad.*

John H. Alexander, whose father had been an Arkansas state legislator during Reconstruction, became the second Black to graduate from West Point. John H. Burrus, who received the B.A. and M.A. degrees from Fisk, became president of Alcorn University in Rodney, Mississippi, in 1883.

Mary "Mollie" Church (1863–1954) was the daughter of prominent Memphis businessman Robert R. Church, Sr., who loaned Ida B. Wells $100 to return to Memphis from Visalia. After graduating from Oberlin in 1884, Mary Church spent two years in Europe before returning to Memphis. Although Wells writes that Church's "ambitions seem so in consonance" with hers, the two women never became friends. In 1899, when Mary Church Terrell gave in to pressure from other women not to place Ida Wells-Barnett on the convention program of the National Association of Colored Women's Clubs, Wells-Barnett wrote in her autobiography that it was a "staggering blow." She added, "I was still more surprised that she had obeyed the dictates of women whom she did

not know against one she did know, who had come from her own home
in Memphis, Tennessee. And that since she had done this I would prom-
ise not to inflict my presence upon the organization" (Duster 1970,
259).

Wendel's Farm, 4 miles west of Woodstock
Wednesday, July 13

Nearly a month has elapsed since I scratched a pen in my diary!
Four days only is lacking to make it out; during that time I have seen
much and got about briskly. On the Tuesday following my last entry, I came out here, and with the exception of last week spent in
town, have been here ever since. Sunday June 19th, an omnibus full
of us went to Raleigh and spent the day very pleasantly and on
Tuesday shook the city dust from my feet. Returned the following
Saturday for my trunk, the next Tuesday for a side saddle and went
to Millington July 2nd in response to a postal from my brother Jim
stating that he was sick & asking me to come to him. Returned here
Sunday & left Monday for Memphis where I went to meet Mr.
Yates and help make his stay a pleasant one. With the exception of
having drawn 5 dollars every time I have gone in town, I have nothing otherwise to regret. I have only $35. in bank now, and with no
school to teach this summer, there is a strong probability of its
being again diminished before school opens.

Dr. S[immons] has placed me on the program of the Press Convention against my consent, and promises to send the wherewithal
so I guess I'll go there & of course will have to prepare, and *prep-*
aration takes money. Last Monday July 4th, Mr. Y[ates] & myself
spent the day talking over old things; that evening we went to the
Asylum & had a very pleasant time. The Cadet, Mr. Alexander's
brother, was out with Miss Church and I was glad of the opportunity to meet him. I also met President Burrus of Alcorn University that evening. Talked to "Charlie," Mark, and Jimmie W. Tuesday. Mr. Yates spent part of the day with me, he and Fan[nie]; Then
came Matt, and after him came Mr. Fleming. We went to Mrs
Hooks' concert that evening. Wednesday ate dinner with Mrs. Wallace, afterward we took a drive, then home to meet an engagement
that was not filled. That morning we called on Miss Church and
found her the most pleasant companion; from there to Mrs Hook's,

thence to Mrs. Cassels. Thursday went to Mrs Cooper's and that evening, Mrs. Hooks gave a quiet entertainment for him & we had a pleasant time with some good music from Miss McCulough. Friday morning we went to the office of the schoolboard but Mr. Collier was out. Mr. Hill though was present & entertained us nicely. Our parting was peculiar to ourselves as we said our goodbys on Main Street while waiting for my car. Miss Mollie was down Friday evening to call and said she wished to have a talk with me. Her ambitions seem so in consonance with mine that I offered to come up the next morning. I did go and I came away after about two hours chat—very much enthused with her. She is the first woman of my age I've met who is similarly inspired with the same desires hopes & ambitions. I was greatly benefited by my visit and only wish I had known her long ago. I shall not let the acquaintance slack. Indeed I shall write & invite her to come out here to see me.

Wrote to Dr. S[immons]—Aunt F[annie]—, Jim & George & Aunt M[argaret] & rode out to Woodstock & mailed my letters Monday. Have gone about so constantly, I've not had time to settle down to regular work yet. I must do something to show for this summer.

Saturday, July 16

This morning I stand face to face with twenty five years of life, that ere the day is gone will have passed by me forever. The experiences of a quarter of a century of life are my own, beginning with this, for me, new year. Already I stand upon one fourth of the extreme limit (100 years), and have passed one third of the span of life which, according to the Psalmist, is alloted to humanity. As this day's arrival enables me to count the twenty fifth milestone, I go back over them in memory and review my life. The first ten are so far away, in the distance as to make those at the beginning indistinct; the next 5 are remembered as a kind of butterfly existence at school, and household duties at home; within the last ten I have suffered more, learned more, lost more than I ever expect to, again. In the last decade, I've only begun to live—to know life as a whole with its joys and sorrows. Today I write these lines with a heart overflowing with thankfulness to My Heavenly Father for His wonderful love & kindness; for His bountiful goodness to me, in

that He has not caused me to want, & that I have always been provided with the means to make an honest livelihood. And as I re-
hearse these measures my soul is singing the glad refrain "Bless the
Lord O my soul and all that is within me, Bless His Holy Name for
all His benefits." When I turn to sum up my own accomplishments
I am not so well pleased. I have not used the opportunities I had to
the best advantage and find myself intellectually lacking. And ex-
cepting my regret that I am not so good a Christian as the goodness
of my Father demands, there is nothing for which I lament the
wasted opportunities as I do my neglect to pick up the crumbs of
knowledge that were within my reach. Consequently I find myself
at this age as deficient in a comprehensive knowledge as the veriest
school-girl just entering the higher course. I heartily deplore the neglect. God grant I may be given firmness of purpose sufficient to
essay & *continue* its eradication! Thou knowest I hunger & thirst after righteousness & knowledge. O, give me the steadiness of purpose, the will to acquire both. Twenty-five years old today! May
another 10 years find me increased in honesty & purity of purpose
& motive!

HERE, *Wells critiques* Les Misérables, *the romantic novel written by
Victor Hugo (1802–85) and published in 1862. Her antipathy to Hugo's romantic heroine, whom she describes as "sweet, lovely . . . but utterly without depth," gives an insight into her attitude toward the passive
and feminine ideal woman of the nineteenth century.*

Friday, July 29

Have just finished reading "Les Miserables." It is a very touching
thrilling story, but the description is somewhat tedious. It is like
climbing mountains & crossing valleys to read some of it. But the
hero is grand, a truly miserable old man and I cannot forgive his
daughter for forgetting him. I do not like his heroine—she is sweet,
lovely and all that, but utterly without depth, or penetration—fit
only for love, sunshine & flowers. He breaks off suddenly from a
certain line of thought and begins on something seemingly foreign
to the subject, but brings it into the main channel finally if in a

round about manner. His moralizing may be of interest to many but not to this reader.

Letters today from Aunt Margaret, Mr. Fleming, and Miss Mollie Church, but none yet from Dr. Simmons. I wonder if he means to disappoint me at the last moment? I have made all preparations to go to M[emphis] & will start tomorrow. I think he is not at home, is why I have not heard from him & and am acting on that belief. If he disappoints me it will not be the first of its kind. However I shall leave nothing undone on my part. A letter from Mr. W. yesterday. He is very stiff—the result of the cold water douche I threw on his first very gushing epistle. I don't like that style & I might as well say so. I won't encourage it.

August 3

Came in town Saturday and have yet received no letter from Mr. S[immons]. Sent him a telegram today. Mrs. S[ettle] is very sick & I have been cooking etc. these very warm days. Drew $10. out of the bank Monday & had my book balanced. Find that I am $5. richer than I thought for as I still have $30. in bank. Got my new seersucker yesterday as well as made a $2.72 bill at Menken's. I didn't want to do it, but my money was running too short.

AT the invitation of Dr. William J. Simmons, president of the National Press Association, Ida B. Wells attended the organization's annual convention in Louisville. Located on a plain adjacent to the Ohio River Falls, Louisville was a thriving industrial and cultural center with a population of close to 25,000 by the mid-1880s. By 1890, the well-established Black community included thirteen doctors, eight attorneys, fifty-nine clergymen, and over a hundred teachers.

The university to which Wells refers was a Black Baptist college located on Kentucky Street between 7th and 8th streets. Originally called Kentucky Normal and Theological Institute, its name was changed in 1879 to State University. In 1887, Dr. Simmons was president of the institution. Mrs. Fitzbutler was the wife of Kentucky's first Black physician, Henry Fitzbutler.

Ida B. Wells about 1893. Courtesy of University of Chicago Library.

The Beale Street Baptist Church. From T. O. Fuller's History of the Negro Baptists of Tennessee, *1936.*

Wells frequently made "cabinets," or photographs of herself. From James T. Haley's Sparkling Gems of Race Pride, 1897.

.ls. ʷhen this portrait was p blished in 1891 rl⌐ˊ enn's The n Press, Wells shed journalist. Moorland-Spingarn ente⸳ Howard University.

Residence of the Settles, with whom Wells boarded. From G. P. Hamilton's The Bright Side of Memphis, 1908.

The State Normal School in Holly
Mississippi. Courtesy of the ——— ——a
County Historical Museum.

A typical Black Holly Springs family in the post-Reconstruction period. Courtesy of the Marshall County Historical Museum.

Memphis businessman Robert R. Church, Sr. From Roberta Church's The Robert R. Churches of Memphis, *1974.*

Mary "Mollie" Eliza Church was an 1884 graduate of Oberlin College. Courtesy of the Moorland-Spingarn Research Center, Howard University.

Isham F. Norris, a Memphis businessman. From T. O. Fuller's Pictorial History of the American Negro, *1933.*

William J. Simmons was a prominent writer and minister. From William J. Simmons's Men of Mark, *1887.*

The Barnett family in 1917. From Alfreda Duster, editor,
Crusade for Justice, *1970.*

Kortrecht Grammar School. From G. P. Hamilton's
Booker T. Washington High School, *1927.*

Julia Britton Hooks was a Memphis musician and teacher. From Historic Black Memphians.

══

T. Thomas Fortune was editor of the New York Age. *From William J. Simmons's* Men of Mark, *1887.*

══

R. C. O. Benjamin was a writer, minister, and editor. From I. Garland Penn's The Afro-American Press, *1891.*

══

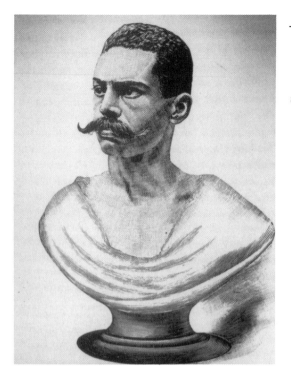

J. A. Arneaux was editor of the New York Enterprise. *From William J. Simmons's* Men of Mark, *1887.*

Edwin P. McCabe was state auditor of Kansas. From William J. Simmons's Men of Mark, *1887.*

Louisville, Kentucky
Friday, August 12

Have been in this city since Monday evening. The Convention is over, my paper read, many men of prominence met, many visitors received, my picture (God save the mark) in yesterdays Courier Journal and I am still here. An answer to a second telegram came Friday evening Aug 5th, telling me my pass was on the way & on Saturday I had everything to do, as Mrs. S[ettle] was still very sick. Sent for Fan[nie] who staid all night with me & helped me all next day. Mr. H[ill] drove me down to the depot—Messrs Savage & Froman came down to see me off & I got here to find no one awaiting me but I found them. Am stopping with a pleasant lady on Centre St. No. 631—Mrs. George Murfree, by name. The convention was but poorly represented north of Mason's & Dixie's line—none of the northern giants were present, but we had a very pleasant session and an earnest one. There were some able debates by P. H. Murray of St. Louis, Bragg & Mitchell of Virginia, Alexander Clark— D. A. Rudd,—Anderson—C. M. Wade and others. I think it accomplished much good and I am glad to be here. Was called on to respond to "Woman in Journalism" at the banquet Wednesday night and was so surprised that I omitted to say many things I should have said. I offered no word of thanks in behalf of my sex— for the flattering encomiums bestowed on them by our editors and the hearty welcome accorded our entrance into this field. I wished & may never have a more favorable opportunity to urge the young women to study & think with a view to taking places in the world of thought & action. The suddenness of the thing drove every thing out of my head but I will remember next time. For visitors I've received Messrs McKinley of this place, Jones of New Orleans, Allensworth of the N.S.A., Bragg & Mitchell of Virginia, Alexander Clark of Chicago, W. J. Simmons our President, Wade of Nashville—and last but by no means least—Mrs. Morris the mother of "Charlie." Mrs. Fitzbutler & Mrs Froman called in the afternoon while I was away at the University where I took supper. So also did Mr. Wade. Wrote to Mr. Ousley & Lily today also sent papers to Mr. Wilkins. Must stop & prepare a toilet to go out. Later: Had a dozen photographs ordered today after we returned from New Albany, Ind. Messrs Bragg & Mitchell called & together with Miss

Cook we went over the river to Indiana. Took in the town & returned on the daisy line. Paid $1.25 for my pictures & am afraid for that reason I shall not be satisfied with them; they are too cheap. Will not receive them till I get home. Have already exchanged with Mr. Mc[Kinley] almost against my will. I hardly know him well enough.

THE following entry was written in Lexington, the second largest city in Kentucky, which is located in the center of the Bluegrass region. There, Wells met Mary "Meb" E. Britton, a teacher and journalist and sister of Memphian Julia A. Hooks; her articles had appeared in several Black newspapers throughout the area. In 1887, the American Catholic Tribune *published her paper "Woman's Suffrage as an Important Factor in Public Reforms."*

Lexington, Kentucky
Wednesday, August 17

One can never tell one day what he will do the next. I had no dreams of coming here twentyfour hours ago, but here I am domiciled in Bro. Ayres' house. Arrived at noon today after leaving this morning at 6.50 A.M. and have had a good sleep since. Have already met "Meb" the correspondent for the paper here & sister of Mrs. Hooks of my town. She & a younger sister called soon after my arrival. I was very much pleased that they did so. Am going to Millersburg tomorrow to see Dr. Berry & think of returning to Louisville Sat. I will have company if I return then, as Messrs Parrish & Gibson who came up this morning with me, will return then. Messrs Bragg & Mitchell, after going down with & having a group picture taken Saturday, left for this place that evening and Mr. B[ragg] preached here last Sabbath. They have gone home now & I am not sure they have not taken a great deal of my interest with them. (P.S. Wrote to Mr. Wilkins & Bertcha tonight.) Bought Lily a pair of earrings $1.50 and Mr. Ousley a volume of "Robinson Crusoe" 70 cts. Myself a Norfolk Jersey jacket $3.00. Had any number of callers last Sabbath, many of whose names I can't remember. Miss Booker, a one time friend of Charlie's, was the only lady. Messrs Perry, Nixon, Childress, Upshaw, Bennett, McKinley, & Minor were a few of those I remember. Dr. Simmons & Miss Cook spent the evening with us. Monday morning in company with Mr. Mc[Kinley], I visited the City Hall & ascended to the cupola—only 147 ft. high & had a splendid view of the city—which is roughly estimated as being seven miles square.

Spent the afternoon at the University but went nowhere at night. Tuesday morning wrote & mailed two letters to the Headlight & Sun, respectively of Ark[ansas]. Monday evening, sent a card each to Messrs Settle & Ousley apprising them of the fact that I had decided staying longer as my ticket was extended to Sept. 1st. Mrs. Dr. Williams is trying to get me in the notion of visiting Mammoth Cave. Might do so if I have any clothes.

On Sunday, Wells visited St. Marks Colored Episcopal Church and the Fifth Street Baptist Church, pastored by the Reverend Andrew W. Heath. The most prestigious Black church in the city at that time, it included among its members public school teachers and faculty of the State University. The Colored Orphan Home, located at 18th and Dumesnil streets, was founded in 1878. It was the first welfare institution established by Blacks in Louisville.

Louisville, Kentucky
Wednesday, August 24

Returned here against the earnest expostulations of Lexington friends, last Saturday night. Went to Millersburg last Thursday from L[ouisville] to see Dr. Berry & wife. My visit was a pleasant surprise to them. Returned that evening & Miss B[ritton] brought her married sister, Mrs. Franklin to call. Spent the next day with them at her country seat & the finest dinner, and most superb I ever ate was served at her house. The cream was excellent. Spent the evening at Miss B[ritton]'s (who had a few friends there) and the night with her. She is a sensible pleasant girl & gave the best recitation of "Ostler Joe" I've heard. Visited Misses Ross, the younger of whom played splendidly, also at Mrs Nelson's. Then home to see if any one had come. Packed my trunk & received a telegram to come on. Had fine fun; coming back. Visited the Christian church Sunday morning, the Episcopalian that night. Came home by Fifth St.

Church & met a number of people, among whom was a Mr. Hackley who is cousin to my Denver one-time-friend.

Monday morning bright & early I went to get my pictures & change my jersey, the neck of which was too large. The pictures were ruined & I would not have them. A $1.25 thrown away, but came down to another gallery and ordered another dozen. Plenty of money. Came home then went out to the University & remained all day—Got here about 3 o'clock & found half Louisville had been to call. Mrs. M[orris] & I then went to the Orphans Home and spent the remainder of the afternoon. Went to Miss Jordan's to a rehearsal that evening & came back by the University. Borrowed 5 from Mr. S[immons] that day. Went buggy riding yesterday morning with a Mr. Jones of New Orleans. A visit from Mr. Gibson & the gentlemen during the day—an excursion up the Ohio River last night, by the light of the new moon & the day for me was done. Miss Bryant called to see me while I was down town buying gloves (69 cts) but I came before she left. Misses Jordan & Davis called today, also the Messsrs Hackley & J[ones]. Went went [*sic*] to look at the proof of my pictures which was very good then went up on the tower of the city hall. Tea at Mrs. Sam Jordan's tonight. Home & bed.

On Wells's return from Louisville, her relationship with her landlords, the Settles, deteriorated because of differences over money. On August 3, Wells had only $30.00 in the bank and, later, had to borrow $5.00 from Mr. Simmons, so she was probably unable to pay her rent for August and September. On June 17, her last payday, she had paid Mrs. Settle $15.00, but her landlady claimed that an additional $18.00 was due. Wells was very proud and diligent about paying her bills, as is evident in the regularity of her payments to Robert R. Church. She was, therefore, quite upset that the Settles "made [her] feel badly" and even locked up her things.

Woodstock, Tennessee
Tuesday, September 6

Have been back from Louisville 11 days and am just making my first entry. Was made to feel badly on my arrival and have been busily hunting a home ever since—but am unsuccessful as yet. Have only stayed at the house two or three of the nights since my return & then my things were locked up, and there was such an air of constraint visible that I have only tarried long enough to write to Dr. S[immons] Mr. G[ibson], & Miss Jordan. I've had no heart to write to any one else, I've been in a state of such depression.

Left L[ouisville] Friday Aug. 26th, at 8 o'clock P.M. accompanied by Miss Britton and arrived in M[emphis] next day at 1 P.M. The friends did not want me to leave apparently & were very kind to me. Quite a number met at the house and entertained me with songs and Messrs Harris and Childress gave very fine elocutionary renditions and the whole body adjourned down to the train with me. Messrs Harris & Gibson & Miss Jordan rode to the last station with us. Thursday.

MRS. SPILLMAN is the wife of William L. Spillman, who is listed in the Memphis city directory as a blacksmith (colored), residing at 17 Wright Avenue. There is no listing for a Mrs. Hawkins.

15 Wrights Avenue
Friday, September 9

Moved here yesterday—at Mrs Spilman's but don't know how I will like it. Only did it as a last resort. On coming back I found every other place objectionable on some account & I had knocked around as long as I cared. Stayed at Bert's that night—went out to see Mr. Mayo also. Letters from Lottie, Lem. Dr. S[immons] and Mr. Mitchell (his picture also) Have answered all but Lem. Also wrote to Charlie, "Meb" & Aunt F[annie]. Lily is at Mrs H[awkins]'s. I earnestly trust we will pull thro' the year all right.

Everything & body is stirred up over the school matters. Mr. W. had a fine article on the question in Sunday's Avalanche that is stirring up a lot of sand. I hope it will be successful. No letter from Mr. G[ibson] yet. I guess Mr. Jones must have been mistaken. I thought I'd write & acknowledge the receipt of the confectionery but on second thoughts I won't.

IN the 1888 Memphis city directory, E. Cooper is listed as the occupant of 20 Goslee Street. Florence P. Cooper, a teacher at the Monroe School, might have been the spouse or a relative of E. Cooper.

20 Goslee Street
Sunday, September 18

Stayed at Mrs. S[pillman]'s 5 days & moved morning. Mr. J. took me another buggy ride & I returned & had a chill almost there was such a change in the atmosphere. Mr. G. took me to see "The Burning of Moscow" that evening. The next day I went nowhere, but received visitors at home. Monday Aug 29th I drew $5. from the bank. Tramped all the week but have no boarding place—yet as I had not seen Lily, my dear little sister—I came out this morning and am here. Mrs. O[usley] greeted me so coldly I was rather hurt and will return tomorrow instead of staying the week as I had intended. Am firmly resolved to go to housekeeping on my own account next year. If Mrs. Hawkins will take Lily & teach her how to cook I will be able to do so and have her to keep house. I am sick & tired begging people to take me to board, and if the Father prospers me, I'll do it no more after this year. Received letters from Meb & Charlie Saturday. Enjoyed & must answer them today.

SEVERAL words in the following entry are illegible, and the date is not clear.

This is the last entry in Wells's Memphis diary, but on September 16 she bought a blank book, possibly of the type that she used for her diary.

. . . here on Tuesday. . . . There is more room, better facilities, and so far am doing very well. Lily is still at Mrs. H[awkins]'s. Couldn't borrow the money to buy aunt F[annie]'s place so shall try to save for it if she will wait. Wrote a statement to her & await her answer. School began the 15th; on Thursday. Went to see the Dr. about a bill of $13.50 he sent me as charges for attending George & he told me George had never been to get the instrument. I wonder if all that money goes for nothing? My pictures came Wednesday after I had written Miss G. on Tuesday. They are very good—the best I ever had I think. Strange to say, no letters from L. yet. I sent a very formal card to him yesterday, also a letter to Mr. Y[ates] & one to Ridie. An invitation to Mr. Bragg's wedding came to me last week also. He is to be married next Tuesday. I don't know how to understand my Louisville friends. I've not heard a thing from Mrs. Murphy yet. I'm anxious to know if she's got her shawl. Must answer Lem's letter.

Aug 29	drew from bank	$5.00
Sept 4th	bought basket at Menken's	1.25
Sept 8th	Stationary at W.s on Acct	1.05
Sept 16	Blank book	.40
Sept 10	Toilet Articles & Menken's	2.15
Sept. 16	Shoes	2.50

The 1893 Travel Diary of Ida B. Wells

*W*HEN Ida B. Wells began her travel diary on April 5, 1893, she was on her way to England and Scotland to enlist international support for the antilynching movement, hoping that pressure from other countries would force the federal government to take a more active role in the elimination of lynching. Wells usually began her first-person narratives during periods of change and movement, so she must have kept a diary throughout this, her first trip abroad. All that remains of that diary, however, is the nine-entry fragment that she published at the beginning of chapter 12, "Through England and Scotland," of her autobiography (see Duster 1970, 87–88). During that trip, she had new experiences that she would have wanted to remember and record: she met distinguished Britons, attended meetings, gave lectures, and traveled throughout England, where the newspapers carried glowing accounts of the speeches of the "American Negro lady."

Wells wrote, as she usually did, in what she had at hand: a small record book given to steamship passengers, probably similar in size and format to the 2½ × 5¼-inch book in which she penned her 1930 diary. The short and cryptic entries conform to the "brief spaces" of the diary, and the style—the informal tone, conversational language, and brief sentences—is distinctly Wellsian. It is a delightfully spirited journal in which she treats the usual topics: the weather, travel, her physical and emotional states, letters written and received, and new friends. She reveals later that her "four traveling companions bound for Africa" include three Liberian men and Dr. Georgia E. L. Patton, who "settled in Memphis . . . and built up a practice there." Patton was the first female to graduate from Meharry Medical Col-

lege, the first Black woman licensed to practice medicine in Tennes-
see, and the first Black woman physician in Memphis. In 1893, she
went to Liberia as a missionary but returned to the States in 1895
when her health failed. In 1897, she married David W. Washington,
who appears briefly in Wells's 1885–87 diary. Both their children
died soon after birth, and Dr. Patton died on November 8, 1900.

In one of the little books furnished passengers on the steamships, I
find in the brief spaces of blank pages left for daily record of the
passage the following entries:

I 8 9 3

First Day, Wednesday, April 5
Sailed for England today. First voyage across the ocean. Day is fine
and trip so far enjoyable. Have four traveling companions bound
for Africa.

Second Day
No seasickness. Hope to get thru alright. At any rate Miss Patton
is with me. She is a doctor and will take care of me, but I don't think
I am going to need her.

Third Day
Seasick. So is Dr. Georgia E. L. Patton. We have a stateroom to ourselves and lie in the two lower berths looking at each other. Ugh.

Fourth Day
Seasick still. Am afraid to lift my head. How I hate the sight of
food.

Fifth Day
Seasicker.

Sixth Day
Seasickest. Ugh. How I wish I was on land. Got better this evening
after swallowing half the ship doctor's medicine chest contents.

Seventh Day

Have eaten a little something but have no appetite yet. Indigestion holds me for its own. I do not advise anybody to start on a sea voyage with a disordered system. Wrote a number of letters today.

Eighth Day

We got to Queenstown this morning and our letters back to the states were mailed. I also received unexpectedly a letter and telegram from Miss Impey telling me to come directly to her home in Somerset. I had cabled her when I sailed. We reached Liverpool too late tonight to land.

Ninth Day

Woke up this morning to find out ship standing in the middle of the Mersey River opposite Liverpool. Landed about 9:30 A.M. Went thru the customs office assisted by the baggage master of Bywater Taugery & Co., who directed us to Shaftsbury Hotel where I shall stay with Miss Patton until she sails Saturday, then go to Miss Impey.

The 1930
Chicago Diary of
Ida B. Wells—Barnett

$\mathcal{A}$LTHOUGH the diary that Ida B. Wells-Barnett kept between January 1 and May 19, 1930, is short—only fifty or so three-line entries over a five-month period—it is important for what it reveals about the sixty-seven-year-old diarist just a year before her death. In 1930, the pattern of her life and the style of her writing parallel in remarkable ways the life and writing style of the twenty-four-year-old woman who began her diary in Memphis in 1885. With the same firm but graceful strokes of the pen, the mature woman records the salient features of her life: family gatherings, visits from friends, conferences with ministers and politicians, meetings of civic and cultural organizations, church attendance, expenditures for clothes and carfare, and her favorite pastimes (books, cards, lovies, concerts, lectures, and the theater). The writing is sparse and cryptic, while the brief entries conform to the size and form of the little book (about 2½ × 5¼ inches) issued by the Ideal Diary Company of New York. Entitled "Ideal Combination Diary or Memorandum Calendar," the book contains four lines for each day's entry as well as maps, reference tables, and cash ledgers. The diary might have been a Christmas gift because the first entry begins on New Year's Day.

In 1930, Wells-Barnett was still a vital and dynamic woman, actively involved in community work: gathering signatures to appeal the U.S. occupation of Haiti and campaigning for election to the Illinois State Senate. The longest and most detailed entries describe her *political campaign, in which she ran as an independent in the Republican primary against Warren B. Douglass and Adelbert H. Roberts. A lifelong Republican, Wells-Barnett was unable to get the support of party officials such as former governor Charles S. Deneen. Deneen, who had appointed Wells-Barnett's husband assistant state's attorney, and who had issued a strong antilynching proclamation after Wells-Barnett's report on a lynching in Cairo, Illinois (see Duster 1970, 320), gave her the cold shoulder in 1930. With little support from party regulars, she ran a poor third in the election.*

Wells-Barnett continued to write: diary entries, reports, personal letters to family and friends, business letters to businessmen and educators, and her autobiography. In her later years, as in the earlier period, money was a problem; on January 1, 1930, for example, she wrote, "Can't understand why my folks have no money." There were other difficulties, too—family problems, similar to those that had plagued her in the 1880s. She was concerned about the gambling of her thirty-three-year-old son, Attorney Herman K. Barnett, who was associated with his father in the law firm of Barnett and Barnett. Her son Herman is to her 1930 diary what her brother Jim was to her 1885–87 diary: the problem "child" about whom she writes at length. But she seems closer to her son than to her daughters, Ida, about whom she writes infrequently, although Ida lived with her parents, and Alfreda, who does not even appear in the diary. One of the first entries, for example, depicts mother and son engaged in an intimate family ritual: "H[erman] & I made a cake for New Year's Day & it was good."

In this diary, we glimpse Mrs. Wells-Barnett at home, baking a cake, washing clothes, and receiving callers in the small apartment to which the family moved when they could no longer keep up the eight-room house on Chicago's Grand Boulevard. Her family—husband, children, stepsons, and sister—are, for the most part, relegated to the background of her text, as they were in her earlier diary. Given the importance of the "gentlemen callers" in her 1885–87 diary, it is somewhat surprising that Wells-Barnett's husband, Attorney Ferdinand L. Barnett, who by all accounts was a loving, attentive, and supportive husband (see Dorothy Sterling's interview with Alfreda Barnett Duster in the "Afterword"), plays such a minor role in this diary. A prosperous lawyer and a prominent newspaperman, Barnett encouraged his wife's journalism, civic activities, and political aspi-

rations throughout their marriage, but Wells-Barnett acknowledges this support only briefly in one entry.

The 1930 diary ends abruptly on May 19, soon after the loss of her election and the disappearance of her son.

PERSONAL

Name	Ida B. Wells-Barnett
Residence	3624 S. Parkway
Res. Phone	Doug 2960
Bus. Phone	"
Emergency, Notify	daughter
	Dearborn 6172

I 9 3 0

January
Spent dry Christmas. Had duck for dinner, Anne was with us. She made egg nog. Ida treated to Hydrox special. We played cards Ferd & his 2 children came in, & the boy & I beat Herman & Ferd. Ida had no coat, so we went nowhere all holiday week, neither did H[erman]. Can't understand why my folks have no money.

Wednesday, January 1
H[erman] & I made a cake for New Year's Day & it was good. Had fried chicken for dinner.

Thursday, January 2
Altho had 3 invitations went nowhere, & received no calls. Meeting Joint Committee Motion Pictures.

Friday, January 3
No club meeting yesterday because the worst blizzard of the winter prevented meeting 4th Thursday at Mrs Cozier's.

Saturday, January 4
Met there yesterday. From there to Bird Cage Tea Room & met Berni Barbour, who promised to call & take me to see Show Boat.

Sunday, January 5
Emancipation Program. W. H. Haynes speaker, Cotton Pickers Quartette sang. Good house, good speech.

Monday, January 6
Wrote introduction to Child Welfare Annual Re[port]. Went to Joliet & before Pardon Board for Fred Nelson & Joseph Jones.

Tuesday, January 7
Home all day resting writing letters. Herman left last night for heven [sic] knows where. Found note to his father on my pillow.

Wednesday, January 8
Bought dress for self 15.00 & a marked down jersey for Ida for $3.00.

Thursday, January 9
Tried to get on to the last chapter of my book, so many interruptions. Worrying about H[erman] from whom I've had no word.

Friday, January 10
Pauline Parker called & paid $5.00 on account. Returned book, changed gloves, got "Compassionate Marriage" to read.

Saturday, January 11
Washed 4 prs hose, 2 prs gloves 1 slip & 1 silk dress, also H[erman]'s silk muffler. Left eye pains.

Sunday, January 12
Got $2.00 from F[erdinand] L. & sent for bread, eggs bacon. Heard H[erman] gone to Los Angeles Calif. Home all day cooked ginger bread. Dr. Ricks called with baby also Dr. Partee & Anne who is grouchy.

Monday, January 13
Ida & I attended meeting of local Negro History club. Reading from Carter Woodson's Book . . . in which is no mention of my anti-lynching contribution.

Tuesday, January 14
Attended Woman's Urban League monthly meeting. Health program very good. Announced Feb program. Had shoes half-soled, heels $1.60.

Wednesday, January 15
Home all day getting house cleaned for club tomorrow. Gave girl 25 cts on acct. Spent $1.00 for refreshments.

Thursday, January 16
Had fine meeting altho janitor was away all day & guests were somewhat uncomfortable 20 present but neither pres, vice nor sec.

Friday, January 17
Bitter cold, so home all day & eve. Ferd Jr here & had nice card game. Wrote letters to all papers anent meetings of I[da] B. W[ells Club].

Saturday, January 18
Shadd gone again altho he was just going to the corner to get tacks & taxi. No word from Herman, but nice letters from Tucker & Page.

Sunday, January 19
Spoke for young people St Thomas on Negro books & plays. Few out but very interested. Dined at Y.M.C.A. while waiting for crowd. Brot cream home.

Monday, January 20
Heard of Fanny Selby's death at County Hospital, thro Marie Hadlin. Alma dressed my feet. Spent eve with Annie, who gave me dinner.

Tuesday, January 21
Doolittle principal refused to co-operate with Parents Ass[ociation]. Paid $4.00 on dresses at Leiter's, $1.00 on acct for lining. Went to 714 E 47th St to see Fannie's corpse.

Wednesday, January 22
Mrs. Williams treated me to cream. Next day went to funeral cemetery, Mrs. Forbes & Ida Clark's carfare 17 cts.

Thursday, January 23
Saw Hallelujah today—good in spots. Went to Y.W.C.A. dinner
tonight; then to annual meeting at Harriet McCormick memorial.

Friday, January 24
Tried to get Deneen over phone all day without success. Thot annual Y.W.C.A. meeting amateurish for a 60 yr celebration. Colored
girls appeared only as "industrials."

Saturday, January 25
Platt paid 1 wks room rent. Shadd out all day—house cold &
dirty—Woman got dress for repair—Also order for Feb 2nd to Mrs.
Millner.

Sunday, January 26
Got to church too late to make announcement of next Sunday's
meeting. Wrote letter to Supt Hogge & took to Mrs M. for typing.
Went to anthrop meeting, had good time.

Monday, January 27
Didn't get to see Deneen—will write. Called on E.H.W. but he is
still stubborn about helping women.

Tuesday, January 28
Saw the Virginian—it's very good. Went to Appomattox & was at
rehearsal of doctors.

Wednesday, January 29
Leiter's announce closing got to get my mdse out. Had interview
with Dr. Shepard of the World's Fair Committee.

Thursday, January 30
Was at Urban League's annual meeting & got their endorsement.
Mayer made good talk, Holsey fair, Jackson, billboard poor. Ar-
nold Hill theoretical Claud[e] B[arnett] punk chairman.

Friday, January 31
Home all day 30th. Wrote Lil, Mrs Carter, John Page. No word yet from Doolittle principal.

Saturday, February 1
31st attended Mrs. Severidge's funeral. Annie to supper. Dr. Davis in & played cards. Ida failed to keep her word—Platt paid $2.00 (at home all day washed).

Sunday, February 2
Church till 1.30 P.M. at Mrs Sweres till 3; Friendship Home till 5, Home to dinner till 7. Meeting at Met 7:30. Great success. Roscoe Simmons made wonderful Douglass speech.

Monday, February 3
Mrs Clarke called with political news. Ordered petitions for state senator $5.00.

Tuesday, February 4
Called on Mrs. D Banks who married white man. Tribune reports effort to annul it. Saw campaign manager who says O.K.

Wednesday, February 5
Got petitions today, gave 5 out. Miss E. Welch agreed to manage for me, being a clerk of election.

Thursday, February 6
Vance did not call for me as per agreement—but wd next day. Went to club at Mrs. Ward's, gave out petitions.

Friday, February 7
Vance neither came nor called. Made a *3rd* appointment for Monday next. Went to moving picture Com. also Show Boat movie.

Saturday, February 8
Shad gone, Platt not returned. Rev Branham came to see me abt campaign, asked me to come to church tomorrow.

Sunday, February 9
Got to Olivet too late to be introduced but B[ranham] had my petition signed. Went to S[aint] P[aul's] M[ethodist] E[piscopal] & Rev. Carroll & Mr Mayer of Urban League signed.

Monday, February 10
Went to Met P.M. to attend U[niversity] of C[hicago] concert. Good. Spoke for B E Natural Club Sun Eve. Got signatures St John Bap[tist] afterward.

HERE Wells-Barnett crosses out dates in the diary and inserts her own handwritten dates.

Monday, February 10

Vance failed again so called on managers Lasalle Hotel & told that col[ored] men had said they wanted W. G. Anderson listed. Had talk with Harrison on way to Baptist min[isters'] meet[ing]. Not many signed. L.K. never gave me chance to see him.

Tuesday, February 11

Had good meeting at movie day. Mrs. Miller made good talk. Mrs. Plummer reviewed "Hallelujah" which was well discussed. Mrs. Caffray brought me home.

Wednesday, February 12

Had caller with novel proposition. Mailed petitions to Springfield over 500 names.

Thursday, February 13

Two women called & brought donation to campaign fund, & sent expense money for Haitian matter. Dictated appeal tonight. Returned waist.

HERE, Wells-Barnett crosses out February 1930 and writes May 19, 1930. She then proceeds to write longer entries with no apparent regard for dates, although she does not cross them out.

May 19

So much has transpired since last entry. Finished Haitian appeal with 85 signatures. Sent to Cong[ressman] Morton D Hull but heard nothing from it save acknowledgement of receipt of petition, & thanks from Mrs Dye.

Called on Dr. Lee Harlan leader of 2nd ward independent group, got his promise of support, he called in man named Cross who accepted my campaign with enthusiasm. He introduced me at Lincoln Center meeting got Fred Morris to endorse me and the fight was on. With money paid me by Mrs D. made a deal with Perry Thompson whereby he gave me $150 worth of printing for $75. I was thus able to distribute

10000 cards
  10000 letters
    600 window cards

Mr B[arnett] helped me, and got out the New Deal Paper—20000 copies & distributed them at his own expense. He also engaged a headquarters at 3449 Indiana but little came of it. Harlan & Melvin had 2 big meetings at Odd Fellows Hall, but little organization. Abraham Lincoln Republican Club had me speak at many meetings but double crossed me & were themselves double crossed as none of their candidates were elected. Douglass Warren B was defeated with 500 odd votes, and Del Roberts is declared winner. He wd be with the veteran machine behind him which always wins because the independent vote is weak, unorganized and its workers purchasable. Have been unable to have conference with my backers— so we may profit by lessons of the campaign.

Few women responded as I had hoped—The outstanding ones were

Mrs. Cora Williams
Halsey
Eddings

Am issuing cards to a tea for Sunday 5-25 which is also a letter of thanks to those who helped. Mrs. McCormick won against Deneen by 200000 majority

Spoke at Orchestra Hall to a large white meeting, at the Lasalle to a luncheon at which all the candidates spoke.

Mrs. D. sent one another contribution to my campaign & J. Tipper got $10 of it and a man named Ewell got $5.00 of it. The rest I used myself. Neither of those contributions helped.

Have been thro hell over revelations of Herman's actions. He used people's money right & left (gambling of course) and went away leaving us the bag to hold. He is up before the Bar Association & there seems nothing in sight save expulsion & disgrace. He fleeced everybody who helped him including his parents. He is in Denver & says he wont come back here, but will try to do so out there. *Mean*while he is doing porter work at $65.00 per mo so he says. He expects us to straighten out his tangle here so he can hang out his shingle there—He doesn't seem to realize that such a record will follow him there & perhaps prevent the realization of his ambitions tho I hope not.

I did not know of his embezzlements till I had announced my candidacy & it was too late to withdraw.

When not engaged in speaking, I read to keep from thinking. I have read

Ex-wife, by Ursula Parrott Rasputin
Catherine the Great
Companionate Marriage Mrs. Mary Baker Eddy

A BLANK half page follows this entry, and then Wells-Barnett resumes writing on the opposite page.

Had no March 1st meeting of our women because of church rally. April meeting meeting [*sic*] choir absent, no explanation unless Harrison's Juvenile Choir was the cause. Shabby treatment but nothing to do about it. Had Mr . . . from Committee of 15 as chief speaker. Spent part of the time reviewing campaign & urging women voters to do their christian duty & vote for race women on Primary Day April 8th.

May meeting on the 4th had Mr Evans of the Joint Service Committee tell of the care of our children by this bureau at Home of the Friendless, Ken 9330? Also Mrs Mamie Mason Higgins whose talk on the Job of Being a Parent was good but not as good as I had hoped. Mrs. Rennie, aunt of Parilee Newton who stabbed another girl on the street—was introduced & told how the girl was defending herself from attack when it happened. I find this joint bureau filling a need that we shd be supplying in giving intelligent care to our young.

May 19th—the Jordan girl was again in Juvenile Court but case was continued.

Letter from Corinne Dean tells me she is married & will be here June 11th. Wish I cd have them stop with me but the house is too dirty & no money to clean it. Will have to give something for her.

Wrote Bishop Barrow asking him to arrange a lecture for me— also Rev J. W. Robinson—B[arrow]'s letter returned stating he was not there. Rev. R[obinson] says I gave him too little time. Perhaps its just as well.

THE *1930 diary ends with this entry. A blank page, dated April 1930, follows, after which Wells records, above the heading "Memoranda and Addresses," the title "Petition holders." Here, she lists the names, addresses, and telephone numbers of one man and eight women. On the opposite page, she notes the addresses of the Imperial Opera Company and the Booklover's Library, both of which she must have frequented.*

On the next two pages, under the headings "Cash—January" and "Cash—February," she lists, in detail, income and expenditures for two months, including many items that she has already recorded in her diary. Her income for January 1930 was $52.50 (but only $11.00 in February), and her expenses for that month totaled $40.65.

Selected Articles,
1885—1888

*T*HE years between 1884, when Ida B. Wells wrote her first "letters" or personal essays to local newspapers, and 1887, when she presented a paper at the National Press Association conference in Louisville, were crucial to her formation as a journalist. It is that process that she traces in the pages of her Memphis diary: joining a literary society and editing its newsletter; selecting topics from her reading and travel; jotting down notes for future articles; submitting "letters," first, to local papers and, later, to national publications; corresponding with Black newspapermen; joining an organization of professional journalists; and, finally, working as a paid correspondent for "the lavish sum of one dollar a letter weekly!" (Duster 1970, 32).

The support of Black male journalists like William J. Simmons was important for her development, as Wells acknowledges in her autobiography: "Dr. Simmons encouraged me to be a newspaper woman, and whatever fame I achieved in that line I owe in large measure to his influence and encouragement" (Duster 1970, 32). Even more important, however, was her own compelling drive to write. With no experience in journalism and little formal education, Wells began, significantly, to portray herself in the pages of her diary as a newspaperwoman, referring to herself as "editress" of the *Evening Star* and adopting the pen name "Iola."

These articles were collected and transcribed by Sarah Ducksworth.

"FUNCTIONS OF LEADERSHIP"
Living Way, September 12, 1885
(Reprinted in the *New York Freeman*)

"FUNCTIONS OF LEADERSHIP," published in the Living Way *on September 12, 1885, was one of Ida B. Wells's earliest articles, written a year after she moved to Memphis. In the article, she challenges Black leaders to help the masses by opening up businesses to employ young people—a theme that also inspired Maria W. Stewart in the 1830s. One of the major values that undergirded Wells's life and that shaped the content of her discourse was the conviction that educated and privileged Blacks had a social responsibility to the less fortunate. As a result, she was outspoken in her criticism of politicians and ministers who did not serve the public or conform to high standards of ethical conduct.*

I came across a letter last week in the Detroit *Plaindealer*, from Washington, signed S.S.R., in which he gave a whole string of names, of men who are famous as orators, politicians, office-holders, teachers, lawyers, congressmen, and an ex-senator—from whom to choose a leader or leaders of the race. "Let me see" mused I, "these men have acquired fame and wealth in their several callings, they have and are now declaring themselves devoted to the interest of the people, and are thereby looked upon as leaders, have impeachable characters, are justly called representative of the race—but since they have by individual energy, gotten the well earned laurels of fame, wealth, individual recognition and influence—how many of them are exerting their talents and wealth for the benefit or amelioration of the condition of the masses?" I look around among those I know, and read up the histories of those I do not know, and it seems to me the interest ceases after self has been provided for. Of those who are amassing, or have wealth I cannot call to mind a single one who has expended or laid out any of his capital for the purpose of opening business establishments, or backing those that are opened by those of limited means; none of them have opened such establishments where the young colored men and women who have been educated can find employment, and yet complain that there is no opening for the young people.

The whites have the young people of their own race to employ, and it is hardly to be wondered at that they do not do for the Negro what his leaders have not done for him; if those who have capital to employ in establishing such enterprises as are needed why— the—the leaders are leaving a great field, whereby their leadership can be strengthened, undeveloped. The ambition seems to be to get all they can for their own use, and the rest may shift for themselves; some of them do not wish, after getting wealth for themselves, to be longer identified with the people to whom they owe their political preferment; if no more. They are able to pay for berths and seats in Pullman cars, and consequently can report that—"railroad officials don't bother me, in traveling," and give entertainments that have but a single representative of their own race present, can see and hear of indignities and insults offered their people because of individual preservation from such, can look and listen unmoved saying, "if it were my wife or daughter or relative I would do so and so," so what real benefit are they to their race any way? "Their example is beneficial, by inspiring others to follow in their footsteps with a hope of similar success," did someone say? True, I had almost forgotten that; example is a great thing, but all of us can not be millionaires, orators, lawyers, doctors; what then must become of the mediocrity, the middle and lower classes that are found in all races? It is easier to say, "Go thou and do likewise," than do it. I would like very much for S.S.R. to tell me what material benefit is a "leader" if he does not, to some extent, devote his time, talent and wealth to the alleviation of the poverty and misery, and elevation of his people?

IOLA

"WOMAN'S MISSION"
New York Freeman, December 26, 1885

Mr. Fortune sent me 10 copies of the paper with my article entitled "Woman's Mission" in it; characterizing it: "a beautiful essay." Sold two copies & will sell the others too. It reads very well, but a little disconnected.
December 29, 1885

After the planet had been thrown in space and chaos resolved into land and water, the earth was prepared for the habitation of the various animal creation, and man was given dominion over them.

Adam, not satisfied with being ruler of all living things and monarch of all he surveyed, still felt a void in his heart. In the vast solitude of the garden of Eden, as far as the eye could reach, could be seen the cattle on a thousand hills, the creeping things of the earth, air and water—all subservient to his will and owning him as master. In all this vast expanse there was no one to dispute his authority or question his sway; still he was not satisfied, for he was alone. Aye, though surrounded by all that was fairest and wonderful in animal and vegetable life, throughout the countless swarm there was no other soul; thus he was alone, for there was no one to share his glory, exult in his magnificence, nor praise his handiwork.

The Grand Architect of the Universe created a being to fill this void, to be the kindred spirit, to help in the work of tending and dressing the garden; in short, to be a companion and helpmeet to man; and when Adam awoke and found this living soul created alike, and yet differently, beside him, he called her woman, and ever since by that name has this being been known. Truly—"The world was sad, the garden was a wild. The man, the Hermit sighed, till woman smiled."

In all histories, biblical and political, ancient and modern, among the names of those who have won laurels for themselves as philanthropists, statesmen, leaders of armies, rulers of empires—we find here and there the name of woman. She has gradually ascended the scale of human progress as men have become more enlightened, until in this 19th century there are few positions she may not aspire to. In colleges she has nobly vindicated her right of equality; in the professions essayed she has borne herself with credit and honor; in positions of trust she has proven her ability and faithfulness.

What is, or should be woman? Not merely a bundle of flesh and bones, nor a fashion plate, a frivolous inanity, a soulless doll, a heartless coquette—but a strong, bright presense, thoroughly imbued with a sense of her mission on earth and a desire to fill it; an earnest, soulful being, laboring to fit herself for life's duties and burdens, and bearing them faithfully when they do come; but a womanly woman for all that, upholding the banner and striving for the goal of pure, bright womanhood through all vicissitudes and temptations. Her influence is boundless. Only the ages of eternity will serve to show the results of woman's influence. A woman's influence gave a new continent to the world. A woman's influence caused man to sin and entailed a curse on all succeeding generations. Woman's influence has been the making of great men, the marring of many more, the inspiration of poets, students and artists, the bane of others. Woman's influence, through "Uncle Tom's Cabin," was indirectly one of the causes of the abolition of slavery. But it is not queens, conscious of power . . . , but yet the many workers and artists who minister to their love of the truthful and beautiful, that most possess this influence for good; of whom men speak with tender love; but woman as embodied in the various characters of daughter, sister, wife, mother. While hallowed associations cluster around all these no earthly name is so potent to move men's hearts, is sweeter or dearer than that of mother. No other blessing can compensate the loss of a good mother. Speak to the hardened criminal of his mother and he is subdued; his defiant look is replaced by one of unutterable longing for the time in the long ago when he was a white-souled child, with no conception of the world outside his home, and no pastime without his mother's face as the central picture.

The masses of the women of our race have not awakened to a true sense of the responsibilities that devolve on them, of the influence they exert; they have not yet realized the necessity for erecting a standard of earnest, thoughtful, pure, noble womanhood, rather than one of fashion, idleness and uselessness. A standard bearing these lines:

> A perfect woman, nobly planned
> To warm, to comfort and command;
> With something of an angel's light
> And yet, a spirit still and bright.

The world labored under a burden of a curse four thousand years, the consequence of one woman's sin. But a promise was given that redemption should come at the hands of a woman, and in the year 4004 there came to a Jewish virgin an angel of the Lord and delivered unto her the tidings that she of all women had been chosen to bear to the world the promised Messiah. Eighteen hundred years ago, as the shepherds watched their flocks by night, came the fulfillment of this prophecy. Suddenly on the astonished eyes of the affrighted shepherds, broke the vision of angels proclaiming "Peace on earth, good will to men!" And this Son born of woman, whose birthnight we celebrate, is owned the world over; and whereever the Christ child is recognized, nations this night join in worship and adoration.

O, woman, woman! thine is a noble heritage! How tenderly He speaks for thee when others censure thee for thy service of love and self-denial! How cheering His invitation to thee to lay thy burdens at His feet! And when thou wast reviled, scorned, outcast, and in danger of being stoned by the multitude, He had only words of pity for thy weaknesses, compassion, pardon and peace. Thou was last at His cross and first at His tomb; in His dying agony thy welfare was His expiring thought. Continue in the good offices that first won His approval; make a living reality of the herald's good tidings of great joy and help men to know this Savior of mankind; to feel that there is a better, higher life and a purer, nobler, more fitting way of celebrating this anniversary of His birth, than in drunken debauchery and midnight carousals; recall to their minds the poor and needy, the halt and blind that are always with us and who stand in the need of Christmas cheer. Teach them this better way of honoring Him who made visible to the world that "by woman came sin and death into the world—by woman, also, came redemption."

Christmas, 1885
IOLA

"A STORY OF 1900"
Fisk Herald, April 1886

Friday I finished and sent off the article I've been preparing for the Fisk Herald, entitled "A story of 1900."
                                        February 23, 1886

Twenty years ago a young girl went from one of the many colleges of our Southland to teach among her people. While she taught for

a livelihood she performed her duty conscientiously with a desire
to carry the light of education to those who dwelt in darkness, by
faithfully instructing her charge[s] in their text-books and ground-
ing them firmly in the rudiments. She was born, reared and educated in the South, consequently the sentiments regarding, and the
treatment of, the Negro were not unknown to her. Justice compelled her to acknowledge sadly that his moral and temporal status
had not kept pace with the intellectual, and while reluctantly ad-
mitting this fact that was so often so exultantly and contemptuously
cited against him she wondered if there were no remedy for a state
of things that she knew was not irremediable. Since it had been am-
ply proven that education alone would not be the salvation of the
race, that his religion generally, was wholly emotional and had no
bearing on his everyday life she thought that if the many ministers
of the gospel, public and professional men of the race would exert
their influence specifically—by precept and example—that they
might do much to erase the stigma from the name. She never
thought of the opportunities she possessed to mould high moral
characters by—as the Episcopalians do their religion—instilling el-
evated thoughts, race pride and ambition with their daily lessons.
One day a gentleman visited the school and mentioned a promising
youth, 18 years old, who had attended that school, as being sen-
tenced to the penitentiary the day before for three years for stealing
a suit of clothes; he concluded his recital by sorrowfully saying:
"That's all our boys go to school for, they get enough education to
send them to the penitentiary and the girls do worse." It flashed on
her while he was talking that the real want was proper home and
moral training combined with mental, that would avert a too frequent repetition of this sad case and that the duty of Negro teachers
was to supplement this lack, as none had greater opportunities.
There came over her, such a desire to make the case in point an impressive lesson that school-work was suspended while she related
the story and for half an hour earnestly exhorted them to cultivate
honest, moral habits, to lay a foundation for a noble character that
would convince the world that worth and not color made the man.
From that time forth, whenever a case in point came up, she would
tell them to illustrate that the way of the transgressor is hard; also
that every such case only helped to confirm the discreditable opinion already entertained for the Negro. These casual earnest talks

made a deep impression, her pupils became thoughtful and earnest, a deeper meaning was given to study; school-life began to be viewed in a new light: as a means to an end; they learned, through her, that there was a work out in the world waiting for them to come and take hold, and these lessons sunk deep in their minds.

Their quiet deportment and manly independence as they grew older was noticeable. This teacher who had just awakened to a true sense of her mission did not stop here; she visited the homes, those where squalor and moral uncleannes [*sic*] walked hand in hand with poverty, as well as the better ones and talked earnestly with the parents on these themes, of laboring to be self-respecting so they might be respected; of a practical Christianity; of setting a pure example in cleanliness and morals before their children. Before, she viewed their sins with loathing and disgust; now she was animated by a lofty purpose and earnest aim and the Son of Righteousness sustained her. She spent her life in the school-room and one visiting the communities to-day in which she labored will say when observing the intelligent happy homes and families, the advanced state of moral and temporal elevation of her one time pupils—that she has not lived in vain, that the world is infinitely better for her having in one corner of the earth endeavored to make it bloom with wheat, useful grain or beautiful flowers instead of allowing cruel thorns, or rank and poisonous thistles to flourish unmolested.

Some may ask, why we have been thus premature in recording a history of twenty years hence. The answer is short and simple that the many teachers of the race may not be content simply to earn a salary, but may also use their opportunity and influence. Finally gentle reader that you and I "may go and do likewise."

IOLA
Memphis Tenn. Feb. 29th 1886

"OUR WOMEN"
New York Freeman, January 1, 1887
(Reprinted from the *Memphis Scimitar*)

WELLS recorded in her diary a conversation with Josiah T. Settle (1850–1915), a former Mississippi state legislator who moved to Mem-

*phis in 1885 to practice law. (At the time, she boarded with Attorney
and Mrs. Settle.) The lawyer informed her that G. P. M. Turner, a former Union officer and editor of the* Memphis Daily Scimitar, *a White
newspaper, had defended the virtue of Black women. In response, Wells
wrote a letter to the* Scimitar, *pointing out that poverty, ignorance, and
immorality were the legacy of involuntary enslavement of Black people,
and asserting that Black women in Memphis and throughout the South
had attained a "true, noble, and refining womanhood."*

> Gen. Turner, editor of the Scimitar, made one of the
> most eloquent pleas in behalf & defense of respectable
> colored people . . . he declared it was not now as it
> had been that colored women were harlots, etc, whose
> virtue could be bought or was a thing of jest—a
> byword & reproach that there were as decent among
> them as among their own race; that there were some
> who were disgraces to their race, but that the white race
> had no room to talk. The same was true of them.
> December 4, 1886

Among the many things that have transpired to dishearten the Negroes in their effort to attain a level in the status of civilized races,
has been the wholesale contemptuous defamation of their women.

Unmindful of the fact that our enslavement with all the evils at-
tendant thereon was involuntary and that enforced poverty, ignorance and immorality was our only dower at its close, there are
writers who have nothing to give the world in their disquisitions
on the Negroes, save a rehearsal of their worthlessness, immorality, etc.

While all these accusations, allowed as we usually are, no opportunity to refute them, are hurtful to and resented by us, none
sting so deeply and keenly as the taunt of immorality; the jest and
sneer with which our women are spoken of, and the utter incapac-
ity or refusal to believe there are among us mothers, wives and
maidens who have attained a true, noble, and refining womanhood. There are many such all over this Southland of ours, and in
our own city they abound. It is this class who, learning of the eloquent plea in defense of, and the glowing tribute paid Negro
womanhood, by G. P. M. Turner in the speech he delivered in the
Bowden case, return him their heartfelt thanks and assure him as a

gentleman, a lawyer and a far seeing economist is inexpressible. Our race is no exception to the rest of humanity, in its susceptibility to weakness, nor is it any consolation for us to know that the nobility of England and the aristocratic circles of our own country furnish parallel examples of immorality. We only wish to be given the same credit for our virtues that others receive, and once the idea gains ground that worth is respected, from whatever source it may originate, a great incentive to good morals will have been given. For what you have done in that respect accept the sincere thanks of the virtuous colored women of this city.

IOLA

"IOLA ON DISCRIMINATION"
New York Freeman, January 15, 1887
(Reprinted from the *American Baptist*)

■

WHEN Wells visited her aunt, Mrs. Fannie Butler, in Visalia, California, she was offered a position in the public schools. In September 1886, she taught for four days in Visalia before returning to Memphis, but she recorded nothing about the experience in her diary. Three months later, however, she wrote a scathing letter to the American Baptist, *denouncing Blacks who "barter the birthright of the race for money, position, [or] self aggrandizement." One of the examples that she cited was the segregated school in California, which she describes in her autobiography.*

> The separation of the two races in [the Visalia,
> California,] school had been asked for by the colored
> people themselves . . . and they had been given the
> second-rate facilities that are usual in such cases. All
> the white, Indian, and half-breed Mexican and Indian
> children went to school in a commodious building up on
> the hill, and I was helping to perpetuate this odious
> state of things by staying and teaching at this school.
> *(Duster 1970, 25–26)*

We howl about the discrimination exercised by other races, unmindful that we are guilty of the same thing. The spirit that keeps

Negroes out of the colleges and places him by himself, is the same that drives him in the smoking car; the spirit that makes colored men run excursions with "a separate car for our white friends," etc. provides separate seats for them when they visit our concerts, exhibitions, etc. is the same that sends the Negro to theatre and church galleries and second class waiting rooms; the feeling that prompts colored barbers, hotel keepers and the like to refuse accommodation to their own color is the momentum that sends a Negro right about when he presents himself at any similar first-class establishment run by white men; the shortsightedness that insists on separate Knights of Labor Assemblies for colored men, is the same power that forces them into separate Masonic and Odd Fellow lodges. Consciously and unconsciously we do as much to widen the breach already existing and to keep prejudice alive as the other race. There was not a separate school in the State of California until the colored people asked for it. To say we wish to be to ourselves is a tacit acknowledgment of the inferiority that they take for granted anyway. The ignorant man who is so shortsighted has some excuse, but the man or men who deliberately yield or barter the birthright of the race for money, position, self aggrandizement in any form, deserve and will receive the contumely of a race made wise by experience.

IOLA
Memphis, Tenn., Dec. 28, 1886

"THE MODEL WOMAN: A PEN PICTURE OF THE TYPICAL SOUTHERN GIRL"
New York Freeman, February 18, 1888
(Reprinted in the *Chattanooga Justice*)

THIS newspaper article was published five months after the last entry of Wells's Memphis diary, and it is significant because, here, she fleshes out in greater detail the model of feminine womanhood that first appears in her entry of June 12, 1886. Both Annie, a young Black student of "ladylike refinement" and "obedient disposition," and Miss Atkinson, a young White teacher, "so fair and pure, so divinely good," epitomize this model of womanhood derived from nineteenth-century ideologies: Romanticism, Victorianism, and the cult of true womanhood. Intellectually, Wells subscribed to this concept of womanhood, which undergirded the racial "uplift" movement, spearheaded in the 1880s and 1890s by "Race" women such as Anna Julia Cooper, Mary Church Terrell, Fannie Jackson Coppin, Josephine St. Pierre Ruffin, and others. It was a model that Wells tried to live up to in her own life, as she explains in her autobiography: "I wanted him to know at least one southern girl, born and bred, who had tried to keep herself spotless and morally clean as my slave mother had taught me" (Duster 1970, 44).

Although there may be girls in our sunny southland to whom the definition in the preceding article may apply, they are not the ideal type. Whatever else she may be, "the typical Southern girl" of to-day is not without refinement, is not coarse and rude in her manners, nor loud and fast in her deportment.

Nor is the stiff, formal, haughty girl the ideal. The field is too broad and the work too great, our people are at once too hospitable and resentful to yield such one much room in their hearts.

The typical girl's only wealth, in most cases, is her character; and her first consideration is to preserve that character in spotless purity.

As a miser hoards and guards his gold, so does she guard her virtue and good name. For the sake of the noble womanhood to which she aspires, and the race whose name bears the stigma of immorality—her soul scorns each temptation to sin and guilt. She counts no sacrifice too great for the preservation of honor. She knows that our people, as a whole, are charged with immorality and vice; that it depends largely on the woman of to-day to refute such charges by her stainless life.

In the typical girl this jewel of character is enriched and beautified by the setting of womanly modesty, dignity of deportment, and refinement of manners; and the whole enveloped in a casket of a sweetness of disposition, and amiability of temper that makes it a pleasure to be near her. She is like the girl of fairy tales, who was said to drop pearls from her mouth as she talked, for her language is elegant from its simplicity and chastity, even though not always in accordance with rules of syntax, is beautiful because of absence of slang.

She is far above mean, petty acts and venomous, slanderous gossip of her own sex as the moon—which sails serenely in the heavens—is above the earth. Her bearing toward the opposite sex, while cordial and free, is of such nature as increases their respect for and admiration of her sex, and her influence is wholly for good. She strives to encourage in them all things honest, noble and manly. She regards all honest toil as noble, because it is ordained of God that man should earn his bread by the sweat of his brow. She does not think a girl has anything of which to be proud in not knowing how to work, and esteems it among her best accomplishments that she can cook, wash, iron, sew and "keep house" thoroughly and well.

This type of Negro girl may not be found so often as she might, but she is the pattern after which all others copy.

In those who recognize in this pen picture the true woman, and desire to model after her, I send this beautiful gem of an acrostic written by a friend for a young lady's album. In its five lines is epitomized all of the above. If young girls would commit and engrave them on their hearts, they would bear with them everywhere a true inspiration and guide:

> Lucille! Since all the world's a stage—
>   Upon which we, the actors
> Come and go in every age,
>   In each act needful factors—
> Live nobly, grandly, aim afar!
> E'er onward, skyward—be a star!

IOLA
Memphis, Tenn.

Afterword

Dorothy Sterling

*B*ORN a slave, Ida B. Wells grew up during the wonderful terrible years of Reconstruction, when any goal seemed attainable for a Black child in Mississippi. During her "butterfly existence" as a schoolgirl, she saw her father cast his first vote and read of the election of Black state legislators, even Black congressmen and senators. Schools for Black children were organized, and a federal Civil Rights Act forbade discrimination in public places. But, by the end of 1885, when she began this diary, the gate to freedom and equality was closing rapidly. Black voters had been driven from the polls by armed bands, and there were no longer federal troops in the South to protect them. The Supreme Court had declared the Civil Rights Act unconstitutional, and Ida B. Wells had been ousted from the ladies' coach of a train and forced to accept Jim Crow accommodations.

Bad as this was, there was worse to come. Before this schoolteacher-turned-journalist could settle down and marry one of her gentlemen callers, the gate to freedom clanged shut with a resounding bang. In 1892, Thomas Moss, one of her closest friends, was lynched in Memphis, not for the "usual" crime of rape, but because he operated a better grocery store than a White competitor. The cry of "rape" as a pretext for lynching had been repeated so often that even Black people had begun to believe it. But the more Wells studied the statistics—726 Black men and women lynched in the preceding ten years—the more she became convinced that these mob murders were still another way to "keep the nigger down" and restore White supremacy in the South.

Traveling alone to small towns in Mississippi in the early 1890s to investigate recent lynchings, she returned with sworn statements from witnesses. Only a small number of the victims of mob violence had even been charged with rape; of those so charged, many were partners in interracial love affairs. With a recently purchased pistol on the desk in front of her, she wrote about these findings in *Free Speech*, her weekly paper. One of her 1892 editorials ended with the statement: "Nobody in this section believes the old threadbare lie that Negro men assault white women. If Southern white men are not careful they will over-reach themselves and a conclusion will be reached which will be very damaging to the moral reputation of their women" (Duster 1970, 65–66).

Before the paper reached its subscribers, Wells went East to attend a conference. She was in New York when her newspaper office was destroyed and the *Memphis Daily Appeal*, Memphis's leading newspaper, printed a front-page story demanding that "the black wretch who had written that foul lie" (Duster 1970, 66) be tied to a stake at the corner of Main Street and publicly burned.

Exiled from the South because of the threats to her life, Ida B. Wells became a crusading journalist, sharpening her denunciation of lynching in the Northern press and in a series of hard-hitting pamphlets. These led to speeches at meetings across the North as well as two trips to Great Britain in which she endeavored to "tell the world the facts." Under her leadership, antilynching leagues were organized in the United States and in England. Slowly, the number of lynchings dropped from a peak of 241 in 1892 to 107 in 1899. This was still far too many, of course, but while Wells never abandoned her crusade, she felt that she could allow herself a modicum of private life.

Although she had four children in fairly rapid succession after her marriage to Ferdinand L. Barnett in June 1893, she continued to write, to protest, and to speak out against injustice. Her first trip back to the South came in her sixtieth year, when she traveled to Elaine, Arkansas, to investigate the case of Black sharecroppers who had dared to form a union. Attacked by armed White men, many had been killed and others arrested as "Black revolutionaries." In a trial lasting less than an hour, twelve leaders of the group had been condemned to death. Posing as a cousin of one of the sharecroppers, Wells-Barnett visited them on death row and heard their story. She gathered enough information for newspaper articles and a pamphlet, *The Arkansas Race Riot.* As a result of the publicity she generated, the Supreme Court ruled that the prisoners had not received a fair trial: over the next year all were set free.

In 1976, my husband and I traveled to Chicago to interview Alfreda Barnett Duster, Ida B. Wells's youngest daughter. A handsome white-haired woman, then in her seventies, Mrs. Duster talked freely, giving a daughter's-eye-view of her illustrious mother. The following are selections from the interviews:

"My mother was very strong willed. She was known as Ida B. Wells, so, when she married, she became Ida B. Wells-Barnett. [Ferdinand Barnett, the freeborn son of slave parents, was a widower with two sons when he met Ida B. Wells.] She kept her own name in order to be remembered for what she had done. She was always introduced that way. Nobody except my father ever called her 'Ida.' Black women had been trying for two hundred years to be called 'Mrs.,' so it was a breach of etiquette to call her by her first name.

"Father was tall, handsome. Women were chasing him while he was a widower. He was just as outspoken and just as militant as Mother, but by nature he was more easygoing. Once he was threatened with jail because he said in a speech that the American flag was a dirty rag if it didn't protect its citizens. Dad had lots of wit and humor, but Mother never kidded around. She was very austere. He was always very supportive of whatever she got into, and she was always out there scrapping for him. She was interested in seeing that he was recognized for his ability.

[Wells-Barnett remained close to her sisters.] "Aunt Annie lived in Chicago. She and her husband established a newspaper, the *Searchlight.* They lived right down State Street. Every Sunday when Mother took us to church, afterwards we came by Aunt Annie's. They were better off financially than we were. Lily married William Daniels. He was on the railroad with a home in Oakland [California], so Lily moved there. She came to Chicago to visit. In that time it took a week from San Francisco to Chicago. [The ties to her brothers were more tenuous.] George later lived in Chicago, but he drank heavily, so I didn't have much to do with him. One of Jim's sons was a mail carrier in Chicago for many years. Jim's other son just walked away—disappeared.

"Father was more prosperous than most folks. We always had a telephone, and our lights were those gas mantels. We had the first fireless cooker, a big container with two aluminum pans in it. Our first washing machine was a Federal. It was square, looked something like what we have today, but it had a wooden tub. It rocked back and forth, and on the side was a wringer.

"Mother used the telephone for business, but didn't talk long. She didn't have any social friends, folks who just came by to talk. They were in a club or organization with her, and she did a lot of talking business about the club and its activities. She didn't have time for gossip. She was really a very positive and controversial person. When she came home from a meeting, she'd be unhappy about the way things had gone because she had plans for the meeting to *do* something. That's the reason why she left the National Association of Colored Women. They weren't *doing* anything. The National Association was top-heavy with social life; they weren't willing to get out into the fray.

"Mother didn't worry about the house. Dad had somebody there to clean it up. At that time it was very easy to get people to come—people who had just come to Chicago and were looking for work. Mother was very displeased by the fact that if you swept the house today, there'd be more dust there tomorrow. That bothered her—the fact that you had to clean up the place today and tomorrow you had to do the same thing. She didn't feel that she was *accomplishing* anything. She said we should always know how to keep house, how to wash, how to iron, so even if we had someone else to do it, we would know how it should be done.

"She used to make bread, but my dad did most of the cooking. He liked to cook—she didn't—so he'd go into the kitchen, put on an apron. He always had to have at least two different kinds of meat on the table—sometimes three. One wasn't enough. Dad loved stews and hash, didn't do too much frying. When I got big enough, I was supposed to help. I made corn pone every night—a mixture of corn meal and water. You make patties and cook them in hot grease. My father usually came home first, on the streetcar. I watched from the window so I could start the corn pone.

"Mother was always busy, always reading, always writing. The dining-room table was stacked up with papers and magazines. She wrote at the table. When she got up in the morning—she slept late [when she wasn't working]—she got up around ten or so. She always had tea and toast for breakfast—got that from England—and not much more. When I came home from school, the cup would be sitting there for me to wash. She didn't even take it to the kitchen.

"She kept us very close. When she went off, she'd always write to us. She arranged that Ida could go with one group and me with another. She kept up with all our activities. We were in largely White schools at that time. At Wendell Phillips High School my graduating class was exactly half and half. She often went to school to see about me, and the report had better be good. She didn't ever spank me after I was old enough to think.

"She came to our high school, and of course she stayed with me all through college and wouldn't let me go away. I had a notion I'd like to go to Howard for a year, for I'd never been to an all-Black school, and we heard there were all sorts of parties and socializing. But she wasn't for that. When I went to the University of Chicago, there were only about twenty-five Negroes there from all over the country. Nobody bothered us. I never encountered any prejudice. I got out in three and a half years, when I was nineteen. It was a fantastic experience.

"When I got married, my mother was very unhappy. She wanted me to marry a professional man. I was supposed to go to law school for three more years. Instead, I worked as a clerk in Dad's office, but it confirmed my desire not to practice law.

"At that time there was no separate Black Belt [in Chicago]. That didn't come along until thousands of people were brought here during World War I to work in the plants and the stockyards. Prior to that, people lived anywhere. The house I remember was a two-story brick house, 3234 Rhodes Avenue, a lovely neighborhood. I was born there, on the second floor, front room. When my parents moved there, there was a lot of consternation. There wasn't any violence, but the people next door showed [their feelings] very plainly. The old 31st Street gang, White boys, they used to beat up the colored boys, so the colored boys formed their own gang. The gangs used to fight each other with fists. They didn't have guns and knives like they do now. They just had a fist fight and maybe got a black eye and that was all. My mother always kept a gun in the house. When the 31st Street gang chased my brothers home one night, she dared anybody to cross [her] doorstep. Everybody knew about the gun. She didn't display it. That wasn't necessary. I never saw it, but I knew it was in the house somewhere.

"In 1919, we moved to 3624 Grand Boulevard (which is now Martin Luther King Boulevard). A beautiful home—all inlaid parquet floors and the kitchen had a big Italian marble sink. They bought it like that. They had eight rooms and a ballroom on the third floor and a full basement. They made the ballroom into an apartment for Herman and his wife until their first child was born. The house is now a national historical landmark. I went there when the designation was made. Diagonally across the street are the Ida B. Wells Homes, the first federal housing project in Chicago['s Black Belt] and the best because it was more individual, no building higher than five stories. When they first started, they had very strict rules about keeping it nice.

"While we were at 3624, Mother ran for the State Senate. That was unusual for a woman to do, but she was unusual. She could have run for representative. [A senator] comes from a much wider district. If she had won the primary, she would still have had to run against the Democrats in the election.

"Even when there was no segregation in Chicago, there were certain places you didn't go because you knew they wouldn't treat you right. After discrimination intensified, Mother went to Marshall Fields department store. She waited and waited, but no clerk would help her. Finally, she took a pair of men's underpants, put them over her arm, and walked toward the door. Immediately, a floorwalker stopped her, and so she was able to buy them.

"She used to tell about this as a funny incident, Ida Wells-Barnett with a pair of underpants dangling over her arm. She was only five feet three or four, and she had grown plump in her fifties, but she walked as if she owned the world. She floated. She always had a dressmaker make her clothes. She was interested in fashions, had some beautiful clothes. One picture of her in a black velvet dress is my favorite. That was taken about 1920, when I had my graduation.

"Women could elect University of Illinois trustees before they could vote in general elections. Mother organized the Alpha Suffrage Club, the first suffrage club in Chicago for Black women. She told them to get out and vote for those three trustees. I remember a big suffrage parade in Chicago; I marched with my mother. I had a white dress and a white streamer across me saying "Alpha Suffrage." We all had banners. We walked all the way down Michigan Avenue. I was about eight years old.

"We had interesting dinner-table conversations. We always had people there. Sunday afternoons and every New Year's everybody came to our house. And every Thanksgiving Mother made it a point to have someone who was away from home and would not have a home-cooked dinner.

"Whenever anyone came around and they were all geared up to do something, my mother was there. I can remember A. Philip Randolph and Chandler Owens when they started the *Messenger* and my mother's support of them. Carter Woodson was here in 1915, when he was just beginning the Association for the Study of Negro Life and History. Mother was a good supporter of his, but she was not one of the five who actually incorporated the society. I remember William Monroe Trotter, a short stocky fellow with a mustache, came to dinner, and we children listened. He was really a militant, so much so that he and Mother got along fine.

[Wells-Barnett attended the founding conference of the National Association for the Advancement of Colored People but was not appointed to the Committee of Forty that set up the permanent organization.] "Mother was with W. E. B. Du Bois in his basic concepts, but she didn't mince words with anybody. She didn't want Mary White Ovington to be on that board, [thought there] should have [been] all Black folks at the head of the NAACP. She took a violent antipathy to Mary White Ovington being the secretary, and of course those who were trying to have peace and quiet would naturally try to go around Ida B. Wells. She was a little ahead of her time. I think there were only two in Chicago to sign the round robin, Dr. [Charles E.] Bentley and Ida B. Wells. So, since she was controversial and Dr. Bentley wasn't, that's why Du Bois thought it better to put Dr. Bentley on there.

"We used to play cards—whist, that was the family game. Mother and Ida played whist as partners against my father and me.

I guess that's the only time she relaxed a little bit. Sometimes in the evening, if we had company, they'd get the card table out and play a game of whist.

"We had a victrola. We had all of the Caruso records, and the sextet from *Lucia* was one of our favorites. Along with the classics, Mother enjoyed the popular music of the day like 'Alexander's Rag Time Band.' I remember especially a humorous record called 'The Preacher and the Bear.' It told about the preacher 'who went out hunting one Sunday morn / And though it was against his religion / He took his gun along.' On his way home he met a great big bear. The preacher prayed, 'Now, Lord, if you can't help me / For goodness sake, don't you help that bear.' We played it often, and every time we played it Mother laughed and laughed. Ida took piano lessons. We had a big old piano. Mother didn't play, but she liked to pick out some things, particularly church tunes. She gave me dancing lessons. I was in the ballet teacher's annual exhibition, and she got my costume made for me. After I got to be eighteen, I was my ballet teacher's helper.

"Mother was interested in the theater, helped budding Negro actors like Abby Mitchell. She took us to the Ziegfeld Follies when Bert Williams did his acts of pantomime and earlier when Williams and Walker were famous cakewalkers. She was one of the first to attend the Avenue Theater when that management featured the Lafayette Players. One of my graduation presents was a theater party to a Negro play at the Avenue Theater.

"By 1930, Mother worried about money. When the Depression came, there was not as much demand for her as a speaker. She'd been so independent and wanted to have her own money. By the time she didn't have her own money, Dad had kind of gotten out of the habit of giving her money—enough for her to do the things she wanted to do. Father had a lucrative practice, but it takes a lot of money to keep a big house. And there were always a lot of folks [going] down to the office [for money]. My two older half-brothers, when they wanted anything, they'd go to the office and get it. And then Herman did things he had no business [doing], and the money situation became very difficult.

"Father continued to practice law until the Depression put him out of business. From the time I can remember, Mother worried what she was going to do when my father died because in those days there was no Social Security, no old-age pension. If you hadn't saved money or made some provisions for your own old age, you were in a very bad situation. He had very heavy insurance, but he lived so long that he cashed it all. So she was worried about what she was going to do, and ironically of course he lived five years after she did.

"She died pretty suddenly. She went downtown on Saturday and came home not feeling well. Sunday she stayed in bed. By Monday she was incoherent. She never came out of the coma and died on Wednesday. My father was pretty much broken up, and it was quite a shock to all of us—so sudden."

Bibliography

Abbott, Carl. 1976. *Colorado: A History of the Centennial State.* Boulder: Colorado Associated University Press.

Andrews, William, ed. 1986. *Sisters of the Spirit: Three Black Women's Autobiographies of the Nineteenth Century.* Bloomington: Indiana University Press.

———. 1988. *To Tell a Free Story: The First Century of Afro-American Autobiography, 1760–1865.* Urbana: University of Illinois Press.

———. 1989. "A Poetics of Afro-American Autobiography." In *Afro-American Literary Study in the 1990s,* ed. Houston A. Baker, Jr., and Patricia Redmon. Chicago: University of Chicago Press.

Aptheker, Bettina. 1982. *Woman's Legacy: Essays on Race, Sex, and Class in American History.* Amherst: University of Massachusetts Press.

———. 1989. *Tapestries of Life: Women's Work, Women's Consciousness and the Meaning of Daily Experience.* Amherst: University of Massachusetts Press.

Bell, Roseann P., Bettye J. Parker, and Beverly Guy-Sheftall, eds. 1979. *Sturdy Black Bridges: Visions of Black Women in Literature.* Garden City, N.Y.: Anchor/Doubleday.

Bennett, Lerone. 1975. *The Shaping of Black America.* Chicago: Johnson.

———. 1982. *Before the Mayflower: A History of Black America.* 5th ed. New York: Penguin.

Benstock, Shari. 1988. *The Private Self: Theory and Practice of Women's Autobiographical Writing.* Chapel Hill: University of North Carolina Press.

Berg, Barbara. 1978. *The Remembered Gate: Origins of American Feminism.* Oxford: Oxford University Press.

Berkeley, Kathleen Christ. 1980. " 'Like a Plague of Locusts': Immigration and Social Change in Memphis, Tennessee, 1850–1880." Ph.D. diss., University of California, Los Angeles.

Berret, Howard. 1905. *Who's Who in Topeka.* Topeka: Adams Bros.

Billington, Ray Allen, ed. 1953. *The Journal of Charlotte L. Forten.* New York: Dryden.

Blodgett, Harriet, ed. 1988. *Centuries of Female Days: Englishwomen's Private Diaries.* New Brunswick, N.J.: Rutgers University Press.

Braxton, Joanne M. 1989. *Black Women Writing Autobiography: A Tradition within a Tradition.* Philadelphia: Temple University Press.

Brown, Andrew. 1976. *History of Tippah County, Mississippi: The First Century.* Ripley, Miss.: Tippah County Historical and Genealogical Society.

Brown, A. Theodore, and Lyle W. Dorsett. 1978. *K.C.: A History of Kansas City, Missouri.* Kansas City, Mo.: Pruett.

Brown, Karen Fitzgerald. 1982. "The Black Press of Tennessee, 1865–1980." Ph.D. diss., University of Tennessee.

Bruss, Elizabeth. 1971. *Autobiographical Acts: The Changing Situation of a Literary Genre.* Baltimore: Johns Hopkins University Press.

Bunkers, Suzanne, ed. 1991. *The Diary of Caroline Seabury, 1854–1863.* Madison: University of Wisconsin Press.

Bureau of the Census. 1872. *Ninth Census of the United States.* Washington, D.C.

———. 1883. *Tenth Census of the United States.* Washington, D.C.

Caraway, Nancie. 1991. *Segregated Sisterhood: Racism and the Politics of American Feminism.* Knoxville: University of Tennessee Press.

Carby, Hazel. 1985. "'On the Threshold of Woman's Era': Lynching, Empire, and Sexuality in Black Feminist Theory." *Critical Inquiry* 12 (Autumn): 262–77.

———. 1987. *Reconstructing Womanhood: The Emergence of the Afro-American Woman Novelist.* Oxford: Oxford University Press.

Carter, Hodding. 1964. "A Proud Struggle for Grace: Holly Springs, Mississippi." In *A Vanishing America: The Life and Times of the Small Town,* ed. Thomas C. Wheeler. New York: Holt, Rinehart & Winston.

Church, Annette E., and Roberta Church. 1974. *The Robert R. Churches of Memphis: A Father and Son Who Achieved in Spite of Race.* Ann Arbor, Mich.: Edwards Bros.

Church, Roberta, and Ronald Walter. 1987. *Nineteenth Century Memphis Families of Color, 1850–1900.* Memphis: Murdock.

Collins, Patricia Hill. 1990. *Black Feminist Thought: Knowledge, Consciousness, and the Politics of Empowerment.* Boston: Unwin Hyman.

Cooper, Anna J. 1892. *A Voice of the South.* Xenia, Ohio: Aldine.

Cox, Thomas C. 1982. *Blacks in Topeka, Kansas, 1865–1915: A Social History.* Baton Rouge: Louisiana State University Press.

Culley, Margo, ed. 1985. *A Day at a Time: The Diary Literature of American Women from 1764 to the Present.* New York: Feminist.

———, ed. 1992. *American Women's Autobiography: Fea(s)ts of Memory.* Madison: University of Wisconsin Press.

Daily Memphis Avalanche. January–April 1886.

Daniel, James Fort. n.d. *Recollections of Things Past.* Holly Springs, Miss.

Daniels, Douglas Henry. 1980. *Pioneer Urbanites: A Social and Cultural History of Black San Francisco.* Philadelphia: Temple University Press.

Davies, Carole Boyce, and Elaine Savory Fido, eds. 1990. *Out of the Kumbla: Caribbean Women and Literature.* Trenton, N.J.: Africa World Press.

Davis, Angela. 1981. *Women, Race, and Class.* New York: Random House.

DeCosta, Miriam. 1973. "The History of Beale Street, 1850 to 1950." In *Feasibility of the Beale Street Cultural Center, Memphis, Tennessee,* vol. 2. Washington, D.C.: Match Institution.

DeCosta-Willis, Miriam. 1991. "Ida B. Wells's *Diary*: A Narrative of the Black Community of Memphis in the 1880s." *West Tennessee Historical Society Papers* 45 (December): 35–47.

Dougherty, Molly C. 1978. *Becoming a Woman in Rural Black Culture.* New York: Holt, Rinehart & Winston.

Dow's City Directory of Memphis. 1886. Memphis.

Dow's City Directory of Memphis. 1887. Memphis.

Dow's Street Directory of Memphis. 1888. Memphis.

Duster, Alfreda M., ed. 1970. *Crusade for Justice: The Autobiography of Ida B. Wells.* Chicago: University of Chicago Press.

———. 1976. Interview by Dorothy Sterling. March 22.

Ellis, Richard N., and Duane A. Smith. 1991. *Colorado: A History in Photographs.* Nuivot, Colo.: University Press of Colorado.

Flexner, Eleanor. 1981. *Century of Struggle: The Women's Rights Movement in the United States.* New York: Random House.

Fortune, T. Thomas. 1893. "Ida B. Wells, A.M." In *Women of Distinction: Remarkable in Works and Invincible in Character*, ed. Lawson A. Scruggs. Raleigh, N.C.

Foster, Frances Smith. 1985. "Adding Color and Contour to Early American Self-Portraitures: Autobiographical Writings of Afro-Americans. In *Conjuring: Black Women, Fiction, and Literary Tradition*, ed. Marjorie Pryse and Hortense Spillers. Bloomington: Indiana University Press.

————. 1993. *Written by Herself: Literary Production by African American Women, 1746–1892*. Bloomington: Indiana University Press.

Fox-Genovese, Elizabeth. 1988. *Within the Plantation Household*. Chapel Hill: University of North Carolina Press.

Franklin, John Hope. 1969. *From Slavery to Freedom: A History of Negro Americans*. 3d ed. New York: Vintage.

Fraser, Leigh D. 1974. "A Demographic Analysis of Memphis and Shelby County, Tennessee, 1820–1972." M.A. thesis, Memphis State University.

Fuller, T. O. 1933. *Pictorial History of the American Negro*. Memphis: Pictorial History.

————. 1936. *History of the Negro Baptists of Tennessee*. Memphis.

Gatewood, Willard B. 1991. *Aristocrats of Color: The Black Elite, 1880–1920*. Bloomington: Indiana University Press.

Gibson, William H. 1897. *Historical Sketch of the Progress of the Colored Race in Louisville, Ky.* Louisville, Ky.

Giddings, Paula. 1984. *When and Where I Enter: The Impact of Black Women on Race and Sex in America*. New York: Morrow.

Griffiths, Mel, and Lynnell Rubright. 1983. *Colorado: A Geography*. Boulder, Colo.: Westview.

Gutman, Herbert G. 1976. *The Black Family in Slavery and Freedom, 1750–1925*. New York: Vintage.

Guy-Sheftall, Beverly. 1990. *Daughters of Sorrow: Attitudes toward Black Women, 1880–1990*. New York: Carlson.

Gwin, Minrose C. 1985. *Black and White Women of the Old South*. Knoxville: University of Tennessee Press.

Haley, James T. 1897. *Sparkling Gems of Race Pride Worth Reading*. Nashville: J. T. Haley.

Hamilton, G. P. 1908. *The Bright Side of Memphis*. Memphis.

————. 1911. *Beacon Lights of the Race*. Memphis: F. H. Clarke.

————. 1927. *Booker T. Washington High School: Retrospective Prospective, from 1889 to 1927*. Memphis.

Hamilton, William Baskerville. 1984. *Holly Springs, Mississippi to the Year 1878*. Holly Springs, Miss.: Marshall County Historical Society.

Harkins, John E. 1982. *Metropolis of the American Nile: An Illustrated History of Memphis and Shelby County*. Woodland Hill, Calif.: Windson.

Harlan, Louis R., ed. 1975. *The Booker T. Washington Papers*. Chicago: University of Illinois Press.

Harley, Sharon, and Roslyn Terborg-Penn, eds. 1978. *The Afro-American Woman: Struggles and Images*. Port Washington, N.Y.: National University Publications.

Hart, James D. 1987. *A Companion to California*. Berkeley and Los Angeles: University of California Press.

Hennig, Margaret, and Anne Jardin. 1977. *The Managerial Woman*. Garden City, N.Y.: Anchor/Doubleday.

Henri, Florett. 1975. *Black Migration: Movement North, 1900–1920*. Garden City, N.Y.: Anchor/Doubleday.

Historic Black Memphians. n.d. Memphis: Memphis Pink Palace Museum Foundation.

Hoffman, Leonore, and Margo Culley, eds. 1985. *Women's Personal Narratives: Essays in Criticism and Pedagogy*. New York: Modern Language Association of America.

Holmes, Jack D. L. 1958a. "The Effects of the Memphis Race Riot of 1866." *West Tennessee Historical Society Papers* 12:58–79.
———. 1958b. "The Underlying Causes of the Memphis Race Riots of 1866." *Tennessee Historical Quarterly* 17:195–225.
Holtzclaw, Robert Fulton. 1984. *Black Magnolias: A Brief History of the Afro-Mississippian, 1865–1980*. Shaker Heights, Ohio: Keeble.
hooks, bell. 1981. *Ain't I a Woman? Black Women and Feminism*. Boston: South End.
———. 1984. *Feminist Theory: From Margin to Center*. Boston: South End.
———. 1989. *Talking Back*. Boston: South End.
Horton, James Oliver. 1986. "Freedom's Yoke: Gender Conventions among Antebellum Free Blacks." *Feminist Studies* 12 (Spring): 51–76.
Houghton, Rick. n.d. "The History of Rust College." Edited by Vera Williams. Holly Springs, Miss.: Rust College.
Hull, Gloria T., ed. 1984. *Give Us Each Day: The Diary of Alice Dunbar-Nelson*. New York: Norton.
Hull, Gloria T., Patricia Bell Scott, and Barbara Smith, eds. 1982. *All the Women Are White, All the Blacks Are Men, But Some of Us Are Brave: Black Women's Studies*. Old Westbury, N.Y.: Feminist.
Hunt, Ruth Wyckoff, ed. 1973. *Raleigh Sesquicentennial Scrapbook*. Memphis: Centennial.
Hutchins, Fred. 1963. Letter to Alfreda M. Duster. July 10.
———. 1965. *What Happened in Memphis*. Memphis.
———. 1968. *Sketch History of Second Congregational Church, Centennial 1868–1968*. Memphis: Johnson Printery.
Jelinek, Estelle C., ed. 1980. *Women's Autobiography: Essays in Criticism*. Bloomington: Indiana University Press.
Johnson, W. D. 1897. *Biographical Sketches of Prominent Negro Men and Women of Kentucky*. Lexington, Ky.
Jones, Jacqueline. 1985. *Labor of Love, Labor of Sorrow: Black Women, Work and the Family, from Slavery to the Present*. New York: Vintage.
Lamon, Lester C. 1977. *Black Tennesseans, 1900–1930*. Knoxville: University of Tennessee Press.
Lapp, Rudolph. 1979. *Afro-Americans in California*. San Francisco: Boyd & Fraser.
Leadabrand, Russ, et al., eds. 1975. *Yesterday's California*. Miami, Fla.: Seemann.
Lensink, Judy Nolte. 1989. *"A Secret to Be Buried": The Diary and Life of Emily Hawley Gillespie, 1858–1888*. Iowa City: University of Iowa Press.
Lerner, Gerda, ed. 1973. *Black Women in White America: A Documentary History*. New York: Vintage.
———. 1979. *The Majority Finds Its Past: Placing Women in History*. New York: Oxford University Press.
Lewis, Selma S., and Marjean G. Kremer. 1986. *The Angel of Beale Street: A Biography of Julia Ann Hooks*. Memphis: St. Luke's.
Litwick, Leon. 1979. *Been in the Storm So Long: The Aftermath of Slavery*. New York: Vintage.
Loewenberg, Bert B. J., and Ruth Bogin, eds. 1976. *Black Women in Nineteenth Century American Life: Their Words, Their Thoughts, Their Feelings*. University Park: Pennsylvania State University Press.
McCormick, John S. 1980. *Salt Lake City: The Gathering Place*. Woodland Hills, Calif.: Windsor.
Meier, August. 1963. *Negro Thought in America, 1880–1915*. Ann Arbor: University of Michigan Press.
Memphis city directory. See either *Dow's* city directory (1886, 1887, 1888) or *Sholes'* Memphis directory (1880, 1884, 1885).

Merrill, Marlene Deahl, ed. 1990. *Growing Up in Boston's Gilded Age: The Journal of Alice Stone Blackwell, 1872–1874.* New Haven, Conn.: Yale University Press.

Neverdon-Morton, Cynthia. 1989. *Afro-American Women of the South and the Advancement of the Race, 1895–1925.* Knoxville: University of Tennessee Press.

Ornelas-Struve, Carole M., and Fredrick Lee Coulter. 1982. *Memphis, 1800–1900.* Vol. 3. New York: Nancy Powers.

Painter, Nell Irvin. 1977. *Exodusters: Black Migration to Kansas after Reconstruction.* New York: Knopf.

Penn, I. Garland. 1891. *The Afro-American Press and Its Editors.* Springfield, Mass.: Wiley.

Perkins, Kathy A. 1981. "Black Women and Racial 'Uplift' Prior to Emancipation." In *The Black Woman Cross-Culturally,* ed. Filomina Chioma Steady. Cambridge, Mass.: Schenkman.

Pruitt, Olga Reed. 1950. *It Happened Here: True Stories of Holly Springs.* Holly Springs: South Reporter.

Pryse, Marjorie, and Hortense J. Spillers, eds. 1985. *Conjuring: Black Women, Fiction, and Literary Tradition.* Bloomington: Indiana University Press.

Qualls, J. Winfield. 1953. "The Beginnings and Early History of LeMoyne School at Memphis, 1871–1874." *West Tennessee Historical Society Papers* 7:5–37.

Quarles, Benjamin. 1964. *The Negro in the Making of America.* New York: Collier.

Rabinowitz, Howard N. 1978. *Race Relations in the Urban South, 1865–1890.* New York: Oxford University Press.

Richardson, Marilyn, ed. 1989. *Maria Stewart, America's First Black Woman Political Writer.* Bloomington: Indiana University Press.

Robb, Frederic H. 1929. *The Negro in Chicago, 1779 to 1929.* Chicago: Atlas.

Rust University Catalogue, 1896–97. Holly Springs, Miss.

Ryan, James Gilbert. 1977. "The Memphis Riots of 1866: Terror in a Black Community during Reconstruction." *Journal of Negro History* 62: 243–57.

Shannon, Samuel. 1983. "Tennessee." In *The Black Press in the South, 1865–1979,* ed., Henry Lewis Suggs. Westport, Conn.: Greenwood.

Shepperd, Gladys Byram. 1954. *Mary Church Terrell, Respectable Person.* Baltimore: Human Relations.

Sholes' Memphis Directory. 1880. Vol. 8. Memphis.

Sholes' Memphis City Directory. 1884. Vol. 11. Memphis.

Sholes' Memphis Directory. 1885. Vol. 12. Memphis.

Sigafoos, Robert A. 1979. *Cotton Row to Beale Street: A Business History of Memphis.* Memphis: Memphis State University Press.

Simmons, William J. [1887] 1968. *Men of Mark: Eminent, Progressive and Rising.* Cleveland: George E. Rewell. 1887. Reprint, New York: Arno.

Simon, Sidonie. 1987. *A Poetics of Women's Autobiography.* Bloomington: Indiana University Press.

Simons, Judy. 1990. *Diaries and Journals of Literary Women from Fanny Burney to Virginia Woolf.* Iowa City: University of Iowa Press.

Smith, Barbara, ed. 1983. *Home Girls: A Black Feminist Anthology.* New York: Kitchen Table Women of Color.

Smith, Valerie. 1987. *Self-Discovery and Authority in Afro-American Narrative.* Cambridge, Mass.: Harvard University Press.

Spacks, Patricia Meyer. *Imagining a Self: Autobiography and Novel in Eighteenth-Century England.* Cambridge, Mass.: Harvard University Press.

Sterling, Dorothy. 1984. *We Are Your Sisters: Black Women in the Nineteenth Century.* New York: Norton.

———. 1988. *Black Foremothers: Three Lives.* 2d ed. New York: Feminist.

Suggs, Henry Lewis, ed. 1983. *The Black Press in the South, 1865–1979.* Westport, Conn.: Greenwood.

Takaki, Ronald T. 1979. *Iron Cages: Race and Culture in 19th-Century America.* Seattle: University of Washington Press.

Tennessee State Gazeteer and Business Directory. 1887. Nashville: Polk.

Terrell, Mary Church. 1940. *A Colored Woman in a White World.* Washington, D.C.: Ransdell.

Thompson, Mildred I. 1990. *Ida B. Wells-Barnett: An Exploratory Study of an American Black Woman, 1893–1930.* New York: Carlson.

Thornbrough, Emma Lou. 1972. *T. Thomas Fortune, Militant Journalist.* Chicago: University of Chicago Press.

Townes, Emilie Maureen. 1993. *Womanist Justice, Womanist Hope.* Atlanta: Scholars.

Tucker, David M. 1971. "Miss Ida B. Wells and Memphis Lynching." *Phylon* 32 (Summer): 112–22.

———. 1975. *Black Pastors and Leaders: Memphis, 1819–1972.* Memphis: Memphis State University Press.

U.S. Congress. 1866. *House Select Committee on the Memphis Riots.* 39th Cong., 1st sess. H. Rep. 101. July 25. (Reprint. *Memphis Riots and Massacres, 1866.* Miami: Mnemosyne, 1969).

Wallace, Phyllis. 1980. *Black Women in the Labor Force.* Cambridge, Mass.: MIT Press.

Waller, Robert Lee. 1974. "Equality or Inequality: A Comparative Study of Segregated Public Education in Memphis, Tennessee, 1862 to 1954." Ph.D. diss., Western Colorado University.

Weeden, Henry Clay. 1897. *Weeden's History of the Colored People of Louisville.* Louisville, Ky.

Wells, Ida B. 1969. *On Lynchings: Southern Horrors* [1892]. *A Red Record* [1895]. *Mob Rule in New Orleans* [1900]. New York: Arno.

———. 1895. *A Red Record: Tabulated Statistics and Alleged Causes of Lynchings in the United States, 1892–1893–1894.* Chicago: Donohue & Henneberry.

———. 1991. *Selected Works of Ida B. Wells-Barnett.* Edited by Trudier Harris. New York: Oxford University Press.

Wells, Ida B., et al. 1893. *The Reason Why the Colored American Is Not in the World's Columbian Exposition—the Afro-American's Contribution to Columbian Literature.* Chicago.

Wharton, Vernon Lane. 1947. *The Negro in Mississippi, 1865–1890.* Chapel Hill: University of North Carolina Press.

Wright, George C. 1985. *Life behind a Veil: Blacks in Louisville, Kentucky, 1865–1930.* Baton Rouge: Louisiana State University Press.

Index

BOOKS OF RELATED INTEREST FROM BEACON PRESS

Gayl Jones
Corregidora

A terse, chilling novel about how the memory of slavery plagues black women and men long after emancipation.

"Gayl Jones has concocted a tale as American as Mount Rushmore and as murky as the Florida swamps."
—Maya Angelou

[0-8070-6315-0, PAPERBACK]

Eva's Man

[0-8070-6319-3, PAPERBACK]

Frances E. W. Harper
With an Introduction by Hazel Carby
Iola Leroy

"This is a book that needs to be read by everyone who wishes to understand the roots of the Afro-American female literary tradition." —Nellie McKay

[0-8070-6317-7, PAPERBACK]

Alice Childress
Like One of the Family: Conversations from a Domestic's Life

[0-8070-0903-2, PAPERBACK]

Jessie Redmon Fauset
Plum Bun: A Novel without a Moral

[0-8070-0909-1, PAPERBACK]

Edited by Frances Smith Foster
Minnie's Sacrifice, Sowing and Reaping, Trial and Triumph: Three Rediscovered Novels by Frances E. W. Harper

"The novels challenge everything we thought we knew about American literature, about African-American culture and about the course of literary history."
—*Women's Review of Books*

[0-8070-8333-X, PAPERBACK]

Ann Petry
Miss Muriel and Other Stories

[0-8070-8311-9, PAPERBACK]

The Narrows

Set in the New England town of Monmouth, Connecticut, in the 1950s, *The Narrows* tells the story of a forbidden love affair between a wealthy white woman and an educated but unemployed black man.

"A story filled with dramatic force, earthy humor, and tragic intensity."
—*Boston Globe*

[0-8070-8303-8, PAPERBACK]

Available at bookstores or directly from Beacon Press, 25 Beacon Street, Boston, Massachusetts 02108-2892